Living the Christ Life

Rediscovering
the Seasons
of the
Christian Year

Louise Mangan
and Nancy Wyse
with Lori Farr

Living
THE
Christ Life

REDISCOVERING THE SEASONS
OF THE
CHRISTIAN YEAR

WOOD LAKE BOOKS

Wood Lake Books Inc. acknowledges the financial support of the Government of Canada, through the Book Publishing Industry Development Program (BPIDP) for our publishing activities.

At Wood Lake Books we practice what we publish, guided by a concern for fairness, justice, and equal opportunity in all of our relationships with employees and customers.

We recycle and reuse and encourage readers to do the same. Resources are printed on recycled paper and more environmentally friendly groundwood papers (newsprint), whenever possible. The trees used are replaced through donations to the Scoutrees for Canada program. A percentage of all profit is donated to charitable organizations.

Editors: James Taylor and Mike Schwartzentruber
Cover and interior design: Margaret Kyle
Cover artwork: Margaret Kyle

Unless otherwise noted, all quotations from the Bible are from the New Revised Standard Version, copyright 1989 by the Division of Christian Education of the National Council of Churches of Christ in the USA. All rights reserved. Used by permission.

Unless otherwise noted, all prayers were written by Louise Mangan, and all poems were written by Nancy Wyse.

**National Library of Canada
Cataloguing in Publication Data**

Mangan, Louise, 1953-
    Living the Christ life
Includes bibliographical references.
ISBN 1-55145-498-X
    1. Church year. 2. Worship programs.
I. Wyse, Nancy, 1953- II. Farr, Lori, 1956- III. Title.
BV30.M36 2001   264   C2001-910828-1

Published by Wood Lake Books Inc.
Kelowna, British Columbia, Canada
www.joinhands.com

Printing 10 9 8 7 6 5 4 3 2 1

Printed in Canada by
Transcontinental Printing

Contents

Introduction

PART ONE
The Christmas Cycle · 17

I. The Advent Season

II. The Christmas Season

III. The Epiphany Season

With thanks

Louise and Nancy first met in the chapel of a little church in Smithers, British Columbia. Both were raising young families. Both were seeking meaning and authenticity for themselves and their children. This book grew out of shared friendship and faith, and the desire to entwine in a meaningful way the seasons of their spirits with the seasons of their everyday lives.

As this project unfolded, Louise (by this time an ordained minister of the United Church of Canada) longed for ways to integrate the wisdom of body, mind, and spirit. At that point Lori joined the team, and brought to the work her expertise in helping others to experience spiritual reality through their bodies. She also brought an invaluable spiritual perspective as a seeker without Christian background.

Nancy, Louise, and Lori are deeply grateful for one another; for the loving support of Simon Nankivell, Liz Shorten, and Graham Truax; for their children Luke, Megan, Kate, Neil, Dan, and Theo; for mentors, colleagues and friends who have given so richly; for Linnea Good who read the first draft when she didn't have time; for the folks at Wood Lake Books who have watered this garden; and for the seed of an idea the Rev. Dr. Thomas Harding shared with Louise years ago. The joy of life in the Spirit together makes everything possible!

INTRODUCTION

Journeying Together

REDISCOVERING FAITH COMMUNITY

As we enter a new millennium, we yearn for the holy and we yearn for communion with each other. Sadly, the way we live can keep us dulled to the sacred; we have little shared language for mystery. Public culture suggests that the life of devotion is too unimportant to share. So we tend to live separately, seeking meaning on lonely private journeys.

With so many competing pressures, and all our comings and goings, how can we recover the holy? And how can we find ways to share it?

This book has emerged from our passionate conviction that whenever we yearn for the Spirit, we are actually praying. Prayer starts with pursuing our spiritual yearning. Sharing that yearning can lead us deeply into love – for God, and for our life, and one another. As we seek and pray together, we rediscover both connection to the holy and the joy of true community.

When we seek and pray together, we put human community back at the center of nurturing whole and holy persons. In faith community we find companions to help us care for what's important, to interpret our experience, and to grow with us in wisdom and courage. With companions on the journey we can share a symbol-language to communicate what can't be explained about the holy, and to pass on the insights of generations. God strengthens us and meets us as teacher, source, and guide through our loving and serving together. Through our mutual commitments, we learn – and by the power of the Spirit, we change the world.

REDISCOVERING SACRED LANGUAGE

Back in the 1930s, psychologist Carl Jung defined symbols of mystery as attempts to express the inexpressible. Jung warned against tampering with the symbols of religion, but over time Christians influenced by the scientific temper attempted to "explain" symbolic actions. Others reacted to modernist thinking by claiming rituals must be understood literally. Either way, the truth of myth was lost. And yet, neither blind faith nor faith that is rationalized seem to speak to the hunger in our souls. We haven't found a shared language for prayer.

The language of prayer is the language of the heart. It nurtures souls. And since our souls are nurtured by who we are and what we do even more than by what we believe, through the ages faith communities have used symbolic actions to communicate truths that are timeless. In the Communist era of the Soviet Union, the Soviet government banned seminaries, Bible study, Sunday schools, and preaching. But the Orthodox Church survived, largely because its liturgy dramatized the stories and poetry of faith through bodily, sensory experience. Symbolic acts rehearse us in transformed ways of being. They open up pathways for our souls. In communal worship, in small groups, or at home with our families, symbolic actions give our whole selves a language for prayer. And prayer changes our lives.

REDISCOVERING THE CHRISTIAN PATH

Christianity has much in common with other major religions, and like others it has its own particular beauty. The readings and rituals, activities and celebrations we have chosen to include in these chapters are drawn from the legacy of Jesus of Nazareth, the Hebrew prophet Christians know as "Christ." Together, they give shape to a spiritual pathway and frame a unique way of being.

Nancy and Louise are practicing Christians. We are also parents, with five children between us. It's our experience, and the experience of Christians through time, that sharing creatively the path we call "the Christ-life" can shape us creatively as disciples – as unique individuals who pray and learn together, and who together form "the body of Christ."

Christ's "body" embraces persons of every age and particularity, including and especially our children. The world of Jesus' day had little use for children. At that time even Jewish society valued children more highly

for who they would someday become, than for the persons they already were. Against this background, Jesus' actions and words are emphatic: "'Let the little children come to me; do not stop them; for it is to such as these that the kingdom of God belongs....' And he took them up in his arms, laid his hands on them, and blessed them" (Mark 10:14–16. See also Matthew 19:13–15 and Luke 18:16–17). In Jesus' view, little children are fully part of faith community. They don't have to be adult to belong; they are "in" as they are.

The Christian path is one that we all walk together with those the rest of the world may exclude. Sharing the Christ-life embodies our yearning for personal and social transformation; indeed, it may be our children who see the way.

The Christ-life unfolds in our lives as "incarnation," as holy presence alive in human flesh. Its readings and rituals, celebrations and activities join the Hebrew story with our community story and join the Christ story with our own. They connect our collective longings for peace and justice for everyone with the longings that God inspired in the people of ancient Israel, and specifically in Jesus of Nazareth. And they associate our inner quest for healing and wholeness with the Spirit unfolding in Jesus and his original disciples. With Christ as the model of God's human image, the Christ-life breathes the Spirit of Christ into us and empowers us to live faith-filled lives. In the amazing truth of a death that transforms us for life, we too can risk commitment to God's dream for creation as we live our real lives in the world.

The Christ-life unites us through open, expansive symbols without requiring us all to think alike. Its readings and rituals, celebrations and activities provide a shared language for holiness. They not only reveal in us the truth of sacred myth, they become the prayer language we crave.

So the Christ-life has more than historical significance; it has community and personal power. It gives structure and freedom to the life we live together, through which the Spirit moves to re-create us. The Christ-life shows that suffering can be turned to holy blessing, and teaches us to love as Christ loves.

REDISCOVERING CHRIST THROUGH SCRIPTURE

The Bible's symbol-language is central to living the Christ-life. For Christians, the ancient texts of Hebrew Scripture and New Testament reveal truth about God and our relationship with God and one another. And they reveal an inner tension, from beginning to end, between a cultural understanding of God as king and victor – a god allied with worldly success – and a subversive understanding of God revealed in the power of compassion. The Jesus we know through scripture comes to us as the Spirit-filled teacher of this second kind of wisdom, the embodiment of a radically inclusive social vision and a healer of bodies and souls. This Jesus invites us into intimate relationship with the boundless, loving grace we call God. This Jesus asks us to die to our old ways of being for the sake of new life without end. Jesus calls us, as friends, to be all that God intends and to share in the power of the Spirit. In all these ways and many more, Christ brings "salvation."

For us as Christians, scripture's symbols and stories are truth, although we know they may or may not be factual. We cherish the miracle of love revealed in Jesus as *more* true than mere facts can show. We cherish biblical traditions with respectful discernment. And we cherish the Christ-life born of scripture and tradition as a sign of the miracle God intends – of peace with justice and harmony for all creation.

REDISCOVERING THE CHRISTIAN YEAR

The ritual patterns of the Christ-life shape the habits of heart through which we come to trust that we are loved. This faith grows in us much the same way a tree grows – by yearly rings. That is why the Jewish and Christian cultures both linked their memories of liberation and renewal to the rhythms of the seasons. Children, in particular, soak up the significance of holy days (holidays!). A three-year-old tree is just as spirit-filled as a tree that is 50 years old; it simply has fewer rings of faith.

Festival days are times when we need to be together in community. With all our different gifts and our diverse ways of being, in the festival experience we can delight in the bonds of common faith and commitment which unite us in the Spirit of Christ. Festivals are perfect times for the whole community to join in worship because they lend themselves to color, movement, and story. Wonder-filled worship re-creates the ancient story through dramatic and holistic ritual patterns. And the test of what's wonderful is whether four-year-old Sarah, her parents, *and* her grandparents are *all* engaged and involved in a flow of symbols.

This creative repetition of ritual pattern is not the same as redundancy. Each time we return to a place we've been before, we remember what we already know and we learn something new. And our capacity to intuit hope and meaning in our lives expands with our symbolic insight.

The Christian year can bless us with rings of faith that strengthen our insight. Two cycles of readings, rituals, activities, and celebrations make up the annual sequence. The Christmas cycle (Advent, Christmas, Epiphany, and the weeks which follow Epiphany) is a pathway to fullness through "becoming." The Easter cycle (Lent, Holy Week, Easter, Pentecost, and the weeks which follow) is a pathway to fullness through "emptying," a path through pain which unfolds in humility, compassion, and community.

These alternating rhythms of self-fulfillment and self-emptying illuminate the holiness of living. Through the lens of the Christ-life, we see the sacred unfolding through real situations and struggles. We learn and change to become the whole selves God intends so we can give of ourselves in joy and sorrow – and all of this in the process of sharing God's dream for our own lives and all of creation.

As we embark on this journey, we hope the wisdom of the Christ-life will be worked out through the seasons of our souls. We pray that honoring the path of Christ will lead us to the life of holy love.

About this book

This book speaks to leaders of Christian groups and communities, to parents, grandparents, and friends in faith. It maps the Christian year as an unfolding cycle of personal and community transformation. It's for living through the year in ways that make the Christ-life visible in our lives and in the world that we share.

These resources are meant to be helpful for worship, for small groups that meet in the community or church buildings, for one-on-one spiritual friendships (prayer partners), and also for families at home. Discussions and prayers have been written for groups with one participant (not necessarily a trained leader) taking a leadership role. They can be easily adapted for worship, prayer partners, or individuals. And families will find it easier, with the help of these resources, to make the Christ-life real every day.

The first half of this book outlines the Christmas Cycle, starting with the Season of Advent and moving on through Christmas and Epiphany, and ending with the weeks between Epiphany and Lent. The second half of the book outlines the Easter Cycle, from Lent through Easter to Pentecost, and the weeks that follow between Pentecost and Advent.

Each seasonal chapter has ten components:
1. The spirit of the season – an overview
2. The beauty of the season – colors, symbols & art
3. Special celebrations
4. Rituals
5. Sharing our story
6. Embodied prayers
7. Written prayers
8. Guided prayers and meditations
9. Inner reflections
10. Activities

These offerings are meant to be sorted, moved, and changed to meet the needs of gatherings and individuals, wherever people are seeking to live their prayer and share it with others.

Notes for leaders, prayer partners, parents, and grandparents

You are in the role of catalyst and guide as you walk with your faith community, your family and/or friends through the cycles of the seasons of the church year. Here are some thoughts about how to use the various sections of each chapter.

IN GENERAL

First, a word about the typefaces. We have used three different kinds. The typeface you are currently reading is used for commentary. **This heavier, darker version of the same typeface is used for instructions to leaders.** Finally, we have used this serif font for material that is meant to be read aloud if used by leaders in group settings.

Worship and group leaders may photocopy prayers and small portions of text for use in worship services or other group settings.

You may find some unfamiliar terms in this book. Christian tradition is a culture like any other – it has words and ideas of its own. Do you need more information? Check the glossary at the end of the book.

Many Christian communities are guided in their use of the Bible by a three-year cycle of readings known as the lectionary. We value the lectionary as both a tool and a discipline. For the sake of simplicity, we have not noted lectionary references in this book. We have, however, been guided by the *Revised Common Lectionary* in selecting readings appropriate to each season.

THE BEAUTY OF THE SEASONS

Special colors and images associated with festival celebrations and worship communicate without need for words. Color can be incorporated in the worship of the church through the stoles of worship leaders, through cloths on the communion table, hangings on pulpit and lectern, and banners hung from the rafters. Banners are especially powerful expressions because they unify color, texture, and symbol. Participants in faith community can work in teams to create a set of colored cloths for each season of the church year, perhaps designing matching stoles for worship leaders as part of each set.

The same colors can be emphasized in the home.

COMMUNITY RITUALS

The rituals we've included are contemporary formulations of traditions important in the western church. They are written for faith communities either large or small, and can easily be adapted for worship, small group, or family use.

Before you begin, plan who will read, who will lead, and who will do which actions. Use your best judgment about how much to "practice" beforehand. Too much practice can stifle creativity and enthusiasm. On the other hand, practicing enough to gain familiarity can deepen learning and meaning for everyone. Particularly for major celebrations in faith community, practicing ahead of time strengthens understanding, confidence, and skills, and makes ritual participation more joyful. Enjoy your practice, too!

Community meals can strengthen the power of storytelling and ritual. When we gather for the sacrament of Holy Communion, our ritual meal re-enacts the sacred pattern of receiving, thanking, and sharing. Everyday meals can do the same! Our motto is "When in doubt – eat!" Eating together is an amazing community-builder.

SHARING OUR STORY

People are spiritually hungry for more than easy answers. Storytelling is a way to integrate sacred stories with real-life stories and our personal lives. The most powerful stories are those which embody the example of a Spirit-led life. Through them, the Christ-life offers new ways to interpret situations and redeem life experiences.

The story sections for each season focus on the Bible's record of God's Spirit at work in persons and communities. The suggestions for exploring stories are written for groups, but they can easily be adapted for use by prayer partners and individuals. When youth and children are included, use words and examples from their experience. Acting out the story can deepen meaning and be great fun as well! Not every young person enjoys this kind of sharing, but many actually crave it – and all can bring wonderful insights. Talking together about scripture and tradition can build crucial bonds of intimacy and acceptance.

EMBODIED PRAYERS

Embodied prayers provide a way to experience the sacred through our physical bodies. While not everyone is familiar with these kinds of prayers, if you are willing to try them they will assist you in relaxing and listening for God's invitation, and in attending to the blessing and spiritual possibilities of living in a physical body.

This book contains two kinds of embodied prayers: some that combine relaxed breathing with visualization, and others that add an element of movement. Choose the prayers that suit you or your group.

Individuals, prayer partners, and groups will find that embodied prayers provide a rich environment for exploring and sharing spiritual experience. Trust your own personal experience of "spirit" in each exercise. If you are leading others, it is your role to nurture this atmosphere of inner trust in the group.

The relaxation and visualization components of embodied prayers may be a new experience for some. If you are leading a group, here are some suggestions to help you attend to questions or concerns that may arise.

- **Remind your group often that they are always personally in control of the visualization and the depth of relaxation they are experiencing. They can open their eyes, move their bodies, or breathe normally at any time they feel the need, especially if they feel distressed or anxious.**
- **When people say, "I can't visualize," reassure them that people experience visualization in many ways. Encourage them to relax and "think about the idea" rather than struggling to "see" an image. A visual image is not necessary to connect to the meaning in the prayer.**

- Present each prayer as an exploration of spirit. Remind the group there is no expectation of achieving anything in particular. We are interested in exploring our experience, not in getting things "right."
- Prayers are a conduit for personal spiritual experience. All experience, even negative, has personal value and should be encouraged to be shared and honored.
- If any members in your group fall asleep, they probably needed it! Sitting forward on the chair so the back does not touch the back rest will help them to stay awake next time.
- When participants worry that their busy minds keep them from focusing, tell them not to judge themselves harshly. They can say to themselves, "Isn't it interesting that I'm thinking about that again." Then they can gently bring their attention back to the prayer. No matter how often they must do this, it is better to be gracious with oneself than to be frustrated. The skill of focusing will come with time.
- Each embodied prayer includes clues on pacing, but these are just suggestions. Your sense of who is with you on a particular day is more important.

Although the Christian year starts with Advent, readers are just as likely to start using this book during the Season of Lent or Pentecost. For that reason, the instructions for embodied prayers (and for the guided prayers and meditations) repeat in each season, and to some extent for each prayer. Even if you have read these instructions before, it's worth looking at them again to be sure you're not overlooking anything.

GUIDED PRAYERS, MEDITATIONS, AND WRITTEN PRAYERS

The purpose of praying intentionally is to become more spontaneously prayerful in our lives. The habit of turning to God in all things leads us into intimate relationship with God, and into the Christ-life of service.

In each season, it helps to build patterns of prayer suited to need and situation. As a group, you may choose to pray one way when you gather, another way in con-templation, and a third way as you leave one another. At home, you may want to pray one way at sunrise, another way at mealtime, and another at the close of the day. Wherever you are, familiarity with different kinds of prayer and meditation will make both discipline and spontaneity easier.

Encourage one another to keep a prayer journal, and to let God speak through your writing, drawing, and emotions as you reflect on each prayer time.

The prayer suggestions, written prayers, and scripture passages provided in this book provide a starting place for shared or personal devotions. The written prayers can be read by individuals privately, used with groups, or included in worship services. The prayer suggestions are primarily written for groups with one participant taking the role of guide, but they can be easily adapted for prayer partners or personal use. Make them your own.

Again, the suggestions for pacing are only clues or hints. Each gathering will find blessing in differing lengths of silence. Timing changes with different moods and seasons. You will learn with each experience, and your sense of your people will guide you.

INNER REFLECTIONS

These meditations also assume that you are working with at least one other person, so that one of your number can read aloud the suggestions to guide your thoughts. At the conclusion of each exercise, however, you will want to reflect on your experience. For this, you will often need blank paper for writing on, or a journal, and a pencil and pen. For some reflections you will also need a candle. Always, you will need a quiet place to be comfortable and alone.

ACTIVITIES

Many of the crafts and activities we suggest will be more fun (and less stressful) if you gather odds and ends that give creativity room to play. Begin with a storage space like a box, drawer or cupboard. Stash paper, crayons, felt pens, glue, and tape, and then be on the look-out for reusable items for the collection – magazines, foil, straws, buttons, yarn and fabric scraps – you know, "stuff"!

Some helpful hints

GENTLENESS

First of all, be gentle with yourself. Don't expect everything to be perfect – you're almost certain to be disappointed! Nancy and her friend Sandy still giggle when they think of their "Advent Project from Hell."

"We wanted to make our Advent preparation more spiritual and more inclusive of our children," Nancy explains. "We planned a mural. We read through the Christmas stories in Luke and Matthew and listed things to add to our mural, one for each day of Advent. We were so proud of our plan. The crowning glory would be the placing of baby Jesus in the manger on Christmas Eve. Just the vision was enough to give us goose bumps. What actually happened? Well, baby Jesus never quite got to Bethlehem that year. Mary did, but no donkey, and no Joseph. We did have a dragon and a few mangy sheep. And lots of trees – and lots of tears and anxiety. Goose bumps were replaced by a rash!"

There's a parable of sorts in that story.

Make use of the ideas in this book in ways that fit your situation. The purpose of these rituals and activities is to add joy and meaning to the journey – not stress! It's generally more helpful to build the Christ-life gradually instead of trying to add too much at once. So be gentle with one another and yourselves.

CARING

Taking seriously the presence of the Spirit each day can open our hearts to the life and the joy that God gives. For some there may also be painful times to move through on the way. The work of faith can be challenging, and important issues can emerge. If you're in a group, some participants may need personal assistance. When you serve as a leader, please take time to assure those present that you can be available later for personal conversation, or to help them find additional resources.

RESPECT

Perhaps the most important attitude is respect – for yourself, for the other participants in these experiences, and for the materials you have to work with. The materials in this book invite personal and collective reflections on the ways of the Spirit. The most intimate contemplations are invited by prayers which can be prayed either privately or with others in a group, with or without verbal sharing. Choose prayer-styles and discussions which match the level of trust and familiarity among those who are present. To honor both privacy and self-determination, introduce the intention of each prayer or discussion before you begin. Provide short breaks often to give people space, and remind participants they are always free to "pass" when invited to speak or pray. Groups which are comfortable sharing personal reflections can develop guidelines for discussion which treat confidentiality as a trust-building spiritual discipline.

THE
Christmas Cycle

The "Christmas cycle" begins with the four weeks of Advent, moves through the seasons of Christmas and Epiphany, and culminates immediately before the start of Lent in the Sunday called Transfiguration. Our spiritual unfolding through this first part of the church year has the same shape and feeling as early chapters in the story of Christ. The Christmas cycle is the cycle of spiritual affirmation. It is the part of the church year which lends itself to growing into the fullness of selfhood, to become the special gift God intends.

- Like Mary and Joseph, through our Advent waiting we make our hearts ready to receive the gift of Christ into our lives.

- When the Christ child comes at Christmas, we delight in Spirit-filled human identity as we welcome the gift of holiness and find God in a particular way through family teachings and faith community.

- In the Epiphany scriptures, the light of incarnation is revealed to the world through the visit of the Magi, the baptism of Christ, the calling of Jesus' disciples, and his ministry of healing. In our day-to-day world, the Christ-light is revealed through our faithfulness as followers of Christ. So, in the Season of Epiphany, we celebrate the holy, learn to live in community with the integrity of disciples, and participate together in miracles.

I

THE
Advent Season

I. The spirit of Advent
– an overview

The four-week period leading to Christmas is called the Season of Advent. During Advent we wait for holiness to come as a baby, the child who comes to be known as Jesus Christ. What a marvelous time of year, and what a challenge! In this age of neon Santas and so many "me first" wish books, how can we find a quiet center of expectancy and await with hope the gift of Jesus Christ? How can we still our busy hearts to welcome Christ into our lives?

In our northern climate, the Advent season falls in the "waiting" time of winter, when much that will soon come into being is hidden from view. One Sunday, a congregation passed a stethoscope around so each person could listen to the heartbeat of an unborn infant inside its mother. That's what Advent is like – listening to the hidden heartbeat of a baby soon to come. The word Advent means "coming."

But Advent waiting is active, not passive. We prepare, consciously and intentionally. Many Christian communities prepare for Christ's coming by giving each of the Advent weeks a theme – hope, peace, joy, and love. Such themes express our longing for the God-given energies through which holiness is rooted in the world. We wait for the Christ child to come through hope, peace, joy, and love. We yearn for hope, peace, joy, and love to be reborn in us. We wait not only for Christmas but for the fulfillment of Christ's presence as harmony for all of creation.

The sacred gift of the Christ child comes to us through Mary and Joseph – through a human family. In our lives, the roots of love are born in us through human families of many kinds. So part of the spiritual deepening of Advent involves our families. It may mean honoring our roots, with all their challenges and blessings.

It may mean giving thanks for the identity, strengths, and hopes that come to us through family, and doing whatever preparation is needed to offer gifts of love and forgiveness.

Advent is a time to remember that we are able to love and forgive because we are loved and forgiven. God has loved us without measure. Our very first home is in God.

Sometimes, to say "hello," we first need to say "good-bye." We may need to let go of parts of the past to welcome God's present and trust in God's promise for the future. For some, there can be a poignant sadness to Advent waiting; perhaps the knowledge that persons we have loved will not be with us, that this Christmas will not be like others we have known and cannot be the way we would wish. These feelings are important to honor. In this season there is always a tension between what has been, what is now, and what will be in the future. Dealing creatively with past and present pain can help us welcome holy gifts still to come.

Through our waiting and preparing to receive God's gift of love, somehow we open to the sacred. And in the mystery of the Christ child – of human flesh that breathes the Spirit – we will come to see the holiness of all creation. Through the unlikely story of unwed parents on a journey, a local inn and stable animals, peasant shepherds and glowing angels, God's amazing creativity in the material world will be revealed. Heaven and earth will unite in our hearts. Human flesh and Holy Spirit will be one.

And so we wait. We wait for the light to return to our world, and for the Spirit to warm our wintry hearts. Like Mary, we wait with pregnant anticipation. We long for the time, we work and pray for the time, when the Spirit will make all things new.

2. The beauty of Advent – colors, symbols, & art

The key to Advent is to heighten the sense of expectancy while avoiding commercial fuss and hype. If you can, save some Christmas carols for the Season of Christmas. Lovely Advent carols are available to us now. We can add them to our repertoire and enjoy them.

Amidst the gathering frenzy of the commercial Christmas season, we seek an Advent time of intimacy, tenderness, and simplicity. Visual symbols might include the angel's trumpet, the root or tree of Jesse, and the plea: "*Maranatha*: Come, Jesus, come." Figures from the journey to Bethlehem can also make their appearance.

ADVENT COLORS

Churches used to associate Advent with a color linked to penitence, the color violet. These days the primary color of Advent decoration is more typically blue, a color we associate with expectancy and devotion, and with Mary, the mother of the Christ child. Advent hangings and banners are crafted plain, in quiet hues. Their fabrics are often left rough and coarsely woven, to remind us of the poverty of Mary and Joseph and the humility of the Bethlehem birth.

In public worship, the attire (or vestments) of worship leaders can help, in the words of the mystic Evelyn Underhill, to "make visible the spirit of worship." Worshiping communities do this in different ways. Whether leaders wear street clothes of a particular color or are attired in historically symbolic robes, it is helpful for new participants to be able to identify who worship leaders are by their clothing. Worship is both something we each do spontaneously and something we all do together. Those who have been called to certain functions in public worship serve as representatives of the community.

The white alb, a simple full-length garment reminiscent of baptismal robes, signals continuity between those who worship now and the community of Christ's disciples through the ages. The simplicity of this apparel can also help worshipers focus their attention on God, and avoid being distracted by a leader's personality or style.

The other common vestment in our era is the stole, which for some has become a symbol of ordered ministry. Others of us prefer the ancient usage of the stole as a sign of worship leadership, whoever wears it. The color of the stole highlights the season. Generally speaking, worship leaders in churches around the world now wear blue to evoke the feeling of Advent. But on special occasions throughout the year, such as baptisms, ordinations, marriages or funerals – whenever we celebrate "new life" in the Spirit – the white or gold of Easter, or even the red of Pentecost, are helpful colors.

THE ADVENT WREATH

The Advent wreath is perhaps the most popular custom for church and home through the Season of Advent. Its roots date back to ancient times in northern Europe, when torches were mounted in evergreen-decorated wagon wheels, to encourage the sun to brighten the dark days of winter. This custom had been Christianized in Germany by the 16th century, and quickly spread throughout Europe.

An Advent wreath usually consists of four colored candles (probably blue) of the same size, arranged around a larger white "Christ" candle. One of the outer candles is lighted the first Sunday of Advent, and another each Sunday, until all four Advent candles are lighted. Through the week, the appropriate candles can be lighted whenever people are gathered together. Finally, on Christmas Eve or during the first worship service of Christmas Day, the Christ candle in the center is lighted with the cry: "Christ is born!"

Here is a simple way to put together an Advent wreath. You will need:

- one round metal tray
- five inexpensive glass candle holders
- some evergreen branches and some brightly colored ribbon or tinsel or Christmas tree ornaments

- five candles. (We suggest four blue candles and one large white "Christ" candle for the center. Many sets of Advent candles have one rose-colored candle for *Gaudete* or Joy Sunday, the third week in Advent, and that's fine.)

Place the white candle in the center of the tray, and the other four candles – one for each week of Advent – around the edge of the tray.

Cover the tray and surround the candle holders with evergreen, ribbon, and tinsel to sparkle in the candlelight. (Keep anything flammable well away from the candles!) You will find a ritual for lighting Advent candles in the section on *Rituals for Advent*.

THE JESSE TREE

Decorating a bare branch with symbols of the ways God prepared for Christ's coming anticipates the "Christmas tree" to come.

Jesse was the father of Israel's King David, and the people of Israel expected their Messiah to be a descendent of King David. So "Son of Jesse" was one of the titles they applied to the Messiah they longed for. The prophet Isaiah (10:33–11:2) wrote that God would cut down all the mighty trees of Israel, but that the Spirit of God would rest upon a shoot "from the stump of Jesse." Another prophet, Jeremiah, also predicted that a "righteous branch" would come from Jesse's line (23:5).

The Jesse tree recalls our history as people God cares for, and it reminds us how Jesus came to us through the history of ancient Israel.

To create a Jesse tree, set a large, bare branch at the front of the church or in a central place in your home. Ask the children to make symbols of God's actions through the history of the Hebrew people. Symbols could include Adam and Eve's apple, Noah's rainbow or ark, a tent for Abraham and Sarah, the basket in which the Pharaoh's daughter rescued Moses, the sandals of John the Baptist, a hammer and saw for Joseph, and a piece of blue cloth for Mary. Hang the symbols on the branch as the stories are told or read from the Bible week by week.

THE ADVENT JOURNEY

A lovely way to make visible the Christmas story during Advent is to make figurines of Joseph, Mary and the donkey, the baby Jesus, the Magi, and several shepherds and their sheep. Start Mary and Joseph on their journey to Bethlehem, moving from a far corner of the sanctuary, or your home, on the first Sunday in Advent. Start the Magi off from another far corner the second Sunday, and move Mary and Joseph a bit closer. Start the shepherds and sheep on their journey the third Sunday, and move all the others closer still. On the fourth Sunday in Advent, move Mary, Joseph, the donkey, and the sheep and shepherds to the front of the sanctuary. Place the baby Jesus in the manger on Christmas Eve. Complete the journey of the Magi during Twelfth Night or Epiphany celebrations (January 6), or on Epiphany Sunday.

3. Celebrations in the Advent season

THE FEAST OF SAINT NICHOLAS: DECEMBER 6

Human beings have always caught glimpses of holiness through certain people. Many cultures call these persons "saints." The original Saint Nicholas, Bishop of Myra, is the origin of our tradition of Santa Claus. St. Nicholas is said to have lived in Asia Minor (the region we now know as Turkey) about 325 C.E.

St. Nicholas was a giver, who did good deeds of love and justice in secret. His feast day comes early in the Season of Advent, as if to help prepare our hearts for the gift God gives in Christ, and the gifts we can give to one another.

St. Nicholas lives among us when we continue the work of secret giving. The spirit of St. Nicholas can fill church and community and every home with mysterious acts of kindness. During Advent, every person can be a "St. Nicholas," engaged in many quiet good deeds.

To this day many children, especially in the Netherlands, find gold coins (or gold-covered chocolate ones) in their shoe on the feast of Saint Nicholas. And many children in North America hang up a stocking on Christmas Eve. The late night gifts come from Sint Nikolass, Sinterklaas, the secret gift-giver we have come to call Santa Claus!

Myth conveys a reality we really can't describe in other ways. It is probably best *not* to confuse the inner truth of St. Nicholas with Santa at the local shopping center. Santa at the store is dressed up in a costume; children will soon consider him not "for real." But we can know all our lives that the loving kindness of St. Nicholas is real every day in our hearts.

The feast of St. Nicholas can fire the spirit of giving, and entice us with a taste of what's to come. On December 6, in the darkness and hush of early morning, gather together around a candle-lit table where each plate is heaped with Christmas goodies. And at each place (courtesy of St. Nick, of course!) let each person find a small gift.

4. Rituals for Advent

These rituals and blessings can be adapted for large gatherings like Sunday morning worship, for small-group meetings, or for families at home. Decide in advance who will lead, who will read, and who will take responsibility for the actions.

Advent candle-lighting rituals

WEEK 1

Prepare the wreath itself in advance. Instructions for creating your own Advent wreath are included in *The beauty of Advent* section. When the people have gathered, you can use the following words, or something similar, to light the first candle.

> **The Advent wreath is a symbol**
> of God's holy love,
> shining like light on the earth.
> It is round because love never ends.
> It is green because love always grows.

The candle in the center is called the Christ candle, a sign of love lighting the world.
Now light the first candle.

> **We light the candle of hope.**
> Hope is like a candle in the night.
> As we light this first candle,
> we celebrate the hope
> that we have in Jesus Christ,
> who came to bring hope to the world.
> We pray for the day when God's hope
> is fulfilled for all creation.
> Come, Jesus, come.

After a few moments, say the blessing for this first week in Advent:

> **Holy Presence, you ask us**
> to open our hearts to the Christ child.
> In this season of waiting,
> we make our hearts ready
> by thanking you for what gives us hope.

Invite those present to remember something which helps them to feel hopeful. Then continue:

> **Blessed Creator,**
> as you share your gifts with us
> may we delight in this time,
> and be strengthened to share
> your gifts with others. Amen.

WEEK 2

During the second week in Advent, use this ritual (or something similar) to light two candles when people gather. You may need to replace the candles from time to time as they burn down. Decide in advance who will lead, who will read, and who will take responsibility for the actions.

Light the first candle, the one lit for the first week of Advent. As you light the candle, read the following:

> **We light this candle of hope.**
> We pray for the day when God's hope
> is fulfilled through the presence
> of Christ in the world.
> Come, Jesus, come.

Pause for a moment, and then light the second candle.

> **We light this candle of peace.**
> Peace is like a candle in the night.
> As we light this second candle,
> we celebrate the peace
> that God promises will come,
> the peace that we have

in Jesus Christ.
We pray for the day
when God's peace is fulfilled
for all creation.
Come, Jesus, come.

After a few moments, say the blessing for the second week in Advent.

Holy Presence, you ask us
to open our hearts to the Christ child.
In this season of waiting,
we make our hearts ready
by thanking you for all that gives
peace.

Invite those present to remember something which gives peace, in themselves, to those they know, or to the world. Then continue:

Blessed Creator,
as you share your gifts with us
may we delight in this time,
and be strengthened to share
your gifts with others. Amen.

WEEK 3
During the third week of Advent, light three candles when people gather. Remember to decide in advance who will lead, who will read, and who will take responsibility for the actions.

Light the first candle, the one lit for the first week in Advent. As you light the candle, read the following:

We light this candle of hope.
We pray for the day when God's hope
is fulfilled through the presence
of Christ in the world.
Come, Jesus, come.

Pause for a moment, then light the second candle.

We light this candle of peace.
We pray for the day
when God's peace is fulfilled
through the presence of Christ
in the world.
Come, Jesus, come.

Pause for a moment, and then light the third candle. If your set of candles has a pink candle, this is the week to light the pink one.

We light this candle of joy.
Joy is like a candle in the night.
As we light this third candle,
we celebrate the joy
of every healing and renewal,
the joy that is ours in Jesus Christ.
We pray for the day when God's joy
is fulfilled for all creation.
Come, Jesus, come.

After a few moments, say the blessing for the third week in Advent.

Holy Presence, you ask us
to open our hearts to the Christ child.
In this season of waiting,
we make our hearts ready
by thanking you for all that gives joy.

Invite those present to remember someone or something which gives joy. Then continue:

Blessed Creator,
as you share your gifts with us
may we delight in this time,
and be strengthened to share
your gifts with others. Amen.

WEEK 4

During the fourth week of Advent, use the ritual which follows to light all four colored candles when people gather. Decide in advance who will lead, who will read, and who will take responsibility for the actions.

Light the first candle, the one lit for the first week in Advent. As you light the candle, read the following:

> **We light the candle of hope.**
> We pray for the day
> when God's hope is fulfilled
> through the presence of Christ
> in the world.
> Come, Jesus, come.

Pause for a moment, and then light the second candle.

> **We light the candle of peace.**
> We pray for the day
> when God's peace is fulfilled
> through the presence of Christ
> in the world.
> Come, Jesus, come.

Pause for a moment, and then light the third candle.

> **We light the candle of joy.**
> We pray for the day
> when God's joy is fulfilled
> through the presence of Christ
> in the world.
> Come, Jesus, come.

Pause for a moment, and then light the fourth candle.

> **We light the candle of love.**
> Love is like a candle in the night.
> As we light this fourth candle,
> we celebrate the love which
> strengthened Mary and Joseph,
> the love that is ours in Jesus Christ.
> We pray for the day
> when God's love is fulfilled
> for all creation.
> Come, Jesus, come.

After a few moments, say the blessing for the fourth week in Advent.

> **Holy Presence, you ask us**
> to open our hearts to the Christ child.
> In this season of waiting,
> we make our hearts ready
> by thanking you for love in our lives.

Invite those present to remember someone they love, or someone from whom they receive love. Then continue:

> **Blessed Creator,**
> as you share your gifts with us
> may we delight in this time,
> and be strengthened to share
> your gifts with others. Amen.

A dramatized candle-lighting ritual

WEEK 1: THE LIGHT OF GOD'S FAITHFULNESS

Child: Why do we light candles when we're waiting for Christmas?

Adult: We light candles during the Season of Advent to remember the ways God brings light to our world.

Child: What is the meaning of this first candle?

Adult lights the first blue candle.

Adult: When we light this candle, we remember God's promises to our fore-parents, Abraham and Sarah.

Child: Tell us the story of Abraham and Sarah.

Adult: Abraham and Sarah were very, very old when God promised them that they would have a baby. Sarah was so surprised she laughed! But she did bear a child and she and Abraham named the baby Isaac. Because Abraham and Sarah were God's faithful servants, God promised them that their descendants would be as many as the stars in the sky. And God promised that all the nations of earth would find blessing through Isaac, through Isaac's children, and his children's children. God promised to be faithful to Abraham and Sarah, and through Abraham and Sarah to all people. In the light of this candle, we remember God's promise to be with us always, as light in every kind of darkness.

Child: Thanks be to God!

WEEK 2: THE LIGHT OF GOD'S PROPHETS

Child lights the first blue candle.

Child: Why do we light candles when we're waiting for Christmas?

Adult: We light candles during the Season of Advent to remember the ways God brings light to our world.

Child: The candle of Abraham and Sarah reminds us that God has promised to be faithful. What is the meaning of the second candle?

Adult lights a second candle.

Adult: When we light this candle, we remember that God sent the prophets to prepare the people of Israel for the coming of Christ.

Child: Tell us the story of the prophets.

Adult: For hundreds of years before Christ was born, God's people were proud and very stubborn. God sent prophets among them to tell them to follow God's way of shalom — the way of peace with justice. The prophets taught that God would send a leader to guide the nations, and to show them how to live a different way. "Live in hope," said the prophets, "God is faithful. Your light will come!" In the light of this candle, we remember the prophets' teaching that God will send a Prince of Peace, to bring light to the darkness of the world.

Child: Thanks be to God!

WEEK 3: THE LIGHT OF GOD'S PROMISES

Child lights two blue candles.

Child: Why do we light candles when we're waiting for Christmas?

Adult: We light candles during the Season of Advent to remember the ways God brings light to our world.

Child: The candle of Abraham and Sarah reminds us that God has promised to be faithful. The candle of the prophets reminds us God has promised a Prince of Peace is coming to the world. What is the meaning of the third candle?

Adult lights a third candle – the pink candle, if there is one.

Adult: When we light this candle, we remember that God sent John the Baptist to prepare the way for the Messiah.

Child: Tell us the story of John the Baptist.

Adult: Mary, the mother of Jesus, had a cousin whose name was Elizabeth. Elizabeth and her husband, Zechariah, were too old to have a baby. But the angel Gabriel came to Elizabeth to tell her that she would have a baby, and that she should call the baby John. When John was a young man, he was inspired by the Spirit to preach on the banks of the Jordan River. John said the people should express their sorrow for their mistakes, and should change how they lived day-to-day. He said they should be baptized as a sign of their new life, that they should share all they had, and do no harm. When the people asked John if he was the Messiah, John said that he baptized with water, but that the Messiah who was coming would baptize with fire and Holy Spirit. In the light of this candle, we remember the words of John the Baptist, that baptism in Christ will bring light to the darkness of our lives.

Child: Thanks be to God!

WEEK 4: LIGHT FOR THE WORLD THROUGH SERVING GOD

Child lights three candles, including the pink candle if there is one.

Child: Why do we light candles when we're waiting for Christmas?

Adult: We light candles during the Season of Advent to remember the ways God brings light to our world.

Child: The candle of Abraham and Sarah reminds us God has promised to be faithful. The candle of the prophets reminds us God has promised that a Prince of Peace is coming to the world. And the candle of John the Baptist reminds us that we are baptized in Holy Spirit. What is the meaning of the fourth candle?

Adult lights the fourth candle.

Adult: When we light this fourth candle, we remember that God came to us as Jesus the Messiah through the faith of a young girl named Mary.

Child: Tell us the story of Mary.

Adult: When Mary was a young woman, before she and Joseph could be married and live together, the angel Gabriel told Mary that she would conceive and have a baby. "You shall call his name Jesus," the angel told Mary, "and God will give him the throne of his ancestor, David, and his kingdom shall be without end." Mary asked the angel how this could be when she had never had a husband. And the angel said to Mary that the child would be the Holy Child of God. Then Mary said she was God's willing servant: "Behold I am the handmaid of God." In the light of this candle, we remember that God's light comes to the darkness of our world through our faith and our willingness to serve.

Child: Thanks be to God!

5. Sharing our story in Advent

The Hebrew people were waiting for a leader they called their Messiah. While they were waiting, some of their prophets described visions of the harmony the Messiah would bring through justice, loving-kindness, and humility. This is the "story" Jesus lived. And it's the story St. Paul passed on to the non-Jewish followers of Jesus who later became the Christian church. Because Greek was the universal language of that time, the Hebrew word "Messiah," which means "anointed leader," became the Greek word "Christ," which means "oil of anointing." In this way, the longings of Israel for a Messiah became the Christ story of the Christian church.

Our Advent stories are rooted in the biblical stories of Israel, in the prophets' expectations of the coming Messiah, in the stories of the church, and in our stories of life and the world.

The exercises which follow have been written for groups with one participant in the role of leader. They can be easily adapted for prayer partners or for personal use. Decide before you start who will read the scripture passages, and who will lead the storytelling today.

When discussing stories that refer to a specific city in the ancient world, it will help participants if you can point out these locations on a map, so that they can connect the story's people and their problems with a particular place.

Remember to choose discussions which match the level of comfort and familiarity among those who are present, and remind participants they are always free to "pass." Let the stories and questions unfold as slowly as needed.

Close the session with prayer. You may find it helpful to hold hands in a circle as you pray. The leader can invite group participants to offer the hopes and prayers of their hearts, and then start the prayer with his/her own words. As the leader finishes, he/she squeezes the hand of the next person in the circle who either prays or passes on the "squeeze" to the next person in the circle.

Hope: the first week in Advent

In the first week of Advent, we share stories of a hope that is rooted in God's faithful love.

ABRAHAM AND SARAH

Genesis 17:1–22 (God's promise to Abraham and Sarah) Read aloud the scripture passage and the following summary. Reflect on each question and share responses.

God makes a covenant with Abraham and Sarah that their God will eventually be the God of many peoples. Nations and worldly rulers would emerge in their midst, but each household would signal its ultimate commitment to God.

- How do our children enter into the covenant that we, as a people, have with God? How can each household show its ultimate commitment to God? What faith traditions do we want to continue for our families? How do faith traditions give us hope?
- When you were born, what did your people hope for you? What did they fear? Where did your people put their trust? Where do you put your trust?
- To which "people" do you feel you belong? How have your people cared for you? What gifts have the values and beliefs of your people given you? What challenges? How does your connection to your people contribute to your sense of who you are in the world?

MIDWIVES SAVE THE INFANT MOSES
Exodus 1:15–2:10 (saving the baby Moses)
Read aloud the scripture passage and the following summary. Reflect on each question and share responses.

The midwives Shiphrah and Puah could not have known that Moses would grow up to lead his people out of slavery. What they did know was that no people should destroy another people by killing their babies. So Shiphrah and Puah disobeyed their ruler's command.
- Think of a modern instance when civil disobedience preserved people from violence and opened the way to new life. How can we know when God wants us to break the rules? What rules did we learn when we were young? Which rules would we want to pass on to our children? Which rules might we wish them to resist?
- Think of a time in your life when you yourself resisted evil. How did resisting evil bring you hope? How can your turning from evil give hope to others?

THE LIGHT OF THE MESSIAH
Isaiah 9:2 ("A people who walked in darkness")
Read aloud the scripture passage and the following summary. Reflect on each question and share responses.

Isaiah speaks of "a people who walked in darkness." The people of ancient Israel longed for a world without exploitation or violence, a world that was open and friendly.
- What are our hopes as a people? Where in our world are other peoples now in need of hope? What would bring light to their lives? How are we connected to these people?
- Remember a time when you felt grieved or afraid. What "light" gave you hope? How can you share hope with others?

Peace:
the second week in Advent

In the second week of Advent, we share stories about making peace.

ISAIAH'S PROPHECY
Isaiah 11:6–9 ("the wolf shall live with the lamb")
Read aloud the scripture passage and the following summary. Reflect on each question and share responses.

Isaiah paints an idyllic picture where even the wolf can live peacefully with the lamb. By extension, people will no longer fear violence from either animals or other human beings.
- What does this passage tell us about how to live with differences? If all the peoples on the earth felt secure and connected, how would the world be different? Suggest some ways we can honor other peoples.
- What is the role of the child in this vision? Can you think of a time when you were able to work through a conflict without fear or anger? What helped you feel safe and loved? How can you help those around you to feel safe and loved?

JOHN THE BAPTIST
Matthew 3:1–12, Mark 1:1–8, and Luke 3:1–18 (John "prepares the way")
Read aloud the scripture passages and the following summary. Reflect on each question and share responses.

John the Baptist declares that he has come to prepare the way for the Messiah. He demands that his hearers repent – turn around, change their ways of living.
- Why is John's good news such hard news? How could the powers of the world "turn around" to make peace? What hardens their hearts?
- Think of a time when a conflicted situation

was resolved in such a way that relationships became stronger. What made it possible for people to "turn" their hearts around? Why is it crucial to acknowledge your own part in a problem? Why is this hard?

- What within yourself would you most want to change, to strengthen your capacity for peace? What would free you to change?
- Where are there conflicts in your life which are hurtful? What prevents you from healing your relationships? What steps can you take?

Joy:
the third week in Advent

In the third week of Advent, we share stories of unexpected joy.

JOY WILL COME THROUGH SHALOM.

Isaiah 61:1–3a ("The spirit of God is upon me")
Read aloud the scripture passage and the following summary. Reflect on each question and share responses.

The Hebrew word *shalom* is often translated as "peace," but the Hebrew understanding of shalom includes all our notions of peace, justice, health, and harmony for creation. The prophets envisioned what shalom would be like when the teaching of the Messiah was fulfilled. Isaiah gives examples of what to expect. Jesus chose this passage to describe his own ministry (Luke 4:18–19).

- What does it mean to be oppressed? (A dictionary might be helpful here!) Which nations of the world could we describe as oppressed? How is their situation like the plight of ancient Israel under Babylon's rule, or Judea under Roman domination?
- Who are the oppressed in our community? What good news would give these people joy?
- When has your own heart been broken? When have you felt like a captive? How has God helped you to heal? How has joy come to you? How have you shared it?

JOY CAME TO ELIZABETH AND ZECHARIAH

Luke 1:5–24 and 57–80 (Elizabeth and Zechariah are promised a child)
Read aloud the scripture passage and the following summary. Reflect on each question and share responses.

In the biblical world, childless women were ostracized and disgraced. So John's miraculous birth restored his mother, Elizabeth, to relationship within her community. With the birth of John the Baptist a new future was born — for his family, his communitys and the world.

- Think of a situation where something unexpected strengthened relationships and transformed sorrow into joy. How was the Spirit at work in the persons involved? What new future was born?
- When has joy come to you in ways you didn't expect? How did trusting God make a difference? How did your joy change the future?

Love:
the fourth week in Advent

In the fourth week of Advent, we share stories of Spirit-led loving.

GOD WITH US

Isaiah 7:14 (the child to be called Emmanuel)
Read aloud the scripture passage and the following summary. Reflect on each question and share responses.

Isaiah presents the image of a young woman with child. The name of the child will be Emmanuel, which means "God with us."

- How is God's dream for creation to be fulfilled?
- How and where is God with us now?
- What is our part in God's unfolding creativity?

MARY AND JOSEPH

Luke 1:26–56 and Matthew 1:18–25 (love stories) Read aloud the scripture passages and the following summary. Reflect on each question and share responses.

When Mary became pregnant and the baby wasn't Joseph's, her own life was very much in danger. Women in those times were often stoned for adultery, and Joseph would have been humiliated by Mary's pregnancy.

- Mary's reaction to the news of her pregnancy links Christ with God's love for the lowly. Why did Mary see herself as "lowly"? What does this say about God's dream of how things should be? How are the lowly treated in our community? In what ways are we ourselves lowly?
- How were Mary and Joseph able to overcome fear and shame? What empowered them to choose love instead? What fears and humiliations are you facing? How are you being asked to change?
- How could trusting God make a difference? Who is God asking you to love? What steps can you take?

6. Embodied prayers for Advent

In this season of waiting, with all its tensions and stress, it is wonderful to remember that holiness comes to the world through a physical body. As the Christ child was conceived in the body of Mary, life and love come to our bodies too.

We long to feel the breath of Spirit in our bodies. The Hebrew word for Spirit also means "breath." The Bible tells us God breathed into the first human's nostrils and the creature became a living being. (Genesis 2:7) When we breathe *in* strength and courage, and breathe *out* fear and pain, God breathes new life into us.

Since all our life systems are interlinked in subtle ways, changing our breathing affects our whole self. Deep, slow breathing is the body's natural way of moving into relaxation, which in turn helps us attend to our experience. Combining breathing and prayer can help us focus and center on the presence of the Spirit, and deepen our awareness of that Spirit in our physical being.

INSTRUCTIONS

These prayers can be part of daily spiritual disciplines. They are written for groups, for prayer partners, or for personal use.

When used by a group, one participant will need to assume the role of guide. Decide in advance who will lead the prayers today, letting each prayer unfold slowly and gently.

For an effective pace, we suggest you take two full breaths whenever you see "…" before you start the next phrase. If a time frame is suggested, remember that one minute equals about eight full breaths. Give your group permission to breathe normally at any time, especially if they feel distressed or anxious. Tell the group never to strain or hold the breath. A deep breath is gentle and relaxed.

PREPARATION

Always begin embodied prayer sessions with this exercise. If you are practicing embodied prayers alone, read through the following instructions carefully before starting. If you are leading a group, read the following slowly and calmly aloud, with appropriate pauses.

Sit comfortably, with your spine fairly straight. Close your eyes. Without changing how you breathe, pay attention to the sensations of breathing … Pay attention to the sensation of breath moving in and out of your nose or your mouth … Can you feel the path of breath as it moves through your body into your lungs? … Can you feel the breath move your chest and rib cage, and then release again as you breathe out? … Continue to follow the flow of your breathing, without straining to do anything …

Now breathe in and send the breath into your abdomen as though you are filling your stomach. Exhale, letting the stomach fall back to normal. Breathing in, your belly rises; breathing out, it falls back. Breathe this relaxed "belly breath" for one minute … Don't strain or force your breath … Relax as you breathe in and your belly rises, and relax as you breathe out …

As you breathe quietly, begin to listen to the sounds in the room … Move your fingers and your toes. Open your eyes when you are ready.

SPIRIT BREATH

Sit comfortably with your eyes closed, and gently focus on your breath … As you relax with your breathing, begin to count silently as you breathe. Breathe in and count slowly, one, two, three, then breathe out, one, two, three. What is your natural counting pattern as you breathe? Focus on this for a few minutes … Now, try breathing in for four counts and out for four counts … Now try breathing in for six counts and out for six counts … Can you lengthen the count and still be comfortable, without forcing the breath? …

Now, go back to a natural rhythm for you … Settle in on a breath that is one count longer breathing out than it is breathing in. Perhaps you will inhale for three counts and exhale for

four … Feel how this breath pattern helps you sense that breathing out is active, and breathing in is passive, that the air simply flows back inside you without any effort. Stay with this pattern of breath for two minutes … Breathe effortlessly … Relax with each exhalation … Feel the Spirit breath coming into your body … Feel how God breathes you …

As you breathe quietly, begin to listen to the sounds in the room … Move your fingers and your toes. Open your eyes when you are ready.

AWAITING CHRIST

Sit comfortably with your eyes closed. Bring your attention to your breath. Let the breath flow in and out with ease … Each exhalation releases tension … Feel how God breathes you and relaxes you … Feel how the breath prepares you for the gift of God's holy love …

As you breathe, silently say to yourself "I fill myself with hope as I await the gift of Christ" … "I fill myself with hope" … "I fill myself with hope" …

Now, as you breathe, silently say to yourself "I fill myself with peace as I await the gift of Christ" … "I fill myself with peace" … "I fill myself with peace" …

Now silently say to yourself "I fill myself with joy as I await the gift of Christ" … "I fill myself with joy" … "I fill myself with joy" …

Now, as you breathe, silently say to yourself "I fill myself with love as I await the gift of Christ" … "I fill myself with love" … "I fill myself with love" …

As you breathe quietly, begin to listen to the sounds in the room … Move your fingers and your toes. Open your eyes when you are ready.

Invite participants to share their experience as they are comfortable. Were their experiences of each word different?

PEACE BREATHING

Close your eyes and gently focus on your breath. Let your breath deepen as you relax and let go of the day … As you inhale, imagine that you breathe peace into your soul. As you exhale, breathe out worry and tension. Focus on this for one minute, breathing in peace, exhaling fear …

As you inhale, imagine that you breathe peace into your heart, and when you exhale you spread peace over your family … Imagine releasing barriers between yourself and those you love. For one minute, inhale peace and exhale peace to your family …

Now, inhale peace into your soul, and as you exhale, imagine spreading peace over your community. For one minute, inhale peace and exhale peace to your community …

Now, as you breathe, find peace in your soul. Feel your peace with God … Say to yourself, "Come, Jesus, come," or find your own words to invite peace to come …

As you breathe quietly, begin to listen to the sounds in the room … Move your fingers and your toes. Open your eyes when you are ready.

A DANCING PRAYER

The traditional Shaker song and dance, "Simple Gifts," helps us express bodily the Advent theme of turning to the light by seeking God in new directions. Youngsters and oldsters can learn this dance easily together. Dance facing each other in a circle, around the edges of your worship space, or around the table at a festive meal. If some are watching while others dance, dancing in a semi-circle facing the watchers may help them to feel more included.

"'Tis a gift to be simple, 'tis a gift to be free."	☞	Everyone take four steps forward, holding both hands about waist high, with palms up. Move the wrists gently up and down, which is the Shaker gesture for receiving grace.
"'Tis a gift to come down where we ought to be."	☞	Take four steps backward, hands out, palms down. Move down-turned wrists gently up and down, the Shaker gesture for turning away evil.
"And when we find ourselves in a place just right, 'Twill be in the valley of love and delight."	☞	Repeat the pattern above, stepping first forward then backward.
"When true"	☞	Raise hands to the open prayer position, at shoulder height with palms turned upward. Take a step to the right with the right foot and bring the left foot to meet the right. Bend both knees slightly when stepping.
"simplicity is gained"	☞	Repeat the pattern of stepping and bending, to the left.
"To bow and to bend"	☞	Repeat the stepping and bending, to the right.
"We will not be ashamed."	☞	Repeat, to the left.
"To turn, and to turn will be our delight"	☞	All make a full turn to the right, ending up facing the center. Keep hands in the open prayer position.
"'Till by turning and turning, we come round right."	☞	All make a full turn to the left, ending up facing the center. Join hands at the end.

7. Written prayers for Advent

These written prayers for the Season of Advent can be used for shared or personal devotions.

Prayers for delighting in God

Turn to God in all things,
and in all things see God. Amen.

(Mechtild of Magdeburg, 1210–1294)

Holy Spirit, you are joy
of breathing creatures
and growing earth.
You are grace of stars and wind
and compassion of the waves of the sea.
Speak to us of promise
as the Christ-light among us.
Come to us, and dwell with us in love.
Amen.

God the Beloved has opened a door;
the Child of Mary hastens to help us.
Christ of Hope, Door of joy,
Golden Sun of hill and meadow,
all is One! At your rising, we await
you! Amen.

(Adapted from Gaelic, 6th century)

God is a circle
whose center is everywhere
and whose circumference is nowhere.
Amen.

(Meister Eckhart, 1260–1327)

Beloved in the Spirit,
the Christ child will soon
turn our shadows to light.
God makes our hearts ready for life!
Amen.

In the power of the Spirit,
light is coming!
May love's pure light in Jesus,
the light which shines for all the world,
the light which no shadow
can ever overcome,
shine upon us this day and forever!
Amen.

By the power of the Spirit,
holy love becomes flesh
through the courage and strength
of the lowly.
Christ comes to heal creation! Amen.

Prayers for transformation and renewal

God who shines upon us
to restore us to wholeness,
grant us grace so to wait for your
promised Messiah,
that molded by your hand we may
reveal your compassion,
and our faith may light the world
with your love.
This we ask in the name of your
Christ child, our Beloved. Amen.

Come to us, Advent God,
with your glorious light,
that our lives may show the joy
of your love.
With Mary, we pray:
may your name be holy,
may the hungry be filled,
may the proud be scattered and
the oppressed lifted up,
may your love be with your people
forever.

Come, Source of our Longing,
with healing on your wings. Amen.

God of the weak and the strong,
come to us
for we, too, have been blind, deaf,
and lame.
Heal us of our infirmities
for we, too, have known fear.
Comfort us with your presence
for we, too, have languished in despair.
Make us whole, to love and serve
in the name of Jesus Christ.
In silence, Holy Presence, we seek you
… *(silence)* … Amen.

Advent God, sustain us
as we journey to the stable.
Strengthen our hands
and make firm our feeble knees,
open our eyes to the dawning of the sun,
and guide our steps on the pathways
of peace. Amen.

Loving God, we believe
in your commitment to the worth
of each creature.
We believe in the compassion of Jesus
who heals the pain of outcasts.
We believe in the Spirit
calling us to ways of justice and peace.
So where some are exploited,
where some are excluded,
where some abuse their power,
there we worship an idol, not you.
Maker of the world,
send your Christ child to change us.
Inspire us to faithfulness,
to generosity, to holy rage,
so we alter the future until it conforms
to the shape of your community of joy.
In silence, Holy Presence, we seek you.
Amen.

Tender God, you send us
to the world
to live your love,
to share your promise,
and be restored by your Spirit.
Refresh our hearts, we pray.
Give us *(hope, peace, joy, love)*
in the coming of the Christ-child
who shows the way of compassion.
Amen.

Holy God, you come to us
in unexpected ways,
through the little and the lowly,
through hearts that are willing to love
as you call us to love.
Help us open our hearts to your
Bethlehem baby,
so the world can be blessed
by the Christ-light
which shines through our lives. Amen.

O Day-spring,
brightness of the light everlasting,
sun of righteousness:
Come and enlighten
them that sit in darkness
and the shadow of death. Amen.

(Traditional, Vespers antiphon)

O God, you have searched us
and known us.
You know when we hunger,
not for kindness or justice,
but for comfort, success and contentment.
You know when our fine words
hide closed, hardened hearts,
when we pass by
the world's hurting people.
Give breath to your Spirit
within us, O God.
Be born in us again, as generosity,
as tenderness, as freedom.
Come, O come, Emmanuel. Amen.

God, grant us grace
to desire you with our whole heart,
that so desiring, we seek and find you;
and so finding we may love you;
and loving you we may turn
from those sins
from which you have redeemed us;
for the sake of Jesus Christ. Amen.

(Adapted from St. Anselm, 1033–1109)

May the God of peace
sanctify you wholly;
and may your spirit and soul and body
be kept sound and blameless
at the coming of Jesus. Amen.

(1 Thessalonians 5:23)

May hope in Christ
free us for service,
May peace in God free us to share,
May joy in the Spirit free us for action,
May holy love free us to care! Amen.

Loving God, you promised
the Messiah would be with us
to show us how to live
in peace with justice.
As the people of Israel
waited long ago,
keep us watchful for your presence
among us.
When we're frightened, remind us
that the night is soon over
and the morning light of dawn
surely comes.
Help us lay aside our shadows.
Make us ready for the Christ child
as all creation waits for fulfillment.
Amen.

Tender God, who offers hope when
we are grieving or afraid,
keep us safely through this night and
help us ready our hearts
to live as people of the light
in the morning. Amen.

Prayers of thanks and dedication

Thank you, God, for
(those we love, God's gifts to us, etc.).
While we wait for Christ's coming,
we give thanks for the hope
you have promised.
We name our hopes for tomorrow
(hopes for ourselves, those we love,
and for the world).
As we prepare for Christ's presence,
help us share hope with others
so your hope for creation is fulfilled.
We pray especially for (name some ways
for us to share hope).
We give the world into your care,
Holy Presence,
trusting your loving light to come.
Come into our lives,
we pray in Jesus' name. Amen.

Thank you, God, for
(those we love, God's gifts, etc.).
While we wait for Christ's coming,
we give thanks for the peace
you have promised.
For tomorrow, we pray for peace
(describe what peace is like).
As we prepare for Christ's presence,
help us share your peace with others
in ways of justice, kindness,
and humility.
We pray especially for (name some ways
for us to share peace).

We give the world into your care,
Holy Presence,
trusting your loving light to come.
Come into our lives,
we pray in Jesus' name. Amen.

Thank you, God, for
(those we love, God's gifts, etc.).
While we wait for Christ's coming,
we give thanks for the joy
you have promised.
For tomorrow, we pray joy will come
(describe your joy).
As we prepare for Christ's presence,
help us share joy with others,
so all may know the joy of your love.
We pray especially for (ways for us to
share joy).
We give the world into your care,
Holy Presence,
trusting your loving light to come.
Come into our lives,
we pray in Jesus' name. Amen.

Thank you, God, for
(those who love us, and those we love).
While we wait for Christ's coming,
we give thanks for the love
you have promised.
For tomorrow, we pray love will come
(describe what love's presence will mean.)
As we prepare for Christ's presence,
help us share your love with others
and strengthen us to love as you love.
We pray especially for (ways for us to
share love).
We give the world into your care,
Holy Presence,
trusting your loving light to come.
Come into our lives,
we pray in Jesus' name. Amen.

God of Promise, we give thanks
for Mary and Joseph,
who told the stories of their people,
who sang the songs of ancient Israel,
who held in their hearts
the burning words of the prophets,
and recognized the truth
of angel voices.
We give you thanks for the Christ
who has come
and is coming,
who is even now among us. Amen.

Let us go to the world
with its pain and its wonder,
go to Bethlehem,
with Mary and Joseph,
go with joy and thankful hearts,
to love and serve. Amen.

Holy Mystery of Love,
we give you thanks for the gift
of your outpouring Spirit,
for the courage of Mary,
for Joseph's willing heart,
for glad tidings of comfort and joy.
Receive the gifts we offer that
your light may shine among us
and your love may be re-born
in the world.
With Christ, in Christ, and through
Christ, in the unity of the Spirit,
all power and possibility is yours,
God most Holy,
now and forever. Amen.

Prayers for the world, ourselves, and others

God of all, we pray to you
for those whom we love,
but see no longer.
Grant them thy peace;
let your light shine upon them forever;
and in your patient wisdom,
let your power work in them
to fulfill the perfect promise
of your love. Amen.

(*Book of Common Prayer,* 1928, restated)

Tender God of courage and comfort,
deal graciously with those who mourn,
that casting every care upon you,
they may know the consolation
of your love;
through Jesus Christ, we pray. Amen.

(*Book of Common Prayer,* 1928, restated)

For an angel of peace,
faithful guardian and guide
of our souls and our bodies,
we beseech you, O God. Amen.

(Orthodox prayer, restated.)

O God of the last and the least
and the homeless,
God of the rejected and betrayed,
Grant in this season that we may
learn the ways of justice
and live together, with kindness,
as your people.
As you watched our souls' shaping,
Look upon us now with love
as we wait for the coming
of the Christ child.
Our hope is in you. Amen.

God, you called John the Baptist
to prepare the way for peace
through the love
revealed in Jesus of Nazareth.
Grant us wisdom to turn
to the new way before us
that we may hear you call our names
and prepare for love to come
through our lives. Amen.

Holy Presence, we pray
for peace between nations,
for peace between neighbors,
and peace between lovers and friends.
We pray for deep peace between
brothers and sisters,
and for peace between parent and
child.
We pray for peace to light the living
of all your creation. Amen.

Lord, make me an instrument
of thy peace.
Where there is hatred, let me sow love;
Where there is injury, pardon;
Where there is doubt, faith;
Where there is despair, hope;
Where there is darkness, light;
Where there is sadness, joy.
O divine Master, grant
that I may not so much seek
To be consoled as to console,
To be understood as to understand,
To be loved, as to love;
For it is in giving that we receive;
It is in pardoning that we are
pardoned;
It is in dying to self that we are born
to eternal life.

(St. Francis of Assisi, 1181–1226)

God, who sent holy angels
to proclaim a new age,
open our hearts to the new age
before us, that the blind may yet see,
and the captives' release may bring
your new creation to birth.
Open our hearts
to your holy possibilities,
that we might be a healed and healing
people in your name,
rejoicing in the coming of the light.
Amen.

Holy God, you ask us to prepare
for the Christ child
with tidings of comfort and joy.
Help us share the word of (hope, peace,
joy, love)
'til the peoples of the earth
see your glory together
and walk in the ways of caring justice.
Amen.

God, of your goodness
give me yourself
for you are sufficient for me.
I cannot properly ask anything less
to be worthy of you.
If I were to ask less, I should always
be in want.
In you alone do I have all. Amen.

(Julian of Norwich, 1342–1443)

Here am I, the servant of my God.
Let it be with me according to your
word. Amen.

(Mary, in Luke 1:38)

Hail, Mary full of grace,
the Lord is with thee.
Blessed art thou among women,
and blessed is the fruit
of your womb, Jesus.
Holy Mary, Mother of God,
pray for us sinners,
now and in the hour of our death.
Amen.

(Angelic salutation, traditional, based on Luke 1)

May the God of love fill us
with joy and peace in our waiting,
that we may hope always
in the power of the Spirit,
and be free to love and serve
in Christ's name. Amen.

In the following prayer, one person should read the light text; all present respond with the dark text.

Advent God,
we have lived so long in darkness.
Shine on your people
with glorious light
that our lives may show the wonder
of your radiance.
We pray for those who follow Christ,
and for all who seek you.
God, in your love,

Come to us.

Advent God, our world awaits you.
We pray for the peoples
and leaders of every nation,
for all displaced persons,
and all who suffer from violence.
We pray for peace with justice
on the earth.
God, in your love,

Come to us.

Advent God, your creation
longs for healing.
We pray for the earth, sea, and sky
and all beings
that humankind may serve respect-
fully as stewards of your bounty.
We pray for harmony in the world
you have made.
God, in your love,

Come to us.

Advent God, your people
seek hope in your presence.
We pray for those who seek relief
from loneliness and fear,
and for those who know sickness,
want and loss.
We pray for all who await the light
and power of holy grace.
God, in your love,

Come to us.

Advent God, we pray with Mary, may
your love be with your people. Amen.

8. Guided prayers & meditations for Advent

After 313 C.E., when Christianity became legal throughout the Roman empire, many Christians started to "water down" the way they lived their faith to suit the secular world. Some men and women reacted against this change by retreating to the deserts of Egypt, Palestine, and Syria, seeking an ideal form of Christ-life.

Two significant types of prayer – the *Lectio Divina* and the "Jesus prayer" – emerged in the western church from the experience of desert fathers and mothers. Both made full use of four functions in prayer: sensing, thinking, feeling, and intuition. The common need of people who had different kinds of temperaments to pray in ways that used all four of these functions probably accounts for the continuing importance of desert spirituality and prayer forms.

Examples are written here for groups, with one participant taking on the role of guide. They can easily be adapted for prayer partners or for personal use. Decide in advance who will read the scripture passages, and who will lead the prayers, letting each prayer unfold slowly and gently. Remember to choose a prayer-style which matches the level of comfort and familiarity among those who are present, and to remind them they are always free to "pass."

Encourage participants to keep a prayer journal and to spend about ten minutes reviewing each prayer-time on paper, letting God speak through their writing or drawing.

LECTIO DIVINA

As we make our hearts ready in the Season of Advent, here is a way to listen for God's invitation through scripture or written prayers. The Latin term *Lectio Divina,* pronounced "lex-ee-oh di-vee-nuh," simply means "divine reading." You can pray this way with others or when you are alone, trusting that God's word carries something beneficial to those who receive it in faith.

When praying as a group, remind everyone that all are responsible to pray for one another. You will also be specifically responsible to pray for the person immediately to your right, that he or she may be able to respond in faith to God's invitation. Invite participants to feel free to share or to be quiet at the close of the prayer.

During Advent, consider using as a reading Psalm 42:1–2, or Isaiah 55:10–11, or other passages of scripture which speak of longing, anticipation, homecoming, or the coming of the Messiah. Offer the following guidance:

Take a few moments to come fully into the present. Sit comfortably, eyes closed. For about two minutes, focus on your breathing … Relax as you breathe, and let go of the tensions of the day … Feel the Spirit breath flowing into your body … Feel how God breathes you …

As you relax with your breathing, listen for the word of God.

Read the prayer or passage through slowly, aloud.

Listen for a word or phrase or image that attracts you. Silently repeat the word or phrase or image in rhythm with your breathing several times, in and out …

Read the prayer or passage through again slowly, aloud.

As you breathe, become aware of what God may be saying to you … What does this word or phrase or image mean to you? … How does it speak to your heart? How does it relate to your life? …

Read the prayer or passage through again slowly, aloud.

Listen to discover an invitation in the words or image, relevant to the next few days … Is God speaking through this word or image? … Through a feeling or an insight? … a desire to do or be? … How or what is God inviting you to change? … How can you respond? …

Rest quietly in God's presence … Focus only on the flow of your breathing, in and out …

Pray silently for yourself, for wisdom and courage and strength … Now pray quietly for the person to your right, that he or she will be able to respond to God's invitation … Pray for those who are in special need today … Close with a prayer or a blessing you know by heart …

As you breathe quietly, begin to listen to the sounds in the room … Move your fingers and your toes. Open your eyes when you are ready.

Invite participants to spend about ten minutes reviewing their prayer time on paper, letting God speak through their writing or drawing.

THE JESUS PRAYER (CENTERING PRAYER)

The second desert prayer which prepares our hearts for God is a form of meditation known as the "Jesus prayer," or "centering prayer." It too engages all four prayer functions to establish a deep and continuous communion with God.

In its original form, the words, "Lord Jesus Christ, have mercy on me, a sinner," are repeated over and over, either in silence or aloud, with the rhythm of breathing (sensing function). This speaking is accompanied by inner meditation on Jesus as God's instrument of salvation in our lives (thinking). Speaking and meditation draw us deeper into personal intimacy with God through Jesus (feeling). And constant repetition of these words, thoughts and feelings, as we physically breathe in and out, draws us into mystical communion (intuition).

When using the Jesus prayer, it's important to find "Jesus words" which are healing and empowering for those who are praying. Some find comfort in "Lord Jesus, have mercy." Others ease their longing with "Christ Jesus, stay with us." Some need words like, "Beloved, bring justice and joy," or "Holy Jesus, fill me and use me." One of the writers once stood with a whole congregation, praying through a time of crisis: "Brother Jesus, attend with us." Another prays throughout the day: "Holy One, grant me the grace that I need."

The only rule is this – make the words as simple as breathing. Speak the holy name on your inhale and your plea on the exhale. Continue this pattern so that every breathing in and breathing out through the day, whether conscious or not, becomes your prayer.

9. Inner reflections for Advent

And so we wait
frenzy surrounds us
our windows reflect the glitter
expectant,
we are filled with such longing
a candle's halo
pushes the shadows
and we glimpse the promise
"Prepare ye the way of the Lord"
ah, so much to do
And so we wait…

These weeks before Christmas are very busy. Both inside and outside, we are buffeted by demands to "get it right." It's easy for us to let our spiritual center slip away and to move into a kind of frenetic activity that's far from the holiness we long to touch.

During Advent, we invite you to create your own pattern of personal retreat. The value in taking quiet time for reflection is enormous. Give yourself this gift.

You will need pages for writing or a journal, and a pencil and pen. And you will need a candle. Find a place of quiet darkness where you can be alone, light your candle, pray, and write.

FIRST WEEK IN ADVENT: HOPE

Sun of the world
ever rising,
which by coming, refreshes creation,
shine into our hearts
so the mists fade away
and we walk with you
the path of holy love.

Use your pencil to draw your burning candle. Write words that describe the flame. Write words that describe what the Christ-light means to you.

- What are your hopes for your spiritual deepening?
- How does Christ's coming touch you with hope?
- How does Christ's coming enable you to share hope with others?

SECOND WEEK IN ADVENT: PEACE

May the peace of God
which passes all understanding
guard your heart and your mind
in Christ Jesus.

(Philippians 4:7, restated.)

Be with your candle in the darkness. Breathe deeply and slowly. Invite the peace of God as you breathe.

- Where do you feel the need for God's peace in your life?
- How does Christ's coming touch you with peace?
- How does Christ's coming enable you to share peace with others?

THIRD WEEK IN ADVENT: JOY

Lord Jesus be my holy guest,
my morning joy, my evening rest.
And with your heavenly love impart
your peace and joy upon my heart.

(Traditional, author unknown.)

Make your candle flame dance and flicker. Create a Joy page. Fill it with situations, places, people, animals, growing things – whatever gives you joy. If you feel inhibited about writing or drawing, make a collage of images from magazines that give you joy.

- How does Christ's coming touch you with joy?
- How does Christ's coming enable you to share joy with others?

FOURTH WEEK IN ADVENT: LOVE

So faith, hope, love abide,
these three;
and the greatest of these is love.

(1 Corinthians 13:13)

Light your candle. Reflect on the ways God comes into the world. Think particularly about your experiences of love.

- Where are you longing for love in your life? In your world?
- How does Christ's coming touch you with love?
- How does Christ's coming enable you to share love with others?

10. Activities for Advent

THE ADVENT WREATH

See the section *The beauty of Advent* for instructions on how to make an Advent Wreath. We have included a ritual for lighting the Advent candles in the section on *Rituals for Advent.*

THE JESSE TREE

See the section *The beauty of Advent* for instructions on how to make and decorate a Jesse tree.

THE NATIVITY CRÈCHE

The vision and feel of a Nativity scene helps to make the Advent story real as it unfolds. (See also *The beauty of Advent – colors, symbols, and art.*) Choose a special corner at the front of the room for a crèche. Week by week, move the characters closer to the Bethlehem scene.

If you don't have a Nativity crèche, there are inexpensive ways to make one. You can purchase a "punch-out" paper crèche or draw your own figures on cardboard. You can use clay or dough to create figures for the nativity scene. Or you can use old-fashioned wooden clothespins for characters, with fine-liner felt-pen faces and cloth-scrap clothing. Or you can make heads out of wooden beads, with felt-pen faces, and wire and cloth for bodies.

MEXICAN *POSADAS*

For nine nights before Christmas, Mexican communities choose one household each evening to host, and to "become," the holy family. Two people dress up as Mary and Joseph (or carry with them little figures of the holy couple). They travel from house to house, in a procession, seeking shelter from the cold.

Over and over, they are turned away and told, "there is no room." But each night one home has been chosen as the place where Mary and Joseph will be welcomed. The persons or the little figures of the holy family are taken in to be tended overnight with hospitality.

Then the party begins, with music and dancing and food. Each evening the party ends with a *piñata* for the children. On Christmas Eve, the pilgrimage ends at the church for midnight worship.

MEXICAN *PIÑATAS*

You will need to start at least a week before a piñata is needed, to give the papier-mâché time to dry. You will need

- a round balloon
- newspaper
- paste, made from flour and water in equal parts, and also glue
- paint and other decorations
- string
- lots of small toys, wrapped candies, and coins.

Prepare a work area, covered with newspapers. Blow up the balloon.

Tear other newspapers into strips about two inches wide. Dip each strip into a flour, water, and glue paste. Wipe off excess paste. Smooth the strip around the balloon. Repeat this process until the whole surface of the balloon has been covered two times.

Allow the papier-mâché to dry. Repeat the whole process two more times.

Burst the balloon. Cut a round hole about five inches across in the top of the piñata. Remove the broken balloon. Attach string to the sides of the hole to make a handle. Paint and decorate the piñata, then fill it with treats.

Hang the piñata from the ceiling.

At the piñata party, each guest is blindfolded, in turn. Then each is asked to try to break the piñata with a stick. When the piñata finally breaks, the goodies shower down, and everyone scrambles to gather them!

FRIDGE COVER-UPS

If you don't normally cover your fridge door with a variety of items, these ideas might not delight you. But if you do have a fridge that looks like ours, these ideas might provide an Advent focus that will greet you and your loved ones many times. (This idea will work for groups other than families – most of us usually have a fridge where we gather!)

Advent word-play

After discussing the meaning of Advent, create and decorate word-plays with the letters that make up the word "Advent." After each letter, write a word or phrase that you feel is part of the Advent season. For example, you might do:

A   A special time of preparing
D   Days of waiting
V   Visions of Christmas to come
E   Everyone has to be counted
N   Not the easiest journey
T   Time to share our faith story

Wish list for the world

What do you wish for this wonderful world, and all creatures great and small? Make and decorate a special wish list for the world.

ADVENT MURAL

To avoid Nancy's horror tale in the *Introduction*, keep it simple. Don't set up a schedule of daily tasks that will frustrate you and lead to inevitable disappointment.

Paint a large piece of brown paper as background – perhaps navy blue sky and brown rolling hills.

Add "stuff" to the background to create the scene of Jesus' birth. For example, dried grasses, twigs, cotton-ball sheep, tin foil stars, cloth shepherds, magazine animals and people, hand-drawn animals and people, a stable, a manger with straw – and on Christmas Eve, baby Jesus.

BABIES ARE BEAUTIFUL

During Advent we prepare for the coming of Jesus as a tiny baby. Each of us was once a tiny baby, innocent and precious – each one a child of God.

Collect a baby picture of each person in your group or family. Share stories and pictures with each other. How was your name chosen? What were you like as a baby?

Together, choose a way to display the baby pictures, to honor the miracle of each life.

SPECIAL BAKING

Wonderful memories can be created around a mixing bowl. Set time aside to be together, to put on special music, and to enjoy one another and the delicious tastes and smells of the season. Choose recipes that you enjoy and that are simple. We, the authors, like recipes with a variety of colors and flavors.

You may want to associate some of your baking with special days in the season. For example, make gingerbread in the shape of stockings to celebrate the feast of St. Nicholas. Remember to make your cookie shapes small and to cut your squares into small portions – your baking will go further, and you'll feel healthier!

ADVENT COLLAGES

Cut out pictures and words from magazines and newspapers that represent the themes of Advent. Arrange and glue your pictures and words on a large sheet of paper. Share the significance of the items you have chosen.

Collage of Hope – first week in Advent
Collage of Peace – second week in Advent
Collage of Joy – third week in Advent
Collage of Love – fourth week in Advent

GREETING CARDS

Sharing our wishes and blessings with others through greeting cards is a tradition worth continuing. It's also something we often have difficulty finding time for. Consider gathering for a "greeting card evening" (breaking now and again to test your special baking!). It doesn't matter whether the cards are store-bought or hand-made. The messages of love will warm our hearts and the hearts of those who receive our greetings.

Potato print cards

For the cards, use large plain file cards, folded in half (or other paper). For the printing, you will need potatoes, paring knives, and water paints. (Oil-based paints will not work, because the surface of the potato is wet.)

Cut unpeeled potato in half across the middle.

On one half of the potato, cut a long candle shape. Cut away other parts of the potato that would touch the paint. On the other half of the potato, cut a flame shape.

Brush or dip paint to cover candle shape. Press the potato onto the cards to print the candle shape. Let dry.

Brush or dip paint onto the flame shape. Add flame above the candle. Let dry.

Add your messages of hope, peace, joy, and love.

Birds-on-a-branch thumb print cards

These are really fun to do with little people!

Use brightly colored paint. We like to use red and green.

Do several thumb prints with one color. Let dry, and repeat with the other color.

Once the prints are dry, have adults or older children draw eyes, beaks, and little feet onto the thumb prints with fine-line felt pen, and branches for the feet to grip.

Add your messages of hope, peace, joy, and love.

DECORATIONS FOR THE CHRISTMAS TREE

Set up an ongoing work space for creating decorations. Put all your "fancy stuff" at the work space for easy access.

A **visitor chain** is both decorative and celebrates those who come to your home. Cut paper for chain links. Invite visitors to write their names on the links, or to draw a picture, or write a wish or a message.

Each visitor adds a link to your chain of love. Hang the chain around your tree.

Handmade ornaments make your tree more personal. Get out library books on Christmas crafts, or remember those you made when you were children. Choose ideas to create decorations for the tree.

ANGELS

In our Advent stories, angels bring tidings of great joy and change things in quite amazing ways. Angels remind us to be open to God's unexpected gifts.

Create wonderful **bands of angels** with doilies, sparkles and "stuff." Put the angels in windows to spread gladness to all who pass by.

Or create **Advent angel cards**. First discuss and list things that make Advent preparation special and meaningful. (For example, patience, simplicity, sharing, laughter, memories, excitement, etc.) Cut small pieces of cardboard, about 2 cm by 4 cm (1 inch by 2 inches) into angel shapes. On each angel piece of cardboard, write one word from your list. Each day, choose one Advent angel card to think about through that day.

WAYS TO CARE

Always, Christ showed compassion for the most vulnerable ones in his world – the lonely, the ill, and the rejected. Who are the most vulnerable in your community? How can you make your Advent activities ways to share the compassion of Christ?

For example, could you visit shut-ins, taking parcels of your special baking? Could you offer an afternoon of free babysitting to busy young parents? Could a group of you volunteer to help a few seniors write Christmas cards or finish Christmas shopping?

God's creation is also vulnerable. How can we all show our caring concern for creation in this season? Could you find or make re-usable decorated gift-bags instead of using disposable wrapping paper? Could you organize a service where you wrap gifts in newspaper decorated with "potato-print" candles? Could you gather a group of friends to travel together for Christmas shopping, instead of each driving a separate car?

II

THE
Christmas Season

I. The spirit of Christmas
– an overview

This is the long awaited moment! Where Advent began in darkness with all creation waiting, now at Christmas God's light is here. The baby Jesus has arrived. In the miracle of the birth, heaven and earth are united.

While Christmas is not always a happy time for every person, we always *want* it to be a happy time. Shining eyes delight in the radiance of the child. Grateful hearts rejoice that the Christ child is among us. Family and friends greet the baby and share a festive meal. Light shimmers from glowing candles and the faces of children as we offer our grateful thanks to God. Now at last, we can give and receive gifts of love. We celebrate the coming of holiness in a child, and holy love lights up our lives.

Although popular culture starts "Christmas" much earlier, the Christmas season of the western Church actually begins Christmas Eve and lasts until the festival of Epiphany on January 6. Through the "twelve days of Christmas," we celebrate the gift of love which comes to us in Jesus of Nazareth.

When Jesus was born, his people were waiting for a leader to bring justice and peace. "Jesus" is a Greek form of the Hebrew name "Joshua" or "Jeshua" which means "God saves." We, too, have been waiting for God's gift of salvation – and now new life is dawning. Christ is born!

The Bible stories that tell of the miraculous birth rejoice that holy wisdom has been born in the form of human flesh. Christ is described as "Emmanuel" which means "God with us." Myth and history come together, and God is with us in the humanness of Jesus. And we, who are made in the image of God, can rediscover the sacred in our humanness. Stories of Jesus' birth long ago and far away waken us to Christ's coming in the present. Christ comes to us now in "the flesh" of our relationships, in the love and freeing power that we share. Seeing each day through the lens of the Christ-life, we see Christ wherever loving kindness lives and breathes in the world.

But God's gift comes in such surprising ways! Christ comes into the shadows of oppression and violence – not in physical might, but in the humble vulnerability of an infant. Christ comes subject to fear and pain and temptation. Christ comes peasant-born, to unwed parents for whom there is "no room" in righteous society. Christ comes to weary, willing travelers on the road, as they struggle with the hardships of their journey. And Christ comes to us as we walk the Christian path, with our griefs and limitations and so-called failures.

There are shadows behind the brightness of every Christmas season, too, of loneliness, sorrow, and loss. Many different feelings flow through us at Christmas, but in Christ, God is with us through it all. In Christ, we find our identity as God's beloved creations. In Christ, we know we unconditionally belong. In Christ's birth, we see the Christ-light in one another and our selves. For where there is compassion for fragile yearning human beings, there we know for sure God is present.

Christmas is the season to give thanks for the presence of holiness in the material world. Now is the time to give thanks for Christ among us. All is one. Thanks be to God!

2. The beauty of Christmas – colors, symbols, & art

Christmas is the time when earth and heaven come together – a time of radiant, extravagant splendor, and gentle, graceful beauty. Christmas is a moment of holy mystery.

At the end of Advent, the visual environment changes dramatically for Christmas Eve. Now, textures, garments, and banners are fine and elegant, shimmering with white and gold brilliance. Symbols can include the manger, angels and shepherds, the star of peace, and images from Christmas carols. If decoration has been ongoing through the Season of Advent, Christmas Eve is the time to turn on shining lights and light all the candles in the room. Refresh the Advent wreath, and lay the infant Christ in the manger. In the warmth and the wonder of exchanging gifts at Christmas, we celebrate the light that is born in human hearts through receiving and sharing the gifts of God. "Light" and "gift" are central symbols of the Christmas cycle.

DECORATIVE EVERGREENS

Evergreens were originally a symbol of everlasting life. In Europe, they were a focus of ancient winter celebrations, and were gradually given Christian significance. The custom of decorating evergreen trees comes from Germany, where mention of an evergreen adorned in a parlor dates back to 1605. Some believe that Martin Luther, the great church reformer, was inspired by starlight on evergreens beneath the night sky. Others believe St. Boniface (an 8th century English monk) was the first to decorate a pine tree. The custom of decorating Christmas trees had reached North America by the late 1700s.

3. Celebrations in the Christmas season

CHRISTMAS EVE – THE CHRISTMAS VIGIL

After decorating gradually through the Advent season, Christmas Eve may be the time when the lights on the Christmas tree are finally lighted. Tonight the Nativity crèche receives the baby Jesus. Music, stories, special foods and candle-lit worship can fill this night of nights with wonder.

These days, many faith communities gather on Christmas Eve to celebrate the coming of the Christ child. Louise and her family have been blessed by opportunities to worship late at night on Christmas Eve, to hear the ancient story, to sing out the ancient songs, and to celebrate the joy of Communion. Louise will always remember the beauty of candle light, stained glass and music, with little children cozy in their sleepers. And though Louise's children now wear jeans and not sleepers, memories of midnight services are deeply rooted. (See suggestions for Christmas Eve worship in the section on *Rituals for Christmas*.)

In past years, fewer churches gathered on Christmas Eve. Nancy's family always found their own ways to worship, sharing Henry Van Dyke's *The Story of the Other Wise Man*. Year after year, Nancy fell asleep listening to her father's voice recounting the story. Her memory glows with the richness of Artaban's jewels and also with the richness of the family pattern. Nancy's father died. His voice no longer puts her to sleep on Christmas Eve. She has developed new patterns with children of her own, and even those patterns have changed with time. But the family fabric is rich, and woven with warm remembrance of tender years.

Although sacred rituals and patterns may change, even these changes have meaning. Choose ways to cherish the sacred gift of Christmas Eve with others in faith community if you can. Delight in the present. Delight in the past. Share your dreams for the unfolding of God's future.

ST. STEPHEN'S DAY – BOXING DAY

St. Stephen's Day, or Boxing Day, is observed on December 26, the day after Christmas.

St. Stephen was the first Christian martyr. Stephen was one of seven church officers appointed by the early church, responsible for caring for the poor. Stephen was beloved for miracles of healing and for his preaching, but his enemies accused him of teachings contrary to the Law of Moses. He was brought to trial before the high court of the Sanhedrin, where he made an impassioned speech in his own defense (Acts 7). He said he was not speaking against the sacred Law, but that those who accused him were disobeying the Law of God themselves. The mob became enraged, attacked Stephen, and stoned him to death. Standing by, and presumably approving this execution, was a young man from Tarsus named Saul (Acts 8:1). After his conversion, this young man became St. Paul, the great Christian apostle to the Gentiles.

Since St. Stephen was responsible for caring for the poor, St. Stephen's Day is associated with giving food, money, or clothes to the needy. In earlier times, alms boxes were passed around in St. Stephen's name – hence the name "Boxing Day." We remember St. Stephen when we sing about "Good King Wenceslas," a ruler who remembered to care for the poor on the feast of Stephen. Make a point of singing this carol on Boxing Day, and consider giving special gifts of charity.

Take turns reading Acts 6:8–8:1. Remembering Saul's presence when Stephen was killed, consider how God helps us turn even our worst wrongs to blessing.

THE FEAST OF THE HOLY INNOCENTS – DECEMBER 28

The beauty and innocence of Christmas is changed today, as later events in Jesus' life are foreshadowed. Reading Matthew 2:13–18, we remember the violence King Herod is said to have unleashed upon the children of Bethlehem. Our sense of Christmas is affected by our awareness of the reality of cruelty. Even the light of holy presence is threatened by evil.

Yet the presence of evil in the world is what makes holy presence among us so potent. Scripture reminds us again and again that innocence is transformed by the sorrow of experience into the courage and strength of compassion. Joseph and Mary, learning Jesus is in danger, trust God and risk acting in love. Trusting and risking, despite the presence of evil, saves human beings from despair.

On the Feast of Holy Innocents, we mourn the loss of the children of ancient Israel. We mourn the loss of the infants in Bethlehem. We mourn the loss of all innocent people who are killed because of fear, abuse of power, and greed. We even lament our own loss of innocence. And at the same time, we trust in the power of God to inspire us and open up new paths before us in times of desolation and danger.

When we pray on this feast day, we give thanks for all those who have suffered that others might live. We seek guidance for our lives – and for the safety of all innocents – in a world where Herod's power is still real. And we ask Christ to walk with us the way of compassion, in a world where there is both light and shadow.

4. Rituals for Christmas

These rituals and blessings for the Season of Christmas can be adapted for large gatherings like Sunday morning worship, for small meetings, or for families at home. Decide in advance who will lead, who will read, and who will take responsibility for actions.

A CHRISTMAS EVE LITURGY

Here is an outline for a traditional Christmas Eve vigil. This liturgy can be adapted to Christmas morning as well, although Christmas Eve offers the more dramatic possibilities of darkness and anticipation.

To emphasize the dramatic shift from Advent to Christmas, the vigil can begin in the Advent mood of longing. Read one of Isaiah's prophecies, or read Matthew 1:18–23, and sing some verses of "O come, O come Emmanuel."

After this, Christmas readings from Matthew and Luke can each be followed by an appropriate carol. It helps to select only verses in songs and scripture which are specific to the unfolding story. For this first part of the service, the congregation can actually stay seated.

At the moment when Jesus is born in the read-ing, invite everyone to stand for the Christmas declaration, "Christ is born!" At this moment, light the large, white Christ candle, and the whole community can sing *Joy to the World!*

After prayers for the coming of health, peace, and justice, exchange "the peace of Christ" and share in the sacrament of Communion. Children should be invited to participate actively, both in serving and receiving the elements. Individual candles can be lighted from Christ's candle and distributed as each person comes forward to receive Communion elements.

As more and more people return to their seats and stand throughout the church with lighted candles, electric lights can gradually be dimmed. By the end of the Communion, the entire sanctuary is lit only by candle light. This is the moment to sing *Silent Night* and to close with a blessing and dismissal.

Other options

Christmas Eve is also an appropriate moment to celebrate the sacrament of baptism, just prior to passing "the peace of Christ" and sharing Communion.

Both sacraments are ancient Christmas Eve celebrations; both involve us in the mysterious incarnation of God's Holy Spirit and in our human transformation for "new life." If a sense of anticipation has been created during Advent, ritual actions on Christmas Eve are especially potent.

Dramatic portrayals

A brief homily can be added to the Christmas Eve vigil. However, letting song and scripture tell the story directly helps to keep the service flowing so participants of every age can enjoy it.

To portray the story visually and also give children dramatic ways to share its beauty, you could have them enact a pageant as the story unfolds through song and scripture. A core group of players can practice beforehand with the reader(s) and members of the choir, so the action moves with confidence and power.

On Christmas Eve, invite all children who are present in the sanctuary to participate in straightforward ways – to join in as shepherds and sheep at the stable, or as angels who light up the night. (Consider saving the Magi for Epiphany, though.) Have simple costumes on hand, if possible, so children can put them on as they arrive. Arrange for youth to work beforehand with the minister of music to strengthen carols with their musical instruments – and this quickly becomes *the* service of the season.

RITUALS AND BLESSINGS
FOR THE CHRISTMAS SEASON

Whenever you gather through the twelve days of Christmas, use the ritual which follows to celebrate the coming of Christ. Turn out electric lights and light a white "Christ candle" (which may be the center candle from your Advent wreath.) As the candle is lighted, share one of the following prayers:

> **Loving Spirit, in Jesus**
> you join earth and heaven.
> In Christ's light,
> we see the holiness of creation.

Invite each person to name where, or in whom, he/she senses holy presence. Then continue with one of the following:

> **Blessed Creator,**
> for the presence of Christ
> and for the gift of compassion,
> we thank you.
> Grant that the love which
> first welcomed the Christ child
> may shine through our lives
> now and always. Amen.

> **Loving God,**
> whose glory outshines the sun,
> open our hearts
> to the inspiration of the Spirit
> so our lives may more fully
> reveal the power and the beauty
> of your presence.
> This we pray in the name
> of Mary's child, Jesus. Amen.

> **Holy Maker, as your child, Jesus,**
> was made in the image of humanness,
> so may we share
> in the image of holiness,
> breathing as your new creation. Amen.

> **Holy God, we thank you**
> for the gift of baby Jesus,
> who shows us how to shine
> with your love. Amen.

Other options

Before a meal, take several minutes to acknowledge the gift of holiness in human flesh. Ask everyone to close their eyes and focus on their breath as God's breathing. Ask them to let life-breath flow in and through them, and to tell themselves silently, "God breathes me." Finish with one of the prayers above.

5. Sharing our story at Christmas

In the Season of Christmas, we share stories of God's presence with us in the world.

The history of the people of Israel is a story of protest and liberation. Beginning with the exodus from slavery in ancient Egypt, the social vision of Moses and of the prophets of Israel declared that people could live without violence. In the Promised Land, the Israelites tried an experiment which lasted for two hundred years. They distributed land fairly and tried to curb abusive power by having no centralized government. Even when kings emerged, and began to act like other kings, the prophets continued to protest any kind of domination. God's "kingdom" was envisioned as the reign of holy love, and God's "judgment" was seen as justice with compassion. The prophets anticipated that the ultimate reign of holy love would become reality through a leader anointed by God. They called this long-awaited leader "the Messiah." In this vision, God joins the sacred with the material world through the initiatives of justice and compassion. This is our Christmas reality, in the coming of Christ.

The stories we share at Christmas are rooted in the biblical stories of Israel, in the prophets' expectations of the coming Messiah, in stories of the church, and our experience of the world and our lives.

The storytelling exercises which follow have been written for groups with one participant in the role of leader. They can be easily adapted for prayer partners or for personal use. Decide before you start who will read the scripture passages, and who will lead the storytelling for today.

When discussing stories located in a specific city in the ancient world, point out these locations on a map if you can, so that participants can connect the story's people and their problems with a particular place.

Remember to choose discussion themes which match the level of comfort and familiarity among those who are present, and remind participants they are always free to "pass." Let the stories and questions unfold as slowly as needed.

Close your session with prayer. You may find it helpful to hold hands in a circle as you pray. The leader can invite group participants to offer the hopes and prayers of their hearts, and start the prayer with his/her own words. As the leader finishes, he/she squeezes the hand of the next person in the circle who either prays or passes the "squeeze" along.

THE MESSIAH COMES TO BRING PEACE
Micah 5:2–5 (about Bethlehem in Judah)

Read aloud the scripture passage and the following summary. Reflect on each question and share responses.

This is the section of scripture that the scribes in Herod's court quoted when the Magi came to Herod, wanting to know where the new king had been born.

- Given their memories of oppression and slavery, why would the people of ancient Israel want a leader who was "great to the ends of the earth?" How would those who expected their leader to be a mighty warrior have understood these words? How would those who expected a spiritual teacher have understood them? How are these different approaches to peace still present in our world today?
- Who do you see as responsible for making the world more peaceful and just? What is your role? How is God with you in this work?

CHRIST COMES TO BRING PEACE

Luke 1:26–38, Luke 2:1–20, and Matthew 1:18–25 (stories about Jesus' birth)

Read aloud the scripture passages and the following summary. Reflect on each question and share responses.

Most scholars agree that the earliest writings about Jesus are those of Paul and Mark, who say nothing about Jesus' birth. Matthew and Luke appear to have written of Jesus' birth about fifty years after his crucifixion.

- What are the differences in "fact" between these stories? If Luke and Matthew knew Micah's vision of the future, what do the details included in these stories tell us about how they understood the ministry of Jesus? What miracles do you see in this birth?
- What "truths" do these stories hold for you? How is God present for you in the Christ child? How do you experience the peace of Christ being "born" in you?

THE CHRIST UNITES SPIRIT AND FLESH

Luke 1:26–38 and Matthew 1:18–25 (angelic announcements)

Read aloud the scripture passages and the following summary. Reflect on each question and share responses.

The angels' announcements reflect the Christian tradition which has insisted that Jesus was both human and divine – neither just a human with some divine qualities, nor a god in human disguise.

- How can we understand the miracle of Spirit united with flesh? If Jesus is conceived by the Spirit of God, how is this the same as being conceived in God's image? Are there differences for you?
- What do the stories of Jesus' birth tell us about the life-force that flows through human beings? What do they say about human possibilities?
- When do you feel the Spirit of God present in your body? In your life? How does opening to awareness of the Spirit affect your health and healing? How does opening to the Spirit affect your ways of being with others?
- When are you aware of God's presence in another human being?

CHRIST'S COMING
THREATENS WORLDLY POWERS

Matthew 1:1–17 and Matthew 2:1–23 (the Magi seek the newborn king)

Read aloud the scripture passages and the following summary. Reflect on each question and share responses.

Matthew's gospel traces Jesus' lineage through a line of kings, to portray Jesus as the "true king" of the Jews.

- Why would the Magi be afraid to return to King Herod? What was King Herod afraid of?
- Where in our world are leaders opposing a Christ-like focus on justice and peace? When has fear led to violence in modern history? Why is fear connected to violence? What alternative does Jesus offer?
- When do you experience a fear of sharing or giving up what you have? How do you cope with your fear? How could Jesus' "way of being" help to free you from fear? How could it help you to be creative in dealing with violent feelings?

CHRIST'S COMING
TRANSFORMS THE SOCIAL ORDER

Luke 2:1–20 and Luke 3:23–38 (the birth and lineage of Jesus)

Read aloud the scripture passages and the following summary. Reflect on each question and share responses.

Jesus was born to a peasant society where social caste was bound by rules of "purity." Carpenters, unwed mothers, and elderly childless women had very low social status in the ancient world – and shepherds were considered untouchable!

- What is Luke saying about Jesus' social vision when he portrays the Messiah coming as an unwed woman's baby? What are the implications of the heavens revealing truth to lowly shepherds instead of to Israel's priests and princes?
- Why would the writer of Luke trace Jesus' ancestors back through a line of social prophets?
- Who are the outsiders in our culture?
- Mary and Joseph were not "at home" when they needed help desperately. What similar experience have you had?
- For what persons does our society have "no room"? How could you include some of these persons in your life? How could you see God in a stranger?

THE HOLY CHILD
IS PRESENTED AND ACKNOWLEDGED

Luke 2:22–40 (Jesus presented at the temple)

Read aloud the scripture passage and the following summary. Reflect on each question and share responses.

While the gospel stories do not tell us much about Jesus' childhood, they do indicate that his spirituality was nurtured by family and faith community. His presentation and ac-

knowledgment at the temple make clear that Jesus was a child of Jewish tradition.

- In our culture, how big a part does spiritual nurture play in family life? What role does the faith community play in nurturing a child's spirituality? Which individuals represent faith community for our children? How do our children acquire an inner sense that they "belong" in their community of faith?
- What were your first experiences of the holy? When you were little, were you confident God loved you? Did you feel acknowledged and accepted by your family and community?
- Who were the individuals who recognized you as special, and helped you know yourself as a child of God? Where do you currently experience belonging?

THE HOLY CHILD BECOMES A LEARNER

Luke 2:41–52 (Jesus in the temple)

Read aloud the scripture passage and the following summary. Reflect on each question and share responses.

As a young boy, Jesus was taken to the temple in Jerusalem. At twelve, Jesus claimed for himself the relationship with God which was symbolized in the stories about his infancy. In the context of faith community, Jesus accepted responsibility for himself as a spiritual "learner" and named the temple as his spiritual home. These stories show that the Christ child sought to learn about God through Jewish tradition. Later, Jesus fought against the corruption he saw in the faith tradition in which he was raised.

- How is holy mystery interpreted for children in our society? Who models the life of thankful service for our children? How is sacred wisdom transmitted from generation to generation?

· At what point in your life did you become conscious of your task as a spiritual learner? What are the most important lessons you have learned through faith community and/or faith tradition? In what ways has your faith community been a spiritual home for you?

6. Embodied prayers for the Christmas season

In this season of incarnation, we delight in the presence of holiness in the body of the Christ child. As holiness dwells in the Bethlehem baby, holiness dwells in us too.

We long to feel the breath of Spirit in our bodies. The Hebrew word for Spirit also means "breath." The Bible tells us God breathed into the first human's nostrils and the creature became a living being. (Genesis 2:7) When we breathe *in* strength and courage, and breathe *out* fear and pain, God breathes new life into us.

Since all our life systems are interlinked in subtle ways, changing our breathing affects our whole self. Deep, slow breathing is the body's natural way of moving into relaxation, which in turn helps us attend to our experience. Combining breathing and prayer can help us focus and center on the presence of the Spirit, and deepen our awareness of that Spirit in our physical being.

INSTRUCTIONS

These prayers can be part of daily spiritual disciplines. They are written for groups, for prayer partners, or for personal use.

When used by a group, one participant will need to assume the role of guide. Decide in advance who will lead the prayers today, letting each prayer unfold slowly and gently.

For an effective pace, we suggest you take two full breaths whenever you see "…" before you start the next phrase. If a time frame is suggested, remember that one minute equals about eight full breaths. Give your group permission to breathe normally at any time, especially if they feel distressed or anxious. Tell the group never to strain or hold the breath. A deep breath is gentle and relaxed.

PREPARATION

Always begin embodied prayer sessions with this exercise. If you are practicing embodied prayers alone, read through the following instructions carefully before starting. If you are leading a group, read the following slowly and calmly aloud, with appropriate pauses.

Sit comfortably, with your spine fairly straight. Close your eyes. Without changing how you breathe, pay attention to the sensations of breathing … Pay attention to the sensation of breath moving in and out of your nose or your mouth … Can you feel the path of breath as it moves through your body into your lungs? … Can you feel the breath move your chest and rib cage, and then release again as you breathe out? … Continue to follow the flow of your breathing, without straining to do anything …

Now breathe in and send the breath into your abdomen as though you are filling your stomach. Exhale, letting the stomach fall back to normal. Breathing in, your belly rises; breathing out, it falls back. Breathe this relaxed "belly breath" for one minute … Don't strain or force your breath … Relax as you breathe in and your belly rises, and relax as you breathe out …

As you breathe quietly, begin to listen to the sounds in the room … Move your fingers and your toes. Open your eyes when you are ready.

CHRIST POSTURE
1 Corinthians 6:19 (your body is a temple)

St. Paul wrote these words to the churches at Corinh: "Do you not know that your body is a temple of the Holy Spirit within you, which you have from God?" Let us begin.

Sit comfortably, with your spine fairly straight. Close your eyes. Focus on how you are breathing … Pay attention to the sensations of breath moving in and out of your nose or your mouth … Relax as you pay attention to the flow of your breathing, without straining to do anything at all …

Now slouch a bit in your chair. Clench your fists and tighten your legs … Wrap your arms around your chest and hold yourself tightly. Close your eyes firmly. Feel how this posture restricts your breathing and closes you off from the outside world. Feel how your whole self is closed …

Loosen your body and relax …

Now sit up with your feet firmly on the ground and your arms loose at your sides or on your lap. Feel that your back is long and tall, not tense, but long and tall and relaxed. Keep your chin tucked in and feel that the energy from your spine extends to the top of your head and beyond … Your shoulders are relaxed … Feel how much easier it is to breathe deeply in this posture … Can you sense divine energy flowing through your body? Do you sense the beauty and dignity of this posture? … Visualize yourself as God's work of art …

Now, continuing to feel divine presence in your body, open your eyes and slowly stand up. Place your feet firmly on the ground. Feel the full length of your back … Relax your shoulders as you feel the back of your neck stretch up to lengthen your spine. Keep your chin tucked in as you feel the spine's energy rising to the top of your head and beyond, as though your body is being held up by holy energy from above … Breathe deeply into your belly as you release excess tension from your body … Allow God's presence to hold you up with dignity and beauty … Can you sense the Christ-life residing in your flesh and bones? Can you walk through your day feeling the Christ-life in your body?…

After the prayer is over, invite participants to share their experience, as they are comfortable.

SPIRIT-BREATHING PRAYER
Close your eyes and gently focus on your breath … Find a natural rhythm for your breathing … Settle in on a breath that is one count longer breathing out than it is breathing in. Perhaps you will inhale for three counts and exhale for four counts … Feel how this pattern helps you to sense that breath flows without effort … Feel the Spirit-breath entering your body … Feel how God breathes you …

Keeping your breathing rhythm steady, exhale and silently say a simple prayer or simple words of scripture. For example, "God be with me," or "Faith, hope, and love abide" or "Be still," or "All is One." Allow the air to flow into your body without effort. With each breathing out, say your prayer silently … With each breathing in, simply let God's life-breath flow inside you … For two minutes, let God's life-breath flow inside you as you repeat your prayer …

As you breathe quietly, begin to listen to the sounds in the room … Move your fingers and toes. Open your eyes when you are ready.

Other options

When praying as a group, try this embodied prayer first with each person repeating a self-selected phrase or prayer. Then find a common prayer that the entire group can repeat silently, and repeat the exercise. Discuss differences in the experiences afterward.

ALL-IS-ONE BREATHING

Sit comfortably, with your eyes closed. Pay attention to your breathing and gradually begin to deepen your breathing ... Relax your body and mind ... Imagine a large wheel turning in your mind. It turns in exact rhythm with your breath ... Focus on one spoke. When it reaches 12 o'clock, begin to breathe out. When it reaches 6 o'clock begin to breathe in ... 12 o'clock exhale, 6 o'clock inhale ... Imagine the wheel turning smoothly and freely ... Imagine that your breath rolls with the wheel. There is no pause or break in the cycle between exhalation and inhalation. Let it happen as a smooth transition, seamless ... As the wheel turns, the breath flows ...

Now, try to imagine who controls the wheel. Do you turn the wheel? ... Can you imagine giving up control of the wheel? ... Can you give the wheel to the One who creates it? ... Imagine God turning the wheel of your breath ... Entrust your breath to God ...

Let the image of the wheel disappear. Simply be here, breathing with God ... Allow yourself to fall into the exhalation ... Let go ... God is here to fill your inhalation ... You and God are breathing together. Rest in that ... Say to yourself, "All is One" ...

As you breathe quietly, begin to listen to the sounds in the room ... Move your fingers and toes. Open your eyes when you are ready.

CHRIST IS BORN

Sit comfortably with your eyes closed and bring your attention to your breath ... Let the breath flow in and out with ease ... Each exhalation releases tension ... Breathe in and out with ease ... Breathe and let go ...

As you breathe gently, imagine that you are surrounded by darkness, but in that darkness shines one bright light, a star in the night sky ... The star beckons you to follow ... Imagine yourself moving closer to the star. Imagine that it grows brighter as you move ... The star shines the light of love, a warm and comforting light ... Spend a minute feeling the warmth of the light and feeling the excitement of knowing that holy love is coming ...

Now begin to see the face of a child forming in the middle of the star ... Imagine that the star becomes the child ... Can you see the glory of God in the face of the child? ... The Christ child is born ... See the innocence ... Feel the awe ... See the vulnerability ... Feel the power of God's love, and breathe it in ... Delight in holy presence ...

Now, as you imagine the Son of Peace, feel the peace within yourself ... As Christ is born, you are born ... Take a deep breath in. Feel how the breath of Christ is born within you ... As the Christ child breathes, you breathe ... Breathe holy love ... You are God's sacred creation ... The Christ-light shines through your own spirit ... Be confident in God's light, in God's love ... Our hope is here ...

As you breathe quietly, begin to listen to the sounds in the room ... Move your fingers and your toes. Open your eyes when you are ready.

STILLNESS IN GOD
Psalm 46:10 (Be still and know…)

This prayer is based on a line from Psalm 46. Sit comfortably, with your eyes closed … Gently focus on your breath … Each time you exhale, let tension release from the muscles of your face … In your silence, invite the words: "Be still and know that I am God" … Slowly, exhale tension from your face and silently repeat, "Be still and know that I am God" …

Now, each time you exhale, let tension release from the muscles of your neck and your shoulders. Listen for, "Be still and know that I am God" … Release your neck and your shoulders …

Now, each time you exhale, let tension fall from the muscles of your arms and your hands. "Be still and know that I am God" … Release your neck and your shoulders …

Now, each time you exhale, let tension release from the muscles of your back and your chest … "Be still and know that I am God" … Release your back and chest …

Now, each time you exhale, let tension release from the muscles of your legs and your feet … "Be still and know that I am God" … Release your legs and feet …

Spend a few moments being aware of the stillness of God that is in you … "Be still and know that I am God" …

As you breathe quietly, begin to listen to the sounds in the room … Move your fingers and toes. Open your eyes when you are ready.

7. Written prayers for the Christmas season

These written prayers can be a starting place for shared or personal devotions through the Season of Christmas.

Prayers for delighting in God

Hope is here, for we have heard
the good news of Christ's coming.
Joy is here, for we have seen
God's compassion.
Love is here, for the angels
are singing around us,
and still there is a star ahead to follow.
May the whole world delight
in the promise of peace.
Christ is born! Amen.

Lamb of God, I look to Thee:
Thou shalt my example be;
Thou art gentle, meek and mild,
Thou wast once a little child. Amen.
(Traditional, source unknown)

Of the Father's heart begotten,
'Ere the world from chaos rose,
Christ is Alpha: from that fountain
All that is and hath been flows:
Christ is Omega, of all things
Yet to come the mystic close.
     Evermore and evermore.
By the word was all created;
Was commanded and 'twas done;
Earth and sky and boundless ocean,
Universe of three in one,
All that sees the moon's soft radiance,

All that breathes beneath the sun.
Evermore and evermore.
O how blest that wondrous birthday
When the Maid the curse retrieved,
Brought to birth mortals' salvation,
By the Holy Ghost conceived;
And the Babe, the world's Redeemer,
In her loving arms received.
Evermore and evermore. Amen.

(4th century Christmas Processional, Prudentius, restated)

God is not only fatherly,
God is also mother
who lifts her loved child
from the ground to her knee.
The Trinity is like a mother's cloak
wherein the child finds a home
and lays its head
on the maternal breast. Amen.

(Mechtild of Magdeburg, 1210–1294)

Deep peace, pure white
of the moon to you.
Deep peace,
pure green of the grass to you.
Deep peace,
pure brown of the earth to you.
Deep peace, pure gray of the dew to you.
Deep peace, pure blue of the sky to you.
Deep peace, of the running way to you.
Deep peace, of the flowing air to you.
Deep peace, of the quiet earth to you.
Deep peace, of the shining stars to you.
Deep peace, of the Son of Peace to you.
Amen.

(Fiona Macleod, 1855–1905)

God is our heart's desire.
God is our deepest power.
All is One. Thanks be to God! Amen.

Christ, be with me,
Christ before me, Christ behind me,
Christ in me, Christ beneath me,
Christ above me,
Christ on my right, Christ on my left,
Christ where I lie, Christ where I sit,
Christ where I arise,
Christ in the heart of every one who
thinks of me,
Christ in the mouth of every one who
speaks of me,
Christ in every eye that sees me,
Christ in every ear that hears me ... .
May your salvation be ever with us.
Amen.

(St. Patrick, c. 389–461)

To the trinity be praise!
God is music, God is life
that nurtures every creature in its kind.
Our God is the song
of the angel throng
and the splendor of secret ways
hid from all humankind,
But God our life is the life of all.
Amen.

(Hildegard of Bingen, 1098–1179)

Prayers for transformation and renewal

Creator God, you have brought
your word of life to birth among us
through the body and the spirit of
Mary.
Bring us to birth
by that same gracious word,
so that we who hunger and thirst
may be filled,
and our world may become
your new creation.
This we ask in the name
of Mary's child, Jesus. Amen.

May Christ touch our eyes
as he did those of the blind.
Then we shall begin to see in visible
things those which are invisible.
May Christ open the eyes of our heart
to contemplate God in Spirit,
through Jesus Christ, to whom belong
power and glory
through all eternity. Amen.

(Origen, 185–254, adapted)

Prayers of thanks and dedication

Blessed are you, O God, for your
faithfulness to Abraham and Sarah;
for the promise of the prophets; for
John the Baptist who prepared the way;
for the courageous love of Mary
and the tenderness of Joseph;
for the song of the angels
and the wonder of the shepherds,
and for the baby, born to be our Savior.
Blessed are you, O God, for the
Bethlehem Christ
who confronted powers of evil,
befriended the unlovely, healed the
sick and dying,
and proclaimed the possibility
of peace on earth and goodwill to all.
For these, and all your gifts,
we give you thanks. Amen.

For the love you have shown
in the gift of the Christ child,
for ties that bind us together
as holy family and community,
for the Christ-light which shines
through your Spirit in us,
we thank you and we offer our selves.
Turn all we have, all we are
and will become,

into gifts for the world you so love.
With Christ, in Christ,
and through Christ,
in the unity of the Spirit,
all power and possibility is yours,
God most holy,
now and forever. Amen.

Tender God, in your wisdom
you reveal yourself to us
in a tiny baby.
In Jesus' humble birth,
we remember our own opportunity
to care for strangers in our midst.
In Jesus' vulnerability,
we remember our own dependence
on your love.
In Jesus' humanness,
we remember that all of your creation
is sacred.
For the mystery of incarnation
and for your gift of holy love,
we give thanks
and we offer our lives. Amen.

Prayers for the world, ourselves, and others

Loving Jesu, gentle lamb,
In thy gracious hands I am,
make me, Savior, what thou art,
live thyself within my heart. Amen.

(Charles Wesley, 1707–1788)

**God, open our hearts
to the hope of the Christ child**
that we may hear again
the song of the angels
and see again the beckoning star.
Dawn in our shadows
and surprise us with wonder,
that we may go in joy
to proclaim the Messiah
in whose love we become
a new creation. Amen.

Shepherd of the stars,
we remember your gentleness,
your humility and courage,
revealed in a mother's trembling
hopes in a stable,
amid the pain and beauty
of human birth.
Once again we believe
that love is stronger than fear;
that violence can be transformed;
that forgiveness is more potent
than rage.
Open our hearts
to your Bethlehem presence
so your love may be known
through our lives.
This we pray in the name
of Mary's child, Jesus. Amen.

This is the night of radiant
promise and joyful song!
Shine on, O holy light,
in the darkness of our world!
Sing, O holy angels,
in the stillness of our hearts!
Glory to God in the highest,
and on earth, peace to all. Amen.

We celebrate the birth
of the Christ child, O God,
joining our voices
with the heavenly choirs of angels,
wondering with the shepherds
at this miracle of love,
bringing all the hurts and hopes
of our world.
In this season of gifts,
we remember those who have little
with which to celebrate.
We remember the poor,
the unemployed,
and those whose dreams have faded ...
In this season of carols,
we remember those who have little
to sing about.
We remember the lonely, the fearful,
and the grieved,
and all who are sick or in pain ...
In this season of festivity,
we remember those who suffer
the violence of oppression
and domination.
We remember those who are excluded,
imprisoned or displaced,
and all who suffer torture or exile ...
In this season of radiance,
we remember that your angels
can still be heard amidst the discord
of our times.
We pray for those working
for justice and peace,
for good will and caring relationships.
We pray for those who seek to bring
your reign of love to birth,
for those who share your light
and sing your song ...
For ourselves, we ask only
that love be born in us
as purpose, strength, courage,
and hope ...
Be with us, we pray. Amen.

8. Guided prayers & meditations for the Christmas season

To help you delight in holy presence through the Christmas season, these prayers are written for groups with one participant in the role of guide. They can be easily adapted for prayer partners or personal use. Decide in advance who will read the scripture passages and who will lead the prayers today, letting each prayer unfold slowly and gently. Remember to choose a prayer-style which matches the level of comfort and familiarity among participants, and to remind them they are always free to "pass."

Encourage participants to keep a prayer journal, and to spend about ten minutes letting God speak through their writing or drawing as they reflect on each prayer time.

A LECTIO MEDITATION ON INCARNATION

2 Corinthians 4:6–10 (the life of Christ visible in us) Remind participants before you start that all are responsible to pray for one another, and that each will be specifically responsible to pray for the person immediately to their right. Encourage everyone to feel free to share or to be quiet at the close of the prayer.

Take a few moments to come fully into the present … Sit comfortably … Close your eyes … For about two minutes, focus on your breathing … Relax as you breathe, and let go of the tensions of the day … Feel the Spirit breath flowing into your body … Feel how God breathes you …

As you relax with your breathing, listen for the word of God. Listen for a word or phrase or image that attracts you …

Read the passage from 2 Corinthians through slowly, aloud.

Choose a word or phrase or image that attracts you. Silently repeat the word or phrase or image with your breathing several times, in and out …

Read the passage through once again. What does this word or phrase or image mean to you now? How does it speak to your heart? How does it relate to your life?

Read the passage through once again.

As you breathe, become aware of what God may be saying … Is God speaking through this word or phrase or image? Through a feeling or an insight? A desire? What is God inviting you to do or be? … How or what is God inviting you to change? … How can you respond? …

Rest quietly in God's presence, focusing only on the flow of your breathing, in and out. Stay open to God's possibilities …

Now pray silently for yourself, for wisdom and courage and strength …

Now pray quietly for the person to your right, that he or she may be enabled to respond to God's invitation … Pray for those who are in special need today … Close with a prayer or blessing you know by heart …

As you breathe quietly, begin to listen to the sounds in the room. Move your fingers and your toes. Open your eyes when you are ready.

Invite participants to feel free to share or to be quiet at the close of the prayer.

PRAYERS OF AFFIRMATION
Isaiah 43:1–4, or Isaiah 49:15–16a (we are God's)

Take a few moments to come fully into the present ... Sit comfortably ... Close your eyes ... For about two minutes, focus on your breathing ... Relax as you breathe, and let go of the tensions of the day ... Feel the Spirit breath flowing into your body ... Feel how God breathes you ...

As you relax with your breathing, hear God speaking directly to you. Listen for words or images that attract you ...

Read one of the Isaiah passages through three times slowly, aloud.

Hear a word or image through which God is speaking to you ... Repeat the words or image in rhythm with your breathing ... Contemplate the blessing which was yours at your birth – and before ...Whenever you feel vulnerable, pray this way to remember whose you are ...

As you breathe quietly, begin to listen to the sounds in the room. Move your fingers and your toes. Open your eyes when you are ready.

A MEDITATION ON LIFE
Remind everyone before you start that all are responsible to pray for one another, and that each will be specifically responsible to pray for the person immediately to their right. Encourage all to feel free to share or to be quiet at the close of the prayer.

Take a few moments to come fully into the present. Sit comfortably, eyes closed ... Focus on your regular breathing pattern, counting silently as you breathe in and out ... Feel the Spirit breath flowing into your body ... Feel how God breathes you ...

As you relax with your breathing, take several moments to recollect one event or situation which was somehow significant in the last few days ... Remember the time of day when this occurred ... Continue breathing quietly, in and out ... Relive the incident as you experienced it, remembering the sights and sounds and smells ... As you breathe, become aware of what feelings are re-created by remembering this incident ... Where was the strongest feeling? ...

Now set aside your reflections, and be open to a phrase or an image from scripture or literature which may emerge spontaneously in your thoughts. As you continue to breathe, remember that any phrase or image which comes to you is a blessing ...

Now bring back to your consciousness the original incident and place your image or phrase alongside it. Rest in God's presence ... Breathe quietly, holding both the incident and your blessing in peace ...

Now offer both the incident and the blessing back to God ... Listen to discover an invitation for the next few days ... How is God speaking through the incident and the blessing? ... What are you invited to do or be? ... How or what is God inviting you to change? ...

Pray silently for yourself, for wisdom, strength, and courage to respond to God's invitation in your life ...

Now pray quietly for the person to your right, that he or she will be enabled to respond to God's invitation ... Pray for those who are in special need today ... Close with a prayer or blessing you know by heart ... Open your eyes when you are ready.

Invite participants to feel free to share or to be quiet at the close of the prayer. Or invite participants to spend about ten minutes reflecting on their prayer time on paper, letting God speak through their writing or drawing.

9. Inner reflections on Christmas

> The wrappings are gone,
> the gift revealed.
> My heart
> still yearning, yet so delighted,
> surprised at the contents
> of the package,
> fearful about the assembly required.
> Where are those missing pieces?
> And then softly, slowly
> Grace enfolds me.
> Thank you.

The gift is revealed. The Christ child is born. The long awaited is in our midst (John 1:14). What does it mean for us to welcome the Christ into our hearts and minds and bodies? What difference does God's gift make in our lives?

God be in my head
and in my understanding.
God be in my eyes and in my looking.
God be in my mouth and in my speaking.
God be in my heart and in my thinking.
God be at my end and in my departing.

(*Sarum Primer*, 1527)

Find your quiet spot, your candle, paper, pen, and pencil. During this retreat time, we invite you to look at the gifts of the season.

MEMORY AS GIFT

Light your candle and let your mind glow with memories of Christmas. Not all memories are happy, but choose to frame your memories as gifts. Write about the memories. Use your pencil to draw simple symbols for each memory (for example, Nancy might draw jewels to remember *The Story of the Other Wise Man*, and Louise might draw children in sleepers to remember Christmas Eve.)

LOVE AS GIFT

Light your candle and, in the warmth of the flame, think of love as a gift.

- Where is love (or where has love been) a gift in your life?
- How have family members and friendships been a gift?

JESUS AS GIFT

Light your candle. Read the first two chapters in the gospels of Matthew and Luke. Consider who Jesus is for you. Seeing Jesus as gift invites us to look at myth, symbol, paradox, and poetry as layers of the infinite.

- What parts of the Nativity stories hold most significance for you?
- Where is the mystery for you?

BREATH AS GIFT

Light your candle, close your eyes, and take several minutes to focus on the sensations of breathing. Let life-breath flow in and through you. Feel your life-breath as gift. When you are ready, draw your image of Spirit flowing into you, and through you to the world.

CREATION AS GIFT

Light your candle and reflect on the blessing of life. Read Genesis 1:1–2:4a. Consider how the scripture joins together creativity and responsibility.

- What are the ways you want to be creative in your world?
- How will you take responsibility for your creativity?

SEXUALITY AS GIFT

Light your candle. Take a few moments to consider how sexuality has been for you a gift and a blessing. Read Genesis 2:18–25. Notice that Adam and Eve were not at first ashamed of their nakedness. Draw your image of our original blessing.

CHRIST-LIFE AS GIFT

Light your candle, and remember the moments on your spiritual journey which have been most powerful for you. Read 2 Corinthians 5:17. Write in your journal about how Christ has come to your life as "new creation."

- How can Christ be born in you in the days and months to come?
- How will the Christ-life change your ways of being in the world?

RELATIONSHIP AS GIFT

Light your candle. Beginning with your childhood, consider the ways you are significantly connected to other persons and to nature. Write about how these connections have been gifts and blessings.

- How have others honored you?
- How have you honored others?

10. Activities for the Christmas season

GIFT GIVING

In the midst of all the planning and preparing for Christmas, take care to place a special gift under the tree for the unexpected guest or a stranger.

HERE WE COME A'CAROLING

Practice so that you are able to sing some carols together, if possible by memory. Bundle up warmly and walk around the community, sharing the Christmas story in song. Christmas Eve or Christmas Day are both good times. We once caroled at the local police station; the dispatcher put our song over the police car radios. It was a wonderful sharing.

BAKING BASKETS

Purchase inexpensive wicker paper plate holders. Using your Christmas baking, create baking basket platters for those you wish to honor at Christmas. During the twelve days of Christmas, deliver your basket and share your best wishes for the season.

STORY SHARING

Gather as a group and take time to savor memories of Christmases past. Nancy remembers one Christmas gathering where she asked each participant to bring a small item somehow related to a Christmas memory. Both the listening and the telling are gifts.

WAYS TO CARE

Always, Christ showed compassion for the most vulnerable ones in his world – the lonely, the ill, and the rejected. Who are the most vulnerable in our community? How can you make some of the activities listed above into ways to share the compassion of Christ?

For example, could you sing Christmas carols at a hospital, seniors' residence, or a prison? Could you deliver poinsettia plants to those who are shut in, and ask to hear stories about Christmas in their childhood? Would you like to take special treats to the pets at the local animal shelter? (In all these suggestions, remember to call first, and ask what would be welcomed.) Find out what agencies in your community support the homeless, and ask how you can help with gifts of time, clothing, or food. Shop with a child for a special gift for a woman or youngster, and have your church leaders arrange for delivery to a women's shelter.

God's creation is also vulnerable. How can you show caring concern for creation in this season? Perhaps you could create a feast for wild birds on a "giving tree." (If you start this, remember to keep it going throughout the winter.) It's especially fun to watch the birds, so try to put your giving tree by a window. Call wildlife workers or bird watching clubs to find out what birds in your area particularly like to eat.

SIMPLICITY

Christmas is often a season when routines are interrupted and people may be tired. Sometimes, "'tis a gift to be simple." Make popcorn together, and watch *It's a Wonderful Life* with Jimmy Stewart. Shalom, and Merry Christmas!

III

THE
Epiphany Season

I. The spirit of Epiphany
– an overview

The Season of Epiphany is a time of dazzling light and revelation. Imag-ine a crowd in the darkness of night, waiting for a fireworks display. When the starbursts begin, there's a collective "Ooh-aah!" That's Epiphany!

The word "epiphany" comes from a Greek term meaning "manifestation" or "showing forth." God's love is shown in Jesus, and the people watch and see – "Ooh-aah!" In the Season of Epiphany we read stories of the mission and the ministry of Jesus, which show us the radiant light of God. Like the people of Israel, we too watch and see – "Ooh-aah!"

The weeks between the Feast of Epiphany and Lent are sometimes called Epiphany season, or in some churches, just "ordinary time." There can be as few as four weeks or as many as nine, depending on the dates of Lent and Easter. In these weeks, the ordinary is transfigured by wonder through stories of the ministry of Jesus. We learn how to *watch* for God, as we *see* Christ at work in the world.

The mystery and magnificence of the Spirit of God shine through Jesus as a "light" for creation. So at Epiphany, and through the weeks which follow Epiphany, we focus on Jesus of Nazareth as light for the world.

On the Sunday immediately before the start of Lent, the revelation of Christ as holy light for the world finds its zenith in the story of Jesus' shining "transfiguration" on a mountain. We are conscious of shadows through the Season of Epiphany, yet we honor the power of light. In Matthew's story about the Magi on their way to Bethlehem, King Herod's foul intentions and the suspicion in Jerusalem alert us to the presence of danger. And yet the story of the wise ones who seek the child by star-light also tells us Jesus' birth is so important to creation that even the night sky – and seekers far away – are transformed and inspired by his coming. So although we have to grapple with fear and losses on the way, we too can dare to follow the star.

The scripture passages suggested in the *Revised Common Lectionary* show the Spirit manifest in Jesus at his baptism, in his "miracle" at Cana, through his ministry with his disciples, and his deeds of healing. The light we anticipated in the Season of Advent, the light which dawned with Jesus' birth on Christmas morning, now spreads through a series of epiphanies.

The epiphanies which show the Spirit unfolding through Jesus reveal a pattern of spiritual transformation for Jesus' followers as well. In this season, scripture shows how Christ's disciples engage their learning – through reverence for the holy, through commitment to God's intentions, through the spiritual disciplines of relationship and contemplation, and by sharing in a ministry of personal and social transformation. We see that Christ's followers are called to live as Christ lives, as revelations of God's boundless love.

During the weeks between Epiphany and Lent, we move with Christ's followers from our Christmas spirituality, where holy love is born in us, to an Epiphany spirituality of discipleship. The word "disciple" actually means "learner." In this season, we too engage our learning. These weeks are "working time" in the Christmas cycle of spiritual affirmation. This is a time to grow into the fullness of selfhood so we can pour ourselves out. As we learn how to live with integrity in community, we learn to act in ways which correspond powerfully with who God intends us to be. As friends and as partners in community with Christ, we learn to share holy love through prayerful service.

So we journey through this season toward fulfillment as instruments of love. When we celebrate the baptism of Christ at the Jordan, we recognize that we ourselves are asked to turn away from everything which thwarts holy love's possibilities. When we answer Jesus' summons with his other disciples, we know we're called to learn how to love. And when we stand with Christ in the mystery of the Spirit, we know love is the power of God.

The journey of discipleship nurtures strength and resilience through ongoing lessons in loving. Love's lessons tend to challenge our worldly sources of security – usually through losses of wealth, family, power, or health. They reveal where and how fear controls us. Like Mary and Joseph, faced with threats to Jesus' safety, or like the Magi who hear a warning in a dream, we sometimes find we have to travel "by another road." The challenge of finding another way in the darkness leads us into deepening awareness of what we trust, and what functions as our ultimate love. The inner work of Epiphany is learning how to be creative with pain along the way, trusting God to light another road.

For us, as for Jesus' original followers, the discipleship journey can be hard. But holy moments of epiphany reveal the grace which makes everything possible. They guide us by Christ-light to fullness as disciples – as co-learners in the Spirit of God. We watch and we see by the light of a star – Ooh-aah!

2. The beauty of Epiphany – colors, symbols, & art

The central symbol of Epiphany is light, and its symbol is the star. Although the weeks after Epiphany may be known as "ordinary time," scripture readings continue to shine with the radiance of Christ-light. Music also carries the theme of light spreading through the world. This is a marvelous opportunity to learn songs from other ethnic traditions.

The basic color for decorations through the weeks after Epiphany is green, the color of growing. Baptism of Christ celebrations, on the first Sunday after Epiphany, and Transfiguration Sunday just before Lent, are exceptions to this general color guideline. The symbolic colors for these two Sundays are either white or gold, the colors of new life and glory.

3. Celebrations in the Epiphany season

Epiphany is often heralded by "Twelfth Night" celebrations (12 days after Christmas), on the evening before the Feast of Epiphany. Some Christian communities prepare Twelfth Night festivities with drama, singing, rituals – and food! Some suggestions for Twelfth Night celebrations are listed below. Sometimes several congregations walk in lines from church to church, carrying candles to symbolize the light of Christ shining and spreading. Other faith communities move from house to house, blessing each home as they search for the Christ child. (You'll find suggestions for blessing homes in the section on *Rituals for the Season of Epiphany.)*

Preparing for Twelfth Night can help us remember that Christmas "incarnation" is a way of life. Twelfth Night celebrations, or Epiphany worship on the first Sunday in January, technically close the Season of Christmas. The real work of Christmas incarnation will continue – but now the light must be revealed through our lives.

Twelfth Night celebrations

SEEKER NIGHT

Matthew 2:1–12 (the journey of the Wise Ones)
When people gather, include among refreshments a "seeker cake" which is served to every person. Inside the cake, place three beans or coins. (Make sure you warn everyone these are somewhere in the cake!) Whichever three persons find the beans or coins will be the three Magi for the evening.

While the three Magi, or Wise Ones, are being costumed for their parts, have the other participants strip the Christmas tree of decorations. Candy canes on each branch may even entice the children to help! Then ceremoniously remove the tree from the room. Some faith communities keep their tree until Lent when, stripped of branches, it can become a Lenten cross.

When the Magi are appropriately dressed for their roles, ask an appointed storyteller to gather people together for the story of the Wise Ones, who followed a star to the baby Jesus. If there is a Nativity crèche in the room, a child can be asked to place the figures of the Magi near the baby. A drama or skit of the Magi's journey to Bethlehem is wonderful, if preparation has been possible. Conclude the evening with a "Feast of Lights" ritual. (See the *Rituals for the Season of Epiphany* section.)

LA BEFANA NIGHT

Those of Italian descent may remember a gift-giving woman called La Befana (from *Epiphania*.) Legend claims that La Befana was so busy with cooking and cleaning her house that when the Magi came looking for Jesus she couldn't stop to go with them. When at last she was ready to go, the Wise Ones were too far away. So La Befana has been wandering the earth ever since, to catch up and give her gifts to the Christ child. She carries a basket of presents and a broom, and leaves a treat for each child she meets – in the hope that this at last is the Christ child. Similar traditions have been adapted in many places in North America.

HOME-BLESSING NIGHT

See the *Rituals for the Season of Epiphany* section.

WASSAIL NIGHT

Wassail is hot fruit punch to share with neighbors in community as we exchange mutual wishes for health and blessing. *Wassail* is an old Anglo-Saxon word for "be whole." The Wassail-bowl, which offers hospitality to visitors on Twelfth Night, is the ancestor of our present day punch bowl.

The Feast of Epiphany – January 6

Epiphany, a time of great joy for Christians, is historically an older festival than Christmas. As we embark on our journey as disciples (learners), we need to discern the direction that offers hope and healing. And this is the Epiphany miracle: a star is still ahead to show the way. You'll find suggestions for Epiphany celebrations in the section on Rituals.

See the *Rituals for the Season of Epiphany* section for suggestions for Epiphany Sunday – usually the first Sunday in January.

Baptism of Christ – first Sunday after Epiphany

Jesus' conscious commitment to serving God's purposes is expressed in his baptism by John the Baptist. On Baptism of Christ Sunday, we remember this momentous starting-point in the ministry of Jesus, and we contemplate the implications of committing ourselves to God's purposes. (For ways to celebrate the baptism of Christ, see the section on *Rituals for the Season of Epiphany*.)

Baptism enacts physically our human experience with the spirit of love, through affirmation, mercy, and opportunity. The concept of baptism itself pre-dates the ministry of John the Baptist. Children raised in the Jewish faith were considered to have "passed through the waters" to freedom, by virtue of their ancestors' experience. The ancient Hebrews were released from their bondage in Egypt when they passed safely through the Reed Sea. But newcomers to Judaism could also be incorporated into this story. By being baptized, they too could experience the refreshing passage to freedom.

Christian baptism builds on this Jewish heritage. Our exodus story is one of release from everything past and present which holds us captive – from the paralysis of guilt or shame or addiction, from fear or lack of self-esteem, or from any other kind of human bondage. For us as Christians, Christ reveals the affirmation, mercy, and opportunity of holy love in our lives. So baptism into "the Body of Christ" frees us for healing and empowerment. Passing through the waters of life and of death, we're born afresh into a transformed relationship with God, with Jesus Christ, and with all creation. Baptism marks our birth into the Christ-life, just as passing through the waters within a mother's womb begins her child's birth into the world.

Baptism is a rite of commitment. The inner strength which frees us to give and receive emerges through commitment to becoming. And central to becoming all of who we are meant to be is owning our spiritual perspective. On a conscious spiritual journey, we grow increasingly aware of interpreting our own experience through the symbols, stories, and meanings we originally learned in our faith communities. As we engage in self-inquiry and start to make active choices, selfhood emerges through the process of accepting our power and responsibility to make decisions.

The commitments we make as adults in the sacrament of baptism (for ourselves or on behalf of our children) or in the adult rite of passage by which we "confirm" vows previously made on our behalf, mark the start of our intentional journey. Baptism is the outward and visible sign of our decision to follow the Christ-light. Baptism is the sign of our conscious commitment to making the Christ-life our own.

Consciousness does not by itself lead to freedom and justice. To be free and just, a people must live with commitment to God, each other, and creation. So when the Hebrews were released from their bondage in Egypt, they were led to Mount Sinai where freedom and justice came to them in the form of a covenant – a committed relationship in which God and the community of faith accepted mutual responsibility. When as Christians we pass through the baptismal waters, we too inherit a covenant of freedom and justice between God and community, a relationship through which we learn how to love as Christ loves.

Learning love's lessons means becoming disciples who can be "in the world" but not "of it." It means becoming resilient so we live deeply in the world without letting its pain drain our souls. It means becoming a community of justice and peace by sharing the Christ-life together. It means living our baptismal covenant. (See also rituals for Baptism of Christ Sunday, in the *Rituals for the Season of Epiphany* section which follows.)

Transfiguration Sunday

Christ-light spreads as Christ's power and presence are made known in the world. On Transfiguration Sunday, we remember the mountain-top experience of those closest to Jesus, for whom holy light blazed into a blinding revelation of who Jesus actually is. In a vision, they see Jesus "transfigured" before them, standing with Moses and Elijah – suggesting that both law and prophecy affirm the mission of Jesus as the long-awaited Messiah or Christ. (For ways to celebrate Transfiguration in worship situations, see the section on *Rituals for the Season of Epiphany.*)

Transfiguration is celebrated on August 6 in Roman Catholic and Episcopal/Anglican churches. Protestant traditions place Transfiguration at the junction between Jesus' ministry in Galilee, and his self-emptying sacrifice in Jerusalem.

Jesus is affirmed on the top of a mountain. Then he comes down from the mountain to enter once more into the suffering and sin of the world. At the level of myth, with Lent and Holy Week soon to come, the Transfiguration of Jesus anticipates his descent into emptiness. Jesus looks down from his mountain-top glory and sees into the valley of shadow. Ahead lies Jerusalem where Israel's prophets have been betrayed, and where Jesus' own role as the "suffering servant" will all too soon play itself out.

Jesus has already begun to speak with his disciples about his sorrow-filled path down the mountain. The unavoidable question for the disciples – and for us – is "Will we follow?" Will we "save our life" or "take up the cross"? Will we stand before the rage of the world bearing only our love? What do we fear?

4. Rituals for the Season of Epiphany

These rituals and blessings for the weeks between Epiphany and Lent can be adapted for large gatherings like Sunday morning worship, for small group meetings, or for families at home. Decide in advance who will lead, who will read, and who will be responsible for actions.

A HOME-BLESSING RITUAL

Carrying lighted candles, proceed from home to home. Gather at the front door of each participating house to bless the entryway and those who live there.

Leader: Blessed be this house.
All: *And all who dwell here.*
Leader: Three wise ones came to
   Bethlehem seeking the Christ child,
   and gave to the child precious gifts:
   Gold for the true king,
   incense for worship, and
   myrrh for the body which someday
   would die like our own.
All: *In your light, we see light.*
   Thanks be to God.
Leader: Let us pray. O God, you led the
   Wise Ones by the light of a star
   to show your peoples the way
   to Jesus Christ.
   May we who seek Christ trust in you
   to light the way
   So we recognize the Christ-light
   in the epiphanies of the lives
   with which you bless us.
All: *In your light, we see light.*
   Thanks be to God.
Leader: Bless, O God, this household,
   and grant that all who live here
   may share the light of love
   within these walls.

May this house be a haven
of hope and hospitality,
for neighbor and stranger in times of
need.
And may the light of love cast its beam
beyond these doors
to bless the world and all of creation.
All: *In your light, we see light.*
   Thanks be to God.

Bless the house and family members with the sign of the cross, saying, "The light of Christ shine upon you, this day and forever. Amen." Then mark the initials of the legendary names of the Magi, the "wise ones" – Caspar, Melchior, and Balthasar – with chalk on the doorframe of the house, framed by the numbers of the new year, like this: 20 C M B 02

Since the names of the Wise Ones have no biblical reference, the CMB initials may originally have stood for *Christe, Mansionem Benedicta,* which means, in Latin, "Christ, bless this house."

FEAST OF LIGHTS LITURGY

John 1:1–18 (the Light shines in the darkness)
If not used on Twelfth Night, the Feast of Lights liturgy can be adapted for morning worship on Epiphany Sunday, the first Sunday in January. If you are in a church building, have everyone enter a darkened sanctuary. Light the Christ candle to represent the light which has come into the world with the birth of Jesus. Read John 1:1–18 as the candle is lit. Then sing *We Three Kings,* and have the Wise Ones enter as each king is mentioned, bearing gifts for the Christ child.

As each of the Wise Ones passes by the Christ candle, have her or him take a small candle, light it from the Christ candle flame, and remain somewhere in the sanctuary with it lighted. Next, remember by name those participants in the faith community who have died since Twelfth Night last year, and have someone light a candle for each one. Now invite each child present (in the company of a parent or adult) to come forward, and have someone light a candle for each of them to hold. Finally, invite youth and adults to come forward to receive a lighted candle.

When the room is full of "Christ-light," give thanks to God (briefly!) for the light of Christ which shines in our lives, and send the group out to "share the light" with others.

EPIPHANY SUNDAY – FIRST SUNDAY IN JANUARY

On Epiphany Sunday, the sanctuary should still be decorated for Christmas. A procession, led by a child carrying a shiny star on a pole, enters the sanctuary to the first verse and chorus of We Three Kings or a similar hymn.

If not used for Twelfth Night, the story/drama of the Wise Ones and the Feast of Lights ritual can be adapted for Epiphany Sunday. Or enact the journey of the Wise Ones physically through the sanctuary – detouring to avoid dangers, held captive by listening to Herod's false promises, assisted by gifts of support and hospitality, etc. Dramatize or tell a short version of Van Dyke's The Other Wise Man. Or dance through the La Befana legend.

You might include a brief homily on our search for the Christ child, or on what it might mean to return to your home "by another road."

If homes have not been blessed during Twelfth Night celebrations, the Sunday congregation can bless baskets of chalk, and send a piece of chalk home with each family to mark a blessing on their doorframe. (See home-blessing ritual above.)

BAPTISM OF CHRIST SUNDAY – FIRST SUNDAY AFTER EPIPHANY SUNDAY

If baptism was not celebrated on Christmas Eve or Christmas Day, the first Sunday after Epiphany Sunday is a wonderful time to offer the sacrament of baptism to those desiring it for themselves or their children.

As an adult profession of faith and intention, Jesus' baptism has much in common with both adult baptism and the rite of passage we know as Confirmation. In infant baptism also, in addition to vows expressed with regard to the child, adult participants make conscious commitments for their own lives and the life of faith community. The context of these commitments, in the situation of infant baptism, is very similar to Mary and Joseph's presentation of the infant Jesus at the temple (Luke 2:22–38). When a child is baptized we give thanks to God for a new holy life, and we commit ourselves to living the life of faith with the child and to raising the child in faith community.

Whether we baptize adults, children, or both, Baptism of Christ Sunday is a time to offer everyone the opportunity to renew baptismal vows.

Members of the faith community (especially the children) can participate in the sacrament of baptism through ritual actions such as helping to pour the water, giving lighted candles to the newly baptized, and casting drops of water over the congregation with evergreen boughs dipped in the font. This latter practice is derived from the ancient ritual called "asperges" and is accompanied by the words, "Remember your baptism and be thankful!" Youngsters never forget it, and will likely play "baptism" at home!

The sacrament of baptism affirms the communal nature of personal faith, and serves as a time of recommitment and learning for everyone. Baptism of Christ Sunday is therefore a good moment to formally launch a series of small-group weekly gatherings to explore faith and discipleship, or the possibility of baptism for oneself or one's children. Those wishing to be part of such gatherings can commit to this quest during Sunday morning worship, and the congregation can bless them on their journey. At the conclusion of this series, another opportunity for baptism and/or confirmation in faith can be offered for those who desire it, at the Easter Vigil or on Easter Sunday morning.

TABLE RITUALS AND BLESSINGS

These rituals and blessings can be adapted for large gatherings like Sunday morning worship, for small-group meetings, or for families at home. Whenever you gather, use the ritual which follows to celebrate Christ-light shining in the world. Turn out electric lights and light a white "Christ candle" (which may be the center candle from your Advent wreath.)

As the candle is lighted, share one of the following passages of scripture:

Jesus said,
"I am the light of the world...
Whoever follows me
will never walk in darkness
but will have the light of life."

(John 8:12)

Jesus said,
"You are like light for the world.
A city built on a hill cannot be hid.
No one lights a lamp
and puts it under a bowl,
but on the lamp-stand,
where it gives light for everyone.
In the same way, your light
must shine before people,
so they will see the good you do
and give thanks to your Father
in heaven."

(Matthew 5:14–16 restated)

In your light, we see light.

(Psalm 36:9b)

After the reading from scripture, invite each person to name where, or in whom, he/she has seen the light of Christ today. Where was love shining in this day? Then continue with one of the following prayers:

Blessed Creator,
for the presence of Christ
and for the light of compassion,
we thank you.
Grant that the star
which led the Wise Ones to Jesus
may shine on us now, to show the way.
Amen.

Grant that the Spirit
which lighted Jesus' life
may shine through our lives
now and always. Amen.

Grant that the love
which changed the lives
of the disciples
may shine in our hearts
and our world. Amen.

Grant, O God, that the brightness
of the presence of Christ
may shine in our hearts and our lives.
Amen.

A LITURGY FOR MID-WEEK GATHERINGS

This liturgy uses the Epiphany language of "light." Its focus on reflection would make it helpful through Lent as well.

Voice One: Jesus said, "Whoever follows me will never walk in darkness but will have the light of life." (John 8:12)

Voice Two *(lighting the Christ candle)*: Christ Jesus, you tell us that wherever two or three come together in your name, you are with us. The light of this candle symbolizes your presence among us. And Jesus, where you are, the Creator and the Spirit are with us also.

Voice One: Let us pray.
Creator God, you made us and placed us here for a purpose. Jesus, you love us and call us to complete your work on earth. Holy Spirit, you help us to carry out the work for which we are created and called. In your presence and name – Creator, Christ, and Spirit – we begin our reflection. May all our thoughts and inspirations have their origin in you, and be directed to the fulfillment of your peace. Amen.

Sing a hymn, perhaps based on the 3rd century *Phos Hilaron*, "O Laughing Light," used in traditional evening vespers. Follow with scripture and a meditation. Share storytelling based on the reading(s). An embodied prayer or one of the prayer suggestions for the season would also work well.

Next, share in prayers of the people. Invite participants to pray in silence or aloud for:
• the people of this faith community
• those who suffer and those who are in trouble
• the concerns of this local community
• the world, its peoples and its leaders
• the church universal, and all who seek to be faithful

Complete each section of petitions with a pattern of response such as the following:

One: Spirit of holiness,
All: *Reveal your love.*

Finish by praying together the prayer Jesus taught us, "Our Father ..."

Sing something tender and gentle. Call participants to mission in Christ's name with words like these:

Voice One: Jesus said to his disciples,
"You are like light for the world.
A city built on a hill cannot be hid.
No one lights a lamp
and puts it under a basket,
but on the lamp-stand
to give light for everyone."
In this same way our light
must shine always for others,
so that they will see through us
the image of Christ, and come to know
the radiance that is God.
(Matthew 5:14–16, adapted)

Voice Two *(extinguishing the candle)*: Though the light of this candle is now extinguished and we must go, may the light of Christ within us shine forever through our lives. My friends, let us share the peace of Christ: "The peace of Christ be with you always."
All: *And also with you. Amen.*

Exchange the peace of Christ with a hug or a handshake before you leave.

5. Sharing our story during the Epiphany season

God asks a radical faith of Christ's disciples. Now, as in the time of the ear-liest church, living the Christ-life often means going against the norms of society, facing persecution and rejection. And now, as it was in the earliest times, the church is made up of imperfect people who argue, compete, and lose perspective. In the Bible, Christ's disciples are por-trayed as ordinary people called by God to extraordi-nary things. In their joys and struggles we can see our own reality as Christ's disciples.

Like Jesus' first disciples, we are called to be instru-ments of healing in the midst of our lives. During the weeks between Epiphany and Lent, we focus on learn-ing *how* to do this.

Epiphany storytelling is rooted in the church's sto-ries about Jesus, in the roots of these stories in the teachings of Israel, and in our stories of the world and our lives.

The storytelling exercises which follow have been written for groups with one participant taking the role of leader. They can be easily adapted for prayer partners or for personal use. Decide before you start who will read the scripture passages, and who will lead the discussion today. When discuss-ing stories located in a specific city in the ancient world, pointing out these locations on a map can help participants to connect the story's people and their problems with a particular place.

Remember to choose discussions which match the level of comfort and familiarity among those who are present, and remind participants they are always free to "pass." Let the stories and questions unfold as slowly as needed.

Close your session with prayer. You may find it helpful to hold hands in a circle as you pray. The leader can invite the group to offer the hopes and prayers of their hearts, and start the prayer with his/her own words. As the leader finishes, he/she squeezes the hand of the next person in the circle, who can either pray or pass the "squeeze" on.

The Feast of Epiphany

Matthew 2:1–12 (Foreign Wise Ones come seeking the Christ child)
Read aloud the scripture passage and the following summary. Reflect on each question and share re-sponses.

This story locates Jesus' birth in a political context, and reminds us many peoples were affected by talk of a Messiah. Some re-sponded with longing and others responded with loathing.

- How do people today demonstrate their longing for the coming of justice and peace? How do fear and politics threaten that com-ing even now?
- What "star" in your life leads you onward? How can you know which way leads to "the light"?
- Are you willing to commit to this journey? Who will accompany you in your search for the holy? What obstacles tend to get in your way? What kind of lies and illusions are you likely to encounter? Have you a sense of any other dangers? What will you do when you're afraid?

Baptism

THE BAPTISM OF CHRIST
Luke 3:21–22, Matthew 3:13–17, Mark 1:9–11 and John 1:29–34 (the baptism of Jesus)
Read aloud the scripture passages. Reflect on each question and share responses.

- What similarities do you hear in these four stories? What are the differences between them?
- How does the sacrament of baptism express the faith of your own faith community?
- What parts of the faith you received as a child are still a source of light for you now? What parts do you choose to leave behind?
- How do you understand the responsibilities of baptismal commitment? What difference could baptism make in how you choose to live your life?

THE MEANING OF BAPTISM
John 3:3–5 (born anew), John 7:37–39 (living water), John 11:25–26 (the resurrection and the life), and Galatians 2:20 (Christ lives in me)
Read aloud the scripture passages. Reflect on each question and share responses.

- What does each of these passages imply about the meaning of baptism? What does each passage say about the Church as a baptized and baptizing people?
- How does a truth in these verses relate to your life? How does it invite you to change?

Discipleship

John 1:29–51 (the lamb of God), Luke 4:14–21 (the spirit of the Lord is upon me), Luke 5:1–11 (catching followers), Luke 8:1–3 (calling women) and Mark 1:14–20 (calling disciples)
Read aloud the scripture passages and the following summary. Reflect on each question and share responses.

Jesus' teachings and actions about spiritual calling were provocative in his own time and are still very challenging for us. The following role-play is meant to help people comprehend the issues of the heart involved with "call."

Depending on the number or participants, break into several groups of three to five people, each group focusing on a separate gospel writer. In the groups, read the verses of that gospel story again, aloud if possible. Have each person choose a different character in the passage. Spend five minutes in silence imagining what would happen in the life of that character if this scene were to play itself out in our own world right now.

- What is your character feeling? How do their partners and families feel? (We know Peter had a wife because Jesus healed Peter's mother-in-law!)
- What will people say to one another? How will they care for one another? How will they decide what's most important?

Now dramatize the scene together, making up your character's dialogue on the spot, as he/she interacts with other characters. If time permits, have the whole group come back together and play each scene through once for everyone.

Alternative wisdom

PERSPECTIVES ON PEOPLE
Mark 2:13–17 (Jesus calls the tax collector)
Read aloud the scripture passage and the following summary. Reflect on each question and share responses.

Jesus often presented an alternative worldview which challenged conventional wisdom.
- Tax collectors in Jesus' day were despised for maximizing their personal profits, at the expense of those less fortunate than themselves. What categories of citizens seem to fit this stereotype now? How are they regarded by others? Why is it difficult in their

situations to "follow" Jesus? What made change possible in this story?

- With which character in this story do you identify most closely? What does this story say to you about your own calling?

- What does this story imply about all Christ's disciples? Who should be excluded from the church? How does this story help to release you from fear?

PERSPECTIVES ON RULES

Mark 2:23–3:6 (the Sabbath was made for humans)
Read aloud the scripture passage and the following summary. Reflect on each question and share responses.

Jesus disobeyed the rules about activities on the Sabbath. The Law of Moses was meant to help the people of Israel stay attentive to health, for the benefit of both individuals and community. Jesus did all he could do to defend the "spirit" of the Law from distortion. But Jesus broke specific rules when he felt it was important to do so.

- How is tension between the spirit of the law and the letter of the law a factor in Christian life today? How is this tension played out in your own faith community? In your secular life?

- Can you think of an instance where you found yourself siding with strict adherence to the law? In what kinds of situations can "the letter of the law" be important? When could it be harmful? How can we tell whether fear or love is guiding our discernment?

PERSPECTIVES ON ATTENTIVENESS

Luke 10:38–42 (Mary and Martha)
Read aloud the scripture passage. Reflect on each question and share responses.

- Throughout the gospels, Jesus teaches that

caring for others is an authentic response to God's love. What do you think is the one thing from which even caring acts of service should not distract us? What happens to even our well-intended efforts if we fail to seek the wisdom of God? How can we hold contemplation and action together?

- What distractions hinder your attentiveness to God? How could the discipline of contemplative listening strengthen your capacity for service? How might you build an intentional pattern of action and reflection into your lifestyle?

PERSPECTIVES ON DEVOTION

Matthew 26:6–13, Mark 14:3–9, and John 12:1–8 (a woman anoints Jesus)
Read aloud the scripture passages and the following summary. Reflect on each question and share responses.

In each of these accounts a woman expresses radical compassion for Jesus as one in need. By anointing him with oil, she enacts the symbolic ritual through which Jesus gains the title "Christ," a Greek translation of the Hebrew word for "Messiah" which means "anointed one." Unlike the disciples who are preoccupied with issues of public charity, the woman at Bethany perceives that Jesus' mission will lead to his death, and responds with extravagant love.

- How does the world tend to deal with those who are vulnerable? How does Jesus critique worldly ways?

- In what ways is the woman at Bethany a model disciple? Name some other gospel moments when women are first to see truth. How do these portrayals express the radical inclusivity of Jesus' ministry?

- Jesus teaches throughout the gospels that public concern for those who are vulnerable and ostracized by society is essential to community morality. What parallel teaching on personal acts of kindness is suggested by Jesus' affirmation of the woman at Bethany? Have you found it hard to honor both these teachings? What steps can you take to honor both?

Witnessing miracles

UNEXPECTED ENDINGS

John 2:1–11 (the wedding at Cana)
Read aloud the scripture passage and the following summary. Reflect on each question and share responses.

This first miracle at Cana shows us the ordinary changed to wonderful, full of wonder. Scarcity becomes abundance, and the "finest wine" is saved for the end.

- In what ways are these phenomena foretastes of the whole of Christ's story?
- In what ways does this story suggest that the Spirit is at work in everyday life? Describe a time when you experienced a miracle.

FREED FROM FEAR

Matthew 14:22–33 (Jesus walks on water)
Read aloud the scripture passage. Reflect on each question and share responses.

- Describe a fearful or dangerous situation in the world, where the saving power of God was not recognized. How did people's faith falter?
- Name some ways things are changed when people are aware of the power and possibility in holy presence.
- When have you acted like Peter and faltered in faith? Were you able to hear Christ assure you? What can you do to strengthen your capacity to recognize the holy in times of trouble?

FEEDING THE HUNGRY

Matthew 14:13–21 (Jesus feeds the multitude who have gathered to hear him speak)
Read aloud the scripture passage. Reflect on each question and share responses.

- The multiplying of loaves and fishes is still important. There is more than enough food to feed everyone who hungers in the world. The problem is distribution. In the story, who does Jesus depend on to distribute God's abundance? What are the implications for us today?
- Describe a time when you experienced hunger. How can you express your solidarity with those who are hungry? What steps can you take to share in the miracle of ending hunger?

Healing

The ministry of Jesus reveals the power of the Spirit to heal dis-ease in human bodies, minds, souls, and relationships. The healing power of the Spirit flows through Jesus of Nazareth, and through those who come to trust in God's love through the love of Jesus Christ.

RESPONSIBILITY FOR HEALING

Matthew 4:12–25 (the first disciples), Luke 6:12–19 (before the Beatitudes), and Mark 1:23–34 (a man with an unclean spirit)
Read aloud the scripture passages and the following summary. Reflect on each question and share responses.

These three narratives describe Jesus' first healings. The centrality of healing in the ministry of Jesus is very clear in the gospels of Matthew, Mark, and Luke, where Jesus calls his disciples and right away begins to share his healing power.

- In the teachings of your church, has Christ's power to heal people physically and spiritually been emphasized or has it been down-played?

- Why do you think some people experience healing quite simply as deeper peace and harmony, while others experience total remission of physical symptoms, gradual improvement, or cure?
- How have your perceptions of what is possible changed through your lifetime?
- Describe a moment of personal healing in your life, when your perspective and attitude were warmed and altered. What or who opened the way to this healing transformation? How was this an experience of the Spirit for you?

HEALING THROUGH PRAYER
Mark 1:40–45 (healing a leper), Mark 8:22–25 (healing a blind man), and Luke 13:10–17 (healing a bent-over woman), and Luke 7:1–10 (healing a slave at a distance)
Read aloud the scripture passages and the following summary. Reflect on each question and share responses.

Disintegration of harmony in body, mind, or relationships can block the natural flow of healing energy. In our time, there is considerable scientific support for the premise that restoring the life-giving flow of the Spirit can heal us of many kinds of "dis-ease." However, touch is not always appropriate and proximity is not always possible. Researchers have been especially excited by evidence that prayer can bring healing without proximity to or awareness by the sufferer.

- How does scientific support help you grapple with the biblical witness that prayer and touch can bring healing?
- Quantum physics suggests that everything, including material objects and bodies, is simply some form of energy. How might this scientific theory be linked to healings that occur when the healed one is physically

separate from the source(s) of prayer? How might God be linked to quantum physics?
- Why would Jesus choose to lay on hands in some instances and not in others? In what kinds of situations can touch be unhelpful or inappropriate?
- Describe your personal experience or knowledge of healings that are related to prayer or healing touch. How do you interpret what happens when such a healing occurs? How are these experiences of the Spirit for you?

HEALING PHYSICAL AILMENTS
2 Kings 5:1–14 (Elisha heals Naaman of his skin disease), and John 5:1–15 (Jesus heals a crippled man) and Mark 2:1–12 (Jesus heals a paralytic person)
Read aloud the scripture passages and the following summary. Reflect on each question and share responses.

We are mortal creatures, and our physical bodies age and die. Not every illness or affliction can be cured by attitudinal change or by easing distress. Even so, spiritual and emotional healing can open the pathway to physical cure.

- What did each of these afflicted human beings need to do to be cured? How could making an active commitment to healing open up new possibilities? What attitude needed transformation?
- Have you a sense or knowledge of what can block your personal healing? In addition to physical wellness, what other kinds of healing do you seek? What would you need to let go in order to heal?
- In what ways is healing frightening for you? What would be gained? What would strength and grace look like in your own situation? What steps can you take to free your spirit for commitment to healing?

HEALING OF MEMORIES

Genesis 37:1–4 (a favorite son), 12–36 (Joseph sold into slavery) and Genesis 45:1–15 (Joseph reconciles with his brothers)

Read aloud the scripture passages and the following summary. Reflect on each question and share responses.

Renewal in body, mind, and soul may depend on healing our memories of hurts in the past and, where possible, restoring health in relationship. Healing the past is a process. Forgiveness takes time. It seems that Joseph understood the power of his history (for good and for ill) in his life. Working creatively with feelings and fears, he found ways to bear his betrayal and loss which made for more love, not more pain.

- How does Joseph interpret the blessing in all that has happened? How does forgiveness, the healing work of loving enemies, hold open the possibility of miracles?
- What relationships in your life require healing? Are you willing to open yourself to healthy intimate relationship? What fears hold you back? How do your past wounds affect you?
- What lessons in loving is God asking you to learn? What strengths could you gain? What blessings could unfold? What steps in regard to this healing can you take for yourself? Who can help you to do this?

MINISTRY TO OTHERS

James 5:14–16 (healing by the elders), Mark 6:7 and 13 (sending out the disciples), and 2 Corinthians 5:17–20 (ambassadors for Christ)

Read aloud the scripture passages and the following summary. Reflect on each question and share responses.

These passages suggest that Christ's healing message has been entrusted to us. In a sense, all Christian ministry is healing ministry. We enact the healing ministry of Jesus, person to person. We also pray and work for social transformation.

- What kind of healing ministry is already happening among you? What kind of healing ministry can you envision? Who will need to work together for this to happen? What next steps can you take?
- At one level, all healing and renewal is personal. It involves personal relationship with God. Name some ways we can help one another toward personal healing. What gifts can you bring to this ministry? Where and how can you find strength and courage? What steps can you take right away?

Transfiguration

Exodus 24:15–17 (Moses goes up the mountain), Exodus 34:29–35 (Moses' face shines), and Matthew 17:1-8 (Jesus' transfiguration).

Read aloud the scripture passages and the following summary. Reflect on each question and share responses.

- Both Moses and Jesus had mountain-top experiences. How were the identity and mission of each of these prophets confirmed on the mountain?
- Describe a mountain-top experience in your own life. How have your identity and sense of purpose been clarified by this experience?

6. Embodied prayers for the Season of Epiphany

In this Season of Epiphany, the light of Christ spreads through the world. And with each epiphany the light of Christ shines through our lives. As we share the light of love as disciples of Christ, the power of love vitalizes our bodies.

We long to feel the breath of Spirit in our bodies. The Hebrew word for Spirit also means "breath." The Bible tells us God breathed into the first human's nostrils and the creature became a living being. (Genesis 2:7) When we breathe *in* strength and courage, and breathe *out* fear and pain, God breathes new life into us.

Since all our life systems are interlinked in subtle ways, changing our breathing affects our whole self. Deep, slow breathing is the body's natural way of moving into relaxation, which in turn helps us attend to our experience. Combining breathing and prayer can help us focus and center on the presence of the Spirit, and deepen our awareness of that Spirit in our physical being.

INSTRUCTIONS

These prayers can be part of daily spiritual disciplines. They are written for groups, for prayer partners, or for personal use.

When used by a group, one participant will need to assume the role of guide. Decide in advance who will lead the prayers today, letting each prayer unfold slowly and gently.

For an effective pace, we suggest you take two full breaths whenever you see "…" before you start the next phrase. If a time frame is suggested, remember that one minute equals about eight full breaths. Give your group permission to breathe normally at any time, especially if they feel distressed or anxious. Tell the group never to strain or hold the breath. A deep breath is gentle and relaxed.

PREPARATION

Always begin embodied prayer sessions with this exercise. If you are practicing embodied prayers alone, read through the following instructions carefully before starting. If you are leading a group, read the following slowly and calmly aloud, with appropriate pauses.

Sit comfortably, with your spine fairly straight. Close your eyes. Without changing how you breathe, pay attention to the sensations of breathing … Pay attention to the sensation of breath moving in and out of your nose or your mouth … Can you feel the path of breath as it moves through your body into your lungs? … Can you feel the breath move your chest and rib cage, and then release again as you breathe out? … Continue to follow the flow of your breathing, without straining to do anything …

Now breathe in and send the breath into your abdomen as though you are filling your stomach. Exhale, letting the stomach fall back to normal. Breathing in, your belly rises; breathing out, it falls back. Breathe this relaxed "belly breath" for one minute … Don't strain or force your breath … Relax as you breathe in and your belly rises, and relax as you breathe out …

As you breathe quietly, begin to listen to the sounds in the room … Move your fingers and your toes. Open your eyes when you are ready.

BREATHING THE LIGHT

In the Season of Epiphany, the light of Christ spreads through the world. The light which flows through our being moves with our bodies, and expands as we share in its power.

Sit comfortably with your spine fairly straight and close your eyes. Notice the way you are breathing …

Imagine that you are surrounded by a shield of white light … Feel the gentle warmth of the light as you relax and lengthen your breath … Spend a couple of minutes resting inside the bubble of light …

Now imagine that you open yourself to the light by inhaling the light into your body through the top of your head. Exhale the light through your feet … Your body becomes a hollow tube as you inhale the light through your head and exhale the light through your feet … See the light flowing through your body … Your body is an open vessel for the light of God … Let the light wash away any fear or worry. Feel the miracle of light and love flowing through you …

Now close the top and bottom of the tube, so that you hold the light inside your body … See your body radiating white light … God shines within you … Take a couple of minutes to experiment with opening the tube, to let the light flow through you, and closing the tube to let the light radiate from within you …

Imagine yourself surrounded by the shield of light … Be aware of the shadows and darkness that exist outside the light … You can find strength and courage in God's shield of light whenever the shadows close in around you … Whenever you feel broken, or you sense a need for healing, you can see and feel the light in your body … The light reveals the boundless love of God … Take a moment to honor the power of the light …

As you breathe quietly, begin to listen to the sounds in the room … Move your fingers and toes. Open your eyes when you are ready.

BAPTISMAL AFFIRMATION

Show the group the hand movements described below, and practice the movements before beginning the embodied prayer. Also read the words of affirmation below, so that participants can choose in advance the words they will repeat to themselves.

Sit comfortably with your back fairly straight. Close your eyes. Pay attention to your breathing and let yourself relax … Feel the Spirit breath flowing into your body … Feel how God breathes you …

Hold your hands like an open cup in front of your belly. As you inhale, make a dipping motion with your hands. Imagine that you are filling your cupped hands with holy water. Bring your cupped hands above your head. Rest the palms of your hands on the top of your head. Exhale as your finger tips trace down the sides of your head and body, and come to rest in your lap …

Repeat this again, inhaling, bringing cupped hands above your head, exhaling tracing fingers down the sides of your head to rest in your lap.

Repeat this motion once more …

Sit still and remember the sensation of your fingers tracing down your head. Imagine this is the nurturing, healing water of your baptism …

As you continue for the next four exhalations, imagine the water trickling down your head. Choose one of the following phrases to say to yourself as words of affirmation:
· I am God's beloved child, or
· I am a disciple of Christ, or
· I am an instrument of Love.

On the next four exhalations, choose one of the following phrases to say to yourself:
· God have mercy, Christ, have mercy, or
· Holy One, renew our hearts, or
· Power of Love, refresh our minds, or
· Child of Earth, bring us peace.

Now, on the next four exhalations, choose one of the following phrases to say to yourself:
- I accept this opportunity to reveal the love of God, or
- I accept this opportunity to learn the ways of compassion, or
- I accept this opportunity to love and serve.

As you breathe quietly, begin to listen to the sounds in the room ... Move your fingers and toes. Open your eyes when you are ready.

AH-HA BREATH

Stand with your arms by your sides. Take a few moments to come fully into the present ...

Stretch your finger tips away from yourself as you circle your arms forward, up, back, and down. Repeat the circle again, this time inhaling as your arms rise forward and exhaling as they descend. Do this four times ...

Add the sound "Ahh" to the inhalation and the sound "Haa" to the exhalation. Continue to circle your arms as you feel the joy of "Ah-ha." Do this four times ...

Continue to inhale saying "Ahh," as you circle your arms upward, then when your arms are straight up, let them go limp and drop heavy by your sides as you say "Ha!" with some force from your belly. Let your knees bend a bit too ... Again, circle your arms up, then let them drop saying "Ha!" ... Notice the joy rising up in your body. Do this four times ...

STANDING TO LISTEN

Daniel 10:1–19 (Daniel receives a message)
Before starting, make sure everyone has a chair ready to sit on when the time comes.

The Christ-life helps us remember that love is enfleshed in our whole being. Through actions, responses, gestures, and bodily attitudes, our bodies speak the intentions of our souls. Every posture evokes feeling, and each posture contributes differently to how we pray and how we worship. With this prayer, we stand to listen as disciples of Christ.

Begin standing with eyes softly open or closed. Breathe comfortably, in and out ... Let go of the tensions of the day ... Feel the Spirit breath flowing into your body ... Feel how God breathes you ...

Listen for the word of God, speaking to the prophet Daniel and to us.

Read Daniel 10:1–19 aloud

The angel commands Daniel to stand so he can listen to a message from God. Although he is fearful, Daniel has to take charge of his physical being in order to collect his inner self ... In silence, consider how standing can help us listen to God. How can an upright outer posture communicate to our deepest inner fears that we are ready and willing to face the angel? That we are ready to listen and act? ...

Let us keep silence for one minute ...

Now sit on your chair with your legs tightly crossed and your arms wrapped closely around you. Close your eyes ... Be aware of the shallowness of your breathing, the tension in your body, the feeling of being cut off from everything around you ...

Now loosen your body ...

Rise and stand firmly on your feet again, with your back long and straight, without tension. Do you feel different? Do you feel you are ready to move? ... Raise your hands comfortably at your sides, palms turned upward and open. Do you feel more open to God? ... Breathe quietly in this position for one minute ...

Close your eyes, if this is comfortable for you, and hear God's messenger say to you, "Do not fear, greatly beloved, you are safe. Be strong and courageous!" ... Breathe slowly and fully, feeling life-breath flowing into you and through you … For one minute, repeat to yourself, "Speak, my God, for you have strengthened me … Speak, my God, for you have strengthened me…"

As you breathe quietly, begin to listen to the sounds in the room … Move your fingers and toes. Open your eyes when you are ready.

After the embodied prayer has ended, invite people to share their experience, as they are comfortable.

In churches that invite everyone (who is able) to stand for the gospel reading, standing is a bodily prayer. You can stand and read the gospel lesson aloud with other people, or in your private devotions.

You can also try standing to pray, with your empty hands open to God. In this position, you greet the Christ who meets us and walks with us on our journey. Try this now… Feel how this position strengthens your sense of communion with Christ, and with "the body of Christ," the church, around the world.

WALKING PRAYER
Give your group ample time to explore each suggestion in silence. The whole exercise, including discussions, could take twenty minutes or more.

Begin standing and keep your eyes open. Pay attention to your breath … Begin to deepen your breath. Count numbers silently to yourself as you breathe in and out … Settle into a comfortable rhythm, with one count longer on breathing out …

Begin to walk. See if you can coordinate your walking with your breathing. Focus on the numbers as you count silently through your inhalations and exhalations … Try stepping with each count … Remember to keep breathing out one count longer than breathing in … Walk around the room until you can relax and breathe and walk at the same time

… Find a comfortable walking pace while you focus on your breathing …

Flow with changes … Keep going … Notice the walking rhythms of others who are with you … Now let's rest …

Take a break to discuss what you have observed, about yourself and others.

Begin again, and this time keep your eyes focused on the ground … Try to find someone else who has the same walking rhythm, and walk beside that person for a while … If other people are also walking in your rhythm, form a larger walking group … Try not to look up or to say anything. Just walk and breathe together … Now, let's rest for a minute or two …

Begin again. This time, incorporate a prayer into your exhalation. Perhaps, "Let there be light," or "Holy Light, guide me," or "Light of Christ, shine on me." Try to link up with someone whose walking rhythm is like yours, and walk with them awhile … Gradually, return to your seats.

Invite participants to discuss their experience, as they feel comfortable, and to share the prayers that they selected.

As possible alternatives, try the prayer above, choosing one common prayer for everyone. During a break, explore how this is different from praying separate prayers. Or decide on a prayer that will be special for this particular group – something you can all remember whenever you are walking, either alone or together. Also try walking and breathing and praying together outdoors.

7. Written prayers
for the Season of Epiphany

These written prayers can be a starting point for collective and personal devotions on Epiphany, and through the weeks between Epiphany and Lent.

Prayers for delighting in God

The fullness of joy
is to behold God in everything.
God is the ground, the substance,
the teaching, the teacher,
the purpose, and the reward for which
every soul labors. Amen.

(Julian of Norwich, 1342–1419)

I have come that they might have
life – life in all its fullness. Amen.

(John 10:10b TEV)

You are love, You are wisdom.
You are humility, You are endurance.
You are rest, You are peace.
You are joy and gladness.
You are justice and moderation.
You are all our riches,
And you suffice for us.
You are beauty.
You are gentleness.
You are our guardian and defender.
You are courage.
You are our haven and our hope.
You are our faith,
our great consolation.
You are eternal life, Great and
wonderful God,
Merciful Savior. Amen.

(St. Francis of Assisi, 1181–1226, restated)

The gifts of the star-child
are healing of heart,
courage in the struggle
for justice and peace,
the abiding presence of the Spirit
in suffering and joy,
and power to live life anew.
Thanks be to God! Amen.

I pray that, according to the
riches of God's glory,
you may be strengthened in your inner
being with power through the Spirit,
and that Christ may dwell
in your hearts through faith,
as you are being rooted
and grounded in love.
I pray that you may have the power
to comprehend,
with all the saints,
what is the breadth and length
and height and depth,
and to know the love of Christ
that surpasses knowledge,
so that you may be filled
with all the fullness of God.
Now to God, who by the power
at work within us is able
to accomplish abundantly far more
than all we can ask or imagine,
to God be glory in the Church
and in Christ Jesus
to all generations,
forever and ever. Amen.

(Ephesians 3:16–21, restated.)

God speaks:
"I am the breeze that nurtures
all things green...
I am the rain coming from the dew
that causes the grasses to laugh
with joy of life...
I am the yearning for good."
(Hildegard of Bingen, 1098–1179)

For with you is the fountain of life;
in your light we see light. Amen.
(Psalm 36:9)

O burning mountain, O chosen sun,
O perfect moon, O fathomless well,
O unattainable height,
O clearness beyond measure,
O wisdom without end,
O mercy without limit,
O strength beyond resistance,
O crown of all majesty,
The humblest you created
sings your praise. Amen.
(Mechtild of Magdeburg, 1210–1294)

Come, all who are weary,
come, all who yearn for joy.
As the waters of the Jordan
washed over Jesus,
so the Spirit washes over you and me!
The source of life and love,
through the power of the Spirit,
changes water to the gladness of wine.
Amen.

You the joy and the rest;
You the delight and the glory;
You the gaiety and the mirth;
and Your grace,
grace of the Spirit of all sanctity,
will shine like the sun in all the saints;
and You, inaccessible sun,
will shine in their midst
and all will shine brightly
to the degree of their faith,
their asceticism,
their hope and their love,
their purification and
their illumination by Your Spirit.
Amen.
(St. Symeon, 949–1022)

Mine are the heavens
and mine is the earth.
Mine are the nations,
the just are mine
and mine are the sinners.
The angels are mine
and the Mother of God
and all things are mine;
and God is mine and all for me,
because Christ is mine and all for me.
What do you ask then and seek,
O my soul?
Yours is all of this and all for you.
Amen.
(St. John of the Cross, 1542–1591, restated)

Your love, Jesus, is an ocean
with no shore to bound it.
And if I plunge into it, I carry with me
all the possessions I have.
You know, Lord,
what these possessions are –
the souls you have seen fit
to link with mine. Amen.
(Therese of Lisieux, France, 1873–1897)

Prayers for transformation and renewal

Eternal Light,
shine into our hearts,
Eternal Goodness, deliver us from evil,
Eternal Power, be our support,
Eternal Wisdom, scatter the darkness
of our ignorance,
Eternal Pity, have mercy upon us;
that with all our heart and mind
with all our soul and strength
we may seek thy face and be brought
by thy infinite mercy
to thy holy presence;
through Jesus Christ. Amen.

(Alcuin of York, c. 732–804)

Grant, O God,
that the brightness
of the presence of Christ
may shine in our hearts and our lives.
Amen.

Holy God, give to your disciples
grace and power to fulfill
to fulfill their holy calling in the
world.
Make them faithful to serve,
ready to teach,
and constant in their witness
to the gospel.
Grant that having trust in you
and abounding in hope,
and being rooted and grounded in love,
they may continue
strong and steadfast
in the joy and peace of Christ,
to whom, with you and the Spirit,
one holy God, be all honor and glory
forever. Amen.

Keeper of our souls,
we seek your way for our lives.
Refresh us in your holy mercy.
So open our hearts
to your power of possibility,
that through joy and sorrow
we may deepen in wisdom
and grow in the light of compassion.
Let us see with the eyes
of the loving Creator,
hear with the ears of Jesus,
and shine with the power
of your Spirit.
Renew us in true community,
as Christ-light for the world.
This we pray as your people. Amen.

Ah, my God, blessed light,
when you come into my soul,
all that is within me rejoices.
You are my glory
and the exultation of my heart;
you are my hope and refuge
in times of trouble.
Set me free from all destructive passions,
and heal my heart
of all distorted affections;
that being inwardly cured
and thoroughly cleansed,
I may be fit to love,
courageous to suffer, and
steady to persevere.
Nothing is sweeter than love,
nothing more courageous,
nothing fuller nor better
in heaven and earth;
because love is born of God,
and cannot rest but in God,
above all created things.
Let me love you more than myself,
nor love myself except for you;
and in you all that truly love you,
as the law of love commands,
shining out from yourself. Amen.

(Thomas à Kempis, 1380–1471, restated)

Come, my Light,
and illumine my darkness.
Come, my Life,
and revive me from death.
Come, my Physician,
and heal my wounds. Amen.
(St. Dimitri of Rostov, 17th century)

God of Compassion,
in your gracious light
we know our sin,
and the sin of our people.
We crave peace in Christ,
yet we divide against ourselves
as we cling to the values of the world.
The profits and pleasures
we pursue for our comfort
lay waste the land
and injure sea and sky.
The fears and jealousies we harbor
set neighbor against neighbor
and nation against nation, in violence.
Renew us, O God.
Set us free to share
the light of the world. Amen.

O God, we have wondered
at the light of your star,
and still we have not always sought
your presence.
We are sometimes reluctant
to offer our gifts,
and often shrink from sharing
what we have.
We know we have treasured
what is not precious in your sight,
and have turned away
from what you love most dearly.
Holy God, on our journey,
we carry burdens from the past:
broken memories, resentments,
and scorn for those
with whom we disagree.

Cleanse from us
this bitter, brooding spirit.
God of new beginnings,
begin again with us.
Set us right by your healing forgiveness.
Open our hardened hearts, and heal us.
Give to our wills new direction.
Lead us in humility
to the light of your love.
This we pray in the name of Christ
in whom we behold You. Amen.

Come, Holy Spirit,
Send from highest heaven
the radiance of your light.
Come, Father of the poor.
Come, Giver of all gifts.
Come, Light of every heart.
Of comforters the best,
Dear guest of every soul,
Refreshment ever sweet.
In our labor, rest.
Coolness in our heat.
Comfort in our grief.
O most blessed light,
Fill the inmost hearts
of your faithful ones.
Without your holy presence,
All is dark, and
nothing free from sin.
What is soiled, cleanse.
What is dry, refresh.
What is wounded, heal.
What is rigid, bend.
What is frozen, warm.
Guide what goes astray.
Give your faithful ones,
who in thee confide,
Sevenfold blessing.
Give goodness its reward.
Give journey safe through death.
Give joy that has no end. Amen.
(13th century hymn, source unknown.)

O God, you sent Jesus
as prophet, teacher and healer
to proclaim your unconditional love.
Guide us home to the peace and
acceptance you offer that –
united as the Body of Christ
in our time –
we may cherish the beauty
of diversity among us
and serve as instruments
of liberation for all.
This we pray in the name of Christ,
to whom with you and the Spirit,
be honor and thanksgiving forever.
Amen.

Holy Creator, you call us
to oneness that includes the many,
to singing your song in many parts.
We confess we are often
impatient or judgmental,
and not respectful of the blessing
of diversity.
Release us from fear,
from our need to control,
and from anxiety
that leads to domination.
Help us grow in certain knowledge
of your unfailing love
so we are free to cherish differences
in your name.
By the power of your Spirit,
help us build a community
which beats with one heart –
with that vision of harmony –
mapped within us as longing for you.
In silence, Holy Presence, we seek you.
Amen.

Prayers of thanks and dedication

Blessed are you, God of Promise,
who brings light to our darkness.
We give you thanks for the ancestors
who received your holy word,
for the prophets who help us
to see the Messiah, and
for Christ who lights the way
to peace and freedom. Amen.

Giver of immortality, we praise you.
You are the source of life and light,
the source of all grace and truth;
You love the poor,
you seek reconciliation with us all,
and you draw all to you
by sending to us your dear Son.
We beg you, make us really alive.
Give us the spirit of light,
that we may know you,
the supremely true,
and your envoy, Jesus Christ.
Give us the Holy Spirit
and give us voice to proclaim
your mysteries.
May Jesus, Christ and Spirit, speak in us
and praise you through us,
for you are high above all powers,
virtues, and dominations,
above everything that can be named,
both in this world
and in the world to come.
Holy, holy, holy God,
heaven and earth are full of your
glory. Amen.

(Bishop Serapion, 4th century, restated)

O Shining Light, we give thanks
for the light of this day,
for the light of eternal love,
for the light of the journey to justice
and peace,

and for the light of your grace
in our lives.
Shine through us, we pray,
that the light of joy may spread
through the world. Amen.

Prayers for the world, ourselves, and others

Star high in the sky
Did you shine in days gone by,
As Mary sang a lullaby?
When I'm in my bed asleep
I pray that Jesus watch will keep,
Till that light so faint and far
Brightens to a morning star.

(Traditional, source unknown)

O Bright Star of Justice,
light of the world,
seeking to make straight
all that is twisted
and put right all that is wrong,
come with power and awesome mercy
into the reluctance of our hearts.
Amen.

As the wise ones sought Jesus
by following a star,
let us follow the star-child
into the Christ-light of peace.
Holy light of God, shine on us.
As the wise ones dared to trust
in the wonders of the sky,
let us walk in the ways
of compassion together,
in the wonder of true community
on earth.
Holy light of God, shine on us.
As the wise ones returned to their
country by another road,
let us travel a new path
to justice and kindness.
Holy light of God, shine on us. Amen.

O perfect promise,
whose wish for all people
is health and peace,
guide us to Christ's holy way
of compassion,
so our lives may be visible signs
of your love,
and the whole world may sing
songs of joy.
This we pray in the name of Christ
who is coming. Amen.

O God Almighty,
Father of Jesus Christ,
grant us, we pray, to be
grounded and settled in your truth
by the coming of the Holy Spirit
into our hearts.
That which we know not, do reveal;
that which is wanting in us, do fill up;
that which we know, do confirm;
and keep us blameless in your service,
through Jesus Christ our beloved.
Amen.

(St. Clement of Rome, c. 100, restated)

God of creative power
and eternal light:
Look favorably on your whole church,
that sacred mystery;
and by the tranquil operation
of your perpetual providence,
carry out your gracious work
of redemption.
Let the whole world know
that the things that were cast down
are being raised up,
that the things that have grown old
are being made new,
and that all things are being fulfilled
through the One
in whom they had their beginning,
even Jesus Christ our Savior. Amen.

(Gelasian *Sacramentary*, 7th Century)

In the prayer below, several voices may take part. A solo voice should read the words in light type, and the rest of the people respond with the words in dark type.

Light of peace, in the name of Christ,
who came as light for the world,
we pray for the faithful
who seek the light
of true community on earth.
God, in your love, **hear our prayer.**
Light of justice,
in the name of Christ,
born a Jew in Roman regions,
we pray for the persecuted
who suffer for reasons
of gender or race,
faith or politics.
God, in your love, **hear our prayer.**
Light of hope,
in the name of Christ
who was born in a stable,
we pray for those who are in need
of shelter, food, and meaningful work.
God, in your love, **hear our prayer.**

Light of compassion,
in the name of Christ
for whom nowhere was safe,
we pray for the fearful, the bereaved,
and the sick,
for all who are in pain
and special need.
God, in your love, **hear our prayer.**
Light of our souls,
call us onward into light,
today and forever. Amen.

Let us be watchful –
for those whose way is fearful;
Let us be ready –
to stand beside the outcast;
Let us be prepared –
to stay the course with those who suffer.
Let us go to the world
in the power of the Spirit
to fulfill our high calling
as disciples of Christ,
who shines on us now and forever.
Amen.

8. Guided prayers & meditations for the Season of Epiphany

Prayer suggestions for the weeks between Epiphany and Lent are written here for groups with one participant taking on the role of guide. They can be easily adapted for prayer partners or for personal use.

Decide in advance who will read the scripture passages, and who will lead the prayers, letting each prayer unfold slowly and gently. Remember to choose a prayer-style which matches the level of comfort and familiarity among those who are present, and remind them they are always free to "pass." Encourage participants to keep a prayer jour-nal and to spend about ten minutes reflecting on paper about each prayer time, by letting God speak through their writing or drawing.

A LECTIO MEDITATION ON SEEKING
Matthew 2:1–12 (the Wise Ones seek Christ)
Remind everyone before you start that all will be responsible to pray for one another, and that each will be particularly responsible for praying for the person immediately to their right.

Take a few moments to prepare. Sit comfortably … Close your eyes … Focus on your regular breathing pattern, counting silently as you breathe in and out … Relax with your breathing … Feel the Spirit breath flowing into your body … Feel how God breathes you …

Listen for the word of God …

Read through the biblical passage slowly, aloud.

Reflect in the silence on the journey of the Magi … Do you want to see the Christ-child for yourself? … Can you trust God to lead you? … What holds you back? … Are you afraid to follow your star? … Are you afraid you might get lost on this path? … What will help you move through your fear? …

Read through the passage once again, aloud.

Who have you known who has traveled this spiritual pathway? … How has this person affected your life? The lives of others? … Who are your companions now on your journey? … How can they honor your life? …

Read the passage once again, aloud.

Consider what changes in your life this journey will require … What might you have to let go? … What dangers might you face? … What might you learn? … What other roads could lie ahead? … Are you willing to commit to this journey? … Where will you place your trust? …

Rest quietly in the presence of God … Pray in silence for yourself, that God will lead you to the Christ child …

Pray quietly for the person to your right, that he or she may be strengthened and encouraged to seek the holy … Pray for those who are in special need today … Finish with a prayer or a blessing you know by heart …

Open your eyes when you are ready.
Invite participants to feel free to share or to be quiet at the close of the prayer.

A MEDITATION ON FEAR

Since strong feelings and memories can emerge during prayer, explain that the intention of this prayer is to help us release our fears into God's care. Take time to assure participants that you are willing to be available for personal conversation, or to help them find additional resources if that would be helpful.

Take a few moments to come fully into the present … Sit comfortably … Close your eyes … Focus on your regular breathing pattern, counting silently as you breathe in and out … Feel the Spirit breath flowing into your body … Feel how God breathes you …

As you relax with your breathing, take several moments in silence to recollect one event or situation from the last few days which aroused in you some kind of fear … Remember the time of day when this occurred. Continue breathing quietly, in and out …

Take a couple of minutes to relive the incident as it happened, remembering the sights and sounds and smells … As you breathe, become aware of what kinds of fears are re-created by remembering this incident … Where was the strongest feeling? …

Now set aside your reflections, and be open to a phrase or an image from scripture or literature which may emerge from your memory … As you continue to breathe, remember that any phrase or image which comes holds some blessing …

With those words or phrases in your mind, bring back to your consciousness the original incident and place your image or phrase alongside it … Rest in God's presence … Breathe quietly, holding both the fearful incident and your blessing in peace …

Now offer both the incident and the blessing back to God ... Listen to discover an invitation for the next few days ... How is God speaking to you through the incident and the blessing? ... What are you invited to do or to be? ...

Pray silently for yourself, for wisdom, strength, and courage to respond to God's invitation ...

Pray quietly for the person to your right, that he or she will be enabled to respond to God's invitation ... Pray for those who are in special need today ... Close with a prayer or blessing you know by heart. Open your eyes when you are ready.

Invite participants to feel free to share or to be quiet at the close of the prayer.

A MEDITATION ON LEARNING

Use the prayer pattern above on fear, but this time ask specifically what God is inviting you to learn. Where is Christ for you in this incident? What part are you being asked to take? To whom do you belong? Is there someone you are meant to forgive? Have you been forgiven, or do you feel you need forgiveness? What strength or insight emerged in you because of this experience?

A CENTERING MEDITATION ON LIGHT

Genesis 1:3, Isaiah 9:2, 49:6b, 60:1, Psalm 36:9 (images of light)

Take a few moments to come fully into the present ... Sit comfortably, eyes closed ... Focus on your regular breathing pattern, counting silently as you breathe in and out ... Feel the Spirit breath flowing into your body ... Feel how God breathes you ... As you relax with your breathing, listen for the word of God ...

Choose one of the following passages and read it through three times slowly aloud. (Don't read the biblical reference.)

- Then God said, "Let there be light," and there was light. (Genesis 1:3)
- Arise, shine; for your light has come, and the glory of God has risen upon you. (Isaiah 60:1)
- The people who walked in the shadows have seen a great light; those who lived in a land of deep shadows – on them light has shined. (Isaiah 9:2 adapted)
- For with you is the fountain of life; in your light we see light. (Psalm 36:9)
- I will give you as a light to the nations, that my salvation may reach to the end of the earth. (Isaiah 49: 6b)

Repeat these words within yourself, in rhythm with your breathing ... As you continue to repeat the words of the passage within yourself, reflect on the ways God's love shines through Christ in the world ...

As you continue to repeat the words in rhythm with your breathing, stay open to your feelings. Invite the Holy Spirit to fill your being ... Sustain this pattern so that every breathing in and breathing out, whether conscious or not, becomes your prayer ...

As you breathe quietly, begin to listen to the sounds in the room ... Move your fingers and toes. Open your eyes when you are ready. Invite participants to feel free to share or to be quiet at the close of the prayer.

A PRAYER FOR COMMITMENT

Take a few minutes to consider your best qualities and to give thanks to God for these gifts and strengths ...

Consider who God calls you to become. Go for a walk outside and choose two kinds of plants. Choose one plant which reminds you of the way you see yourself now, and another which reminds you of the kind of person God (and you) would want you to become.

Decide what changes in your life would help you to become even more the person you (and God) would like you to be.

It doesn't have to be plants. Choose two kinds of rocks, or two kinds of clouds! Or you could think of two different animals. Indoors, choose different colors, different textures, or different shapes.

A CENTERING MEDITATION ON BAPTISMAL COMMITMENT
Isaiah 6:8, 42:1a, 42:6 (on serving)

Take a few moments to come fully into the present ... Sit comfortably, eyes closed ... Focus on your regular breathing pattern, counting silently as you breathe in and out ... Feel the Spirit breath coming into your body ... Feel how God breathes you ...

As you relax with your breathing, listen for God in the following passage of scripture.

Choose one of the following passages and read it through three times slowly aloud. Do not read the biblical reference.
• Then I heard the voice of God saying, "Whom shall I send...?" And I said, "Here am I; send me!" (Isaiah 6:8)
• Here is my servant, whom I uphold, my chosen, in whom my soul delights. (Isaiah 42:1a)
• I, your God, have called you to serve the cause of right. *(Isaiah 42:6 adapted)*

Repeat the words within yourself, in rhythm with your breathing ... As you continue to repeat these words within yourself, reflect on Jesus as your teacher and guide ... What does Jesus invite you to do or to be or to change? ...

As you continue to repeat the words in rhythm with your breathing, stay open to your feelings and invite the Holy Spirit to fill your being ... Sustain this pattern so that every breathing in and breathing out, whether conscious or not, becomes your prayer ...

As you breathe quietly, begin to listen to the sounds in the room ... Move your fingers and toes. Open your eyes when you are ready.

Invite participants to feel free to share or to be quiet at the close of the prayer.

A LECTIO PRAYER ON OBEDIENCE
Psalm 1:1–3, 119:33–37; Nehemiah 8:1–3, 5–6, 8–10 (on obedience)
Remind everyone before you start that all are responsible to pray for one another, and that each will be particularly responsible for praying for the person immediately to his or her right.

Take a few moments to come fully into the present ... Sit comfortably ... Close your eyes ... Focus only on your breathing ... Relax as you breathe, and let go of the tensions of the day ... Feel the Spirit breath flowing into your body ... Feel how God breathes you ...

As you relax with your breathing, listen for the word of God in the following passage. Listen for words or images that attract you ...

Choose one of the following passages and read it aloud, slowly.
• Psalm 1:1–3 (the way of the righteous)
• Psalm 119:33–37 (a plea for guidance)
• Nehemiah 8:1–3, 5–6, and 8–10 (the wisdom of scripture)

Silently repeat the words or image that attracts you in rhythm with your breathing, in and out ...

Read the passage through again slowly.

As you breathe, become aware of what God may be saying to you ... What does the word or image you have chosen mean to you? How does it speak to your heart? ... How does it relate to your life? ...

Read the passage through again slowly.

Listen to discover an invitation in these words, for the next few days ... Is God speaking through words or an image? ... Through a feeling or an insight? ... A desire to do or be? ... How or what does God invite you to change? ... How can you respond? ...

Rest quietly in God's presence with your word or image ... Focus only on the flow of your breathing, in and out ...

Pray silently for yourself, for wisdom, courage, and strength to fulfill God's invitation in your life ... Now pray quietly for the person to your right, that he or she will be able to respond to God's invitation ... Pray for those who are in special need today ... Close with a prayer or a blessing you know by heart ...

As you breathe quietly, begin to listen to the sounds in the room ... Move your fingers and toes. Open your eyes when you are ready.

Invite participants to feel free to share or to be quiet at the close of the prayer.

LECTIO PRAYERS ON MISSION

Pray the Lectio prayer above, substituting one of the following passages:

- Isaiah 42:1, 5–7 (to be a light to the nations)
- Isaiah 41:17–18 (caring for the poor and needy)
- Psalm 147:1–6 (caring for outcasts)

LECTIO PRAYERS ON INDWELLING SPIRIT

Pray the Lectio prayer above, substituting one of the following passages:

- Ephesians 3:7–21 (an apostle's mission)
- 1 Corinthians 6:19 (the body as a temple of the Spirit)
- 1 Corinthians 12:4–11 (varieties of gifts)

LECTIO PRAYERS ON ALTERNATIVE WISDOM

Pray the Lectio prayer above, substituting one of the following passages:

- Romans 12:2 ("Do not be conformed to this world")
- 1 Corinthians 1:18–31 (the foolishness of the cross)
- Matthew 5:1–12 (the Beatitudes)

AN AFFIRMATION ON ALTERNATIVE WISDOM

Take a few moments to come fully into the present ... Sit comfortably, eyes closed ... For about two minutes, focus on your breathing ... Relax as you breathe, and let go of the tensions of the day ... Feel the Spirit breath coming into your body ... Feel how God breathes you ...

As you relax with your breathing, listen for Jesus speaking directly to you ... Listen for words or phrases that compel your attention strongly ...

Read one of the following passages through twice, slowly, aloud.

- Matthew 5:38–48 (retaliation and love for enemies, see also Luke 6:27–38)
- Matthew 6:19–21 (store up treasures in heaven)
- Matthew 6:24–34 (about wealth, worry for tomorrow)
- Matthew 5:21–26 (concerning anger, see also Luke 12:57–59)
- Matthew 7:1–5 (judging others, the log in your own eye, see also Luke 6:39–49)

Choose a word, or an image of Jesus, through which God is speaking to you now ... Repeat the word or image in rhythm with your breathing ... How does it speak to your heart? ... How does it relate to your life? ... What changes are you being asked to make? ... How can you begin? ... Contemplate the power and responsibility which is yours as Christ's disciple ... Hear God affirm your best self ...

Friends, pray this way to remember whose you are … Let us keep silence for a minute or two …

As you breathe quietly, begin to listen to the sounds in the room. Move your fingers and your toes. Open your eyes when you are ready.

Invite participants to feel free to share or to be quiet at the close of the prayer.

As a variant, invite people to study carefully each verse in one of the passages above. Invite them to consider what changes they could make to follow Christ's teachings more closely. Ask them to note these on paper, or in their journal. Follow with two minutes of silent meditation.

A MEDITATION ON PERSISTENCE IN PRAYER

Matthew 15:21–28 (a woman changes Jesus' mind) Remind everyone before you start that all are responsible to pray for one another, and that each will be specifically responsible to pray for the person immediately to his or her right.

Take a few moments to prepare … Sit comfortably, eyes closed … Focus on your regular breathing pattern, counting silently as you breathe in and out … Relax with your breathing … Feel the Spirit breath coming into your body … Feel how God breathes you …

Read through the biblical passage three times slowly, aloud.

Play this scene through in your mind, taking on the persona of the woman … What empowers you to keep speaking so persistently to Jesus, the healer? … What are you feeling? …

Now, play the scene through in your mind, taking on the persona of Jesus … How are you led to change your mind? … What are you feeling? …

Invite people to share their responses. Allow five minutes or so for discussion together.

Then continue with the following questions.
- Why is it significant that the woman in this story is not an Israelite?
- How is Jesus' perspective on the limits of his ministry altered by this conversation?
- How is your perception of Jesus affected by the fact that he "learns" through this encounter?

Now take a few moments to settle into silence again … Sit comfortably, eyes closed … Focus on your regular breathing pattern, counting silently as you breathe in and out … Relax with your breathing …

Do you ever want to argue with Jesus? What kinds of things would you like to talk to him about? … How might you be changed by talking with Jesus? … How can you imagine Jesus changing as a result of your meeting? … What could you and Jesus learn together? …

Now pray in silence for yourself, that you will retain both humility and integrity in your relationship with Jesus … Pray quietly for the person to your right, that he or she may be persistent in prayer … Pray for those who are in special need today … Finish with a prayer or a blessing you know by heart … Open your eyes when you are ready.

Invite participants to feel free to share or to be quiet at the close of the prayer.

DISCIPLESHIP CHECK-IN

Romans 12:15 (rejoice with those who rejoice, weep with those who weep)Read the passage through slowly, aloud. Invite participants to pair off with the person they know the least.

- Share with one another "a joy I have experienced" recently.
- Share "a fear or concern that is in my heart now."
- Pray for one another, first silently, then aloud … Pray for those who are in special need today … Finish by saying the "The Lord's Prayer" (also called "The Disciples' Prayer") together.

A MEDITATION ON EXTRAVAGANT LOVE

John 12:1–8 (Mary anoints Jesus)

Remind everyone before you start that all are responsible to pray for one another, and that each will be specifically responsible to pray for the person immediately to their right. Encourage all to feel free to either share or be quiet at the close of the prayer. Move gently through the questions, leaving quiet spaces for contemplation.

Take a few moments to prepare … Sit comfortably … Close your eyes … Focus on your regular breathing pattern, counting silently as you breathe in and out … Relax with your breathing … Feel the Spirit breath coming into your body … Feel how God breathes you … Listen for the word of God …

Read the biblical passage through slowly, aloud.

Reflect in the silence on Mary's love for Jesus. See how she acts out of the power of her compassion, honoring the suffering of her friend … Recollect a moment in your own life when you felt such love strongly, but failed to act on your feeling …

Read through the passage once again, aloud.

Feel the courage and strength of Mary's love … Now feel the courage and strength of Mary's love inside you, flowing from your heart through your body … Listen to your own heart's desires … Now, replay the moment in your life when you feel you failed to act in love. Replay it as you wish it could be …

Decide what changes you could make in your life, to free you for extravagant love … What might you have to let go? … What dangers might you face? … What might you learn? … Are you willing to commit to these changes? … How can you begin? … Where will you place your trust? …

Rest quietly in the presence of God … Pray in silence for yourself, that God will bless you with strength and courage to love …

Pray quietly for the person to your right, that she or he may be freed to love with the extravagance of Mary … Pray for those who are in special need today … Finish with a prayer or a blessing you know by heart … Open your eyes when you are ready.

A LECTIO PRAYER ON THE HEALING SPIRIT

Since strong feelings and memories can emerge during prayer, explain that the intention of this prayer is to help us open to God's healing spirit. Take time to assure participants that you are willing to be available later, if personal conversation would be helpful, or to help them find additional resources if they ever feel the need. Remind them they can feel free to share, or to be quiet, at the close of the prayer.

Take a few moments to prepare … Sit comfortably, eyes closed … Focus on your regular breathing pattern, counting silently as you breathe in and out … Relax with your breathing … Feel the Spirit breath flowing into your body … Feel how God breathes you …

Listen for God in the following passage of scripture. Listen for words or an image of God that attracts you strongly …

Read one of the following passages through slowly, aloud.

- Psalm 19 (The law of the Lord is perfect, reviving the soul)
- Psalm 31:1–5, 19–24 (Into your hand I commit my spirit, let your heart take courage)
- Psalm 37:1–11, 39–40 (Trust in the Lord and do good)
- Psalm 62:5–8 (For God alone my soul waits in silence)
- Psalm 71:1–6 (Upon you I have leaned from my birth, who took me from my mother's womb)
- Psalm 103 (God heals and works justice, slow to anger and abounding in love)
- Psalm 130 (Out of the depths I cry)
- Psalm 131 (My soul is like the weaned child that is with me)

Repeat the word or image that you have chosen, silently to yourself … Repeat the word or image in rhythm with your breathing, in and out …

Read the passage through again slowly, aloud.

What does this word or image promise you now? How does it speak to your heart? … How does it relate to your life? …

Read through the passage once again, aloud.

As you breathe, become aware of how God may be speaking to you through these words … What expression of love is God offering? … Can you receive this expression of love? …

What fears keep you from receiving God's fullness in your life? … Name your fears, one by one … Now, place your word or phrase describing God beside your fears. Offer them both back to God … Ask God to help you to work with your fears, to help you turn frailty into strength and courage …

Now imagine that you open the door to your heart, and your self is wide open to God … Feel the Spirit of life flowing in … Feel the healing Spirit flow from the center of your being through every cell of your body … releasing tension … releasing anxiety … bringing peace … Continue to breathe, in and out … Breathe in strength and courage … Breathe out fear and pain … Continue to breathe the healing Spirit of God through your body …

Rest quietly in the presence of God … Pray in silence for yourself, that God will bless you with healing … Pray quietly for the person to your right, that she or he may be freed to receive the healing Spirit of God … Pray for those who are in special need today … Finish with a prayer or a blessing you know by heart … Open your eyes when you are ready.

As an alternative, invite people to remember a time in their life when they experienced an inner sense that God was present and would help them, when anxiety and distress were somehow wonderfully eased. Invite them to find someone else with whom to share these experiences, as they feel comfortable. Invite them to pray for one another, for continuing courage, with joy and confidence in the Spirit.

A MEDITATION ON FORGIVENESS

Matthew 18:21–35 ("seventy times seven")
Remind everyone before you start that they should feel free either to share or be quiet at the close of this prayer. Invite each person to make a short list of people they want to pray for, before the meditation starts.

Take a few moments to prepare … Sit comfortably, eyes closed … Focus on your regular breathing pattern, counting silently as you breathe in and out … Relax with your breathing ... Feel the Spirit breath coming into your body ... Feel how God breathes you ... Listen for the word of God ...

Read the biblical passage through three times slowly, aloud.

Jesus says we must be willing to forgive seventy times seven times, that forgiveness is our spiritual work. As you breathe quietly, name within yourself all those you feel have treated you unkindly, those who have betrayed you, ignored you, or criticized you unfairly ... As you continue to breathe, become aware of any continuing source of pain in these relationships ... Is there anyone in your life you have not yet been able to forgive? ... As you continue to breathe quietly, consider what would change if you were able to forgive ... What would you have to let go? ... What dangers might you face? ... What might you learn? ... Are you willing to forgive? ... How could you begin? ... In what areas do you need to forgive yourself?...

Now decide what changes in your life could help you free your heart for forgiveness ... Decide what you can do about this now ... Where will you place your trust? ...

Rest quietly in the presence of God ... Pray in silence for yourself, asking God to forgive you and to help you forgive yourself ... Ask God to help you release your heart from resentment and bitterness ... Ask God to help you find peace with your memories and relationships ...

Now pray silently for each person on your list by name, seeking for each one the healing, forgiving love of Christ ... Pray for those who are in special need today ... Close with a prayer or blessing you know by heart ... Open your eyes when you are ready.

Invite people to share their prayer experience, as they are comfortable.

Another opportunity
1 John 4:7–21 (Let us live)
Instead of the Matthew reading above, you could read this passage through twice slowly, aloud. Invite participants to think of the person they like least of everyone they know. Ask them to consider how God's goodness and beauty is present and possible in that person. Ask them how they themselves could help to strengthen and support this holy presence. Ask them to decide whether and how they will begin.

A MEDITATION ON TRANSFIGURATION
Mark 9:2–8 (the Transfiguration)
Remind everyone before you start that all are responsible to pray for one another, and that each will be specifically responsible to pray for the person immediately to their right. Remind them they should feel free either to share or be quiet at the close of the prayer.

Take a few moments to prepare ... Sit comfortably, eyes closed ... Focus on your regular breathing pattern, counting silently as you breathe in and out ... Relax with your breathing ... Feel the Spirit breath coming into your body ... Feel how God breathes you ... Listen for the word of God ...

Read the biblical passage two times slowly, aloud.

Reflect in silence on a mountain-top experience in your own life ... How did this experience shape your sense of yourself and your future? ... Were you aware of the presence of God? ...

Read through the passage once again, aloud.

Who was with you when you were on the mountain-top? Did those who were with you understand what was happening for you? ... Did any or all of you want to stay up on the mountain? ...

Were you aware at the time that you would have to come down from the mountain? ... Did you have trouble facing the problems of the everyday world? ... Did the radiance of the mountain-top inspire you or disillusion you? ...

What learning or insight can you bring to the everyday world from your mountain-top experience? ... How will this learning make a difference in your life? ... How can your mountain-top gift be a blessing for others? ...

Rest quietly in the presence of God ... Pray in silence for yourself, that you will be strengthened to share the gifts of the Spirit ... Pray quietly for the person to your right, that she or he may be strengthened and encouraged by experience of the holy ... Pray for those who are in special need today ... Finish with a prayer or a blessing you know by heart ... Open your eyes when you are ready.

9. Inner reflections for the Season of Epiphany

Star
Shine
for all to see
your light
that will not
be clouded
your glow
that shimmers and warms
to the core
of our darkness
exposing the brokenness
illuminating the edges
showing a pathway.

In the context of our after-commercial-Christmas feelings, Epiphany can be a time of the great exhale, the let-down after the build-up. In the context of our Christian seasons, however, Epiphany marks the climax of the Christmas cycle.

These reflections on Epiphany invite you to contemplate some of the powerful images and stories of this season. You will need pages for writing, a special booklet you could create, or a larger journal. You will also need a pencil and pen (felts or crayons are fun). And you will need a candle. Find a place of quiet darkness where you can be alone, light your candle, pray, and write.

Creator, God of Radiance,
be with me
in the glowing of my life,
in the quiet, shady places
of my heart,
the flashing dappled questions
of my mind.
Still me, hold me.
Help me see
the wisdom of your way.
Help me live
the brilliance of your love. Amen.

Starlight reflections

THE STARS OF CREATION

> God said, " Let there be lights in the dome of the sky to separate the day from the night; and let them be for signs and for seasons and for days and years, and let them be lights in the dome of the sky to give light upon the earth." And it was so. (Genesis 1:14–15)

On a clear night, prepare your writing space inside and then bundle yourself warmly and go outside. Find a safe place to be with the vastness. Sit and look at the starlit sky. Be still and know God. Return to your writing space.
- Write words or phrases to describe your star watch.
- What signs do you see?

THE STAR OF THE MAGI

> When they saw that the star had stopped they were overwhelmed with joy. On entering the house, they saw the child with Mary his mother; and they knelt down and paid him homage…And having been warned in a dream not to return to Herod, they left for their own country by another road. (Matthew 2:10–12)

The Magi recognized danger looming even as they celebrated the birth of baby Jesus. We recognize darkness and light in our own lives, our own journeys.

On a clear night, prepare your writing space inside and then bundle yourself warmly and go outside. Find a safe place to be with the vastness. Sit and look at the starlit sky. Be still and know God. Return to your writing space.
- Write as one of the Magi. Include both delight and despair in your response to the Christ child.

- Can you name places of despair in your life?
- What delight has your life-journey brought you?
- How can you share this delight?

Candle-light reflections

ONE REFLECTION

> And may the light shine out of the eyes of you, like a candle set in the window of a house, bidding the wanderer to come in out of the storm.
> (An Irish blessing, source unknown)

Light your candle and be aware of its glow in the darkness.
- How did the light of God shine through you today?
- How could the light of God shine through you tomorrow?
- Who might the wanderer be?

ANOTHER REFLECTION

> There is not darkness enough in all the world to put out the light of one little candle.
> (From a baby's gravestone)

Light your candle and be aware of its glow in the darkness.
- Write of a time in your life when darkness seemed overwhelming.
- Was there a "little candle" that shone?
- What were you invited to do or be?

Christ-light reflections

THE LIGHT OF CHRIST

I am the light of the world.
Whoever follows me will never walk in
darkness
but will have the light of life.

(John 8:12)

Light your candle and be aware of its glow in the
darkness.
- How is the light of Christ part of your life?
- How is the light of Christ part of your relation-
ships with others?
- How is the darkness dispelled by this light?

THE LIGHT OF CHRIST IN YOU

Let your light shine before others,
so that they may see your good works
and give glory to your Father in
heaven.

(Matthew 5:16)

Light your candle and be aware of its glow in the
darkness.
- Christ invites us to let our light shine as a sign of
God's goodness.
- What would that shining mean for you in your life?
- In your family? your work? your community?

Healing-light reflections

HEALING FROM PARALYSIS

Which is easier to say
to the paralyzed one,
"Your sins are forgiven" or to say
"Stand up and take your mat and walk"?

(Mark 2:9)

Light your candle. Open your heart.
- In what places in your life are you paralyzed?
- How does acknowledging limitation free you to
move?
- Do you need forgiveness? Do you feel forgiven?
- Is there someone you need to forgive?
- Are you open to giving and receiving this healing?

HEALING FROM FEAR

But I say to you, love your enemies
and pray for those who persecute you.

(Matthew 5:44)

Light your candle. Open your heart.
- When have you known you were deeply beloved,
with all of your failings and flaws?
- Have you ever felt yourself to be a channel of
unconditional love?
- What freed you to let God's love through?
- What frees you to share it with others?

10. Activities for the Epiphany season

STARS

The star is a beckoning symbol, calling to us from afar. It invites us to leave whatever else might be demanding our attention, and to focus on the light and power of God.

Star-gazing

Go for a star-gazing walk. Choose a starry spot on a starry night. Bundle up. You might even pull smaller people in a sled or a wagon. Tell "star stories" of the angels and shepherds and Magi. Soak in the wonder. Go home, drink hot chocolate or hot apple cider and eat "star" cookies.

Star candle

You will need a clean, paperless tin can, a nail, a hammer, and a felt-pen.

Fill your tin can with water and freeze it. When it is frozen solid, draw a dot-to-dot star on each side of the tin can. Pound a nail hole on every dot. (The ice will keep the can from collapsing.) Remove the ice with hot water.

Put a candle inside the tin can. Turn out all the lights and see the star shape shine!

EPIPHANY BOARD GAME

Create and decorate a board game called "The Journey of the Wise Ones." You will need a sheet of cardboard, magazine cut-out pictures, and perhaps paints and crayons.

On the cardboard, draw a pathway through scenes and pictures of biblical and imaginary incidents on the way to Bethlehem. (Use your imagination – creating the board can be as much fun as playing the game!) The end-point on the journey is the Bethlehem scene of Mary and Joseph with the baby Jesus. Throw dice or draw cards to decide how much to move at each turn. Go ahead five steps when you find the right star. Stop for one turn to water your camel. Go ahead three steps when you are welcomed at an inn with hospitality. Miss one turn when you are misled by Herod, etc. Use buttons or stones to mark each player's place on the journey to Bethlehem.

THE BEATITUDES

Matthew 5:3–11 (the Beatitudes)
Read the Beatitudes, a beautiful collection of teachings, tied to faithful living.

Choose one of the Beatitudes that is particularly meaningful to you. Create a small poster with a special border.

Make a Beatitudes poster as a gift for a friend who may find the words helpful. For example, a friend dealing with loss may enjoy, "Blessed are those who mourn, for they will be comforted."

FLOWERS IN WINTER

Matthew 6:28b–29 (the lilies of the field)
Read the biblical passage.

Go to the library, or gather your own resources – magazines, watercolor paints, origami materials – and surround yourself with pictures of beautiful flowers.

Create a garden, or just one blossom, imaginary or real, with watercolor paints, or as a magazine collage, or as origami.

Make "flower" cards or pictures to take to hospitals or extended care facilities and prisons, with messages of hope and healing.

HEALING MINISTRY

Create a prayer circle or prayer tree. Gather a group who will commit themselves to the spiritual discipline of praying for healing persons or communities, whenever a need is expressed. With your group, make decisions around calling times, prayer times and even feedback times.

To create a prayer circle with a small group, link each name and telephone number to the next in a circle. A prayer request can then begin from anywhere in the circle. Make "prayer request" telephone numbers known in your faith community.

To create a prayer tree, find two or three people to join you in receiving prayer requests. Each person is connected to two or three others, and so on. This model can be extended to include an entire faith community.

BAPTISMAL MINISTRY

Galatians 3:27–29
Read the biblical passage.
Pray regularly for those who are preparing for baptism, and pray for the newly baptized.

Arrange for each person who is preparing for baptism to be mentored by a caring church companion. This mentor will share what it means to him/her to be a Christian, will make personal introductions to other members of the church, be available to answer questions, etc.

Make bread to share in Communion with the newly baptized.

Make simple symbolic garments for those being baptized. (Galatians 3:27–29)

Present each person who is being baptized with a candle (to be lighted from the flame of the Christ-candle. Plan this with your worship leaders.)

Learn to sing a new song for the newly baptized.

Host a party following the baptism.

WAYS TO CARE

Always, Christ showed compassion for the most vulnerable ones in his world: the lonely, the ill, and the rejected. Who are the most vulnerable in our community? How can you make the activities above ways to share the compassion of Christ? Could you keep a gift-box for Epiphany, to share the "light" of food and clothing with those in need? Could you make opportunities to share hospitality with strangers? (They may be "wise ones" on their "journey" to the Christ child.) Could you make an Epiphany Board Game for a child who is ill? Or take the children of a busy couple out star-gazing one evening, so their parents can have time alone?

God's creation is also vulnerable. How can you show your caring concern for creation in this season? The color of Epiphany is green, to signify growing. Are there naturalist organizations which need support? Are there ways to advocate for the environment in your community? How strong is your local recycling program?

PART II

THE
Easter Cycle

The Easter cycle begins with Ash Wednesday during the week after Transfiguration, and moves through the seasons of Lent, Easter, and Pentecost. Where the Christmas cycle is about expansiveness and holiness, the Easter cycle is about limitation and humanness. Where a Christmas spirituality moves through fullness to the holiness of selfhood, an Easter spirituality moves through emptiness to the compassion of community. Together, these alternating cycles of self-fulfillment and self-emptying shape within us the strength and resilience of character which make for wholeness and capacity to love.

Through our Lenten contemplations, like Jesus in the wilderness, we voice our need for God's love and we surrender self-will to the divine. The "Great Fifty Days" of Easter expands our conscious awareness of the power of Christ's continuing presence through the Spirit. And in the weeks which follow Pentecost, we embody our Christian hope for transformation.

IV

THE
Lenten Season

I. The spirit of Lent –
an overview

Our 40 days of inner testing in the Season of Lent are like Jesus' 40 days in the wilderness. After Jesus committed himself to the mission God intended, and expressed his commitment through baptism, the gospel of Mark says the Spirit "drove him out into the wilderness." (Mark 1:12)

It's really not so different for us. The Spirit drives us into wilderness, too, where we contemplate God's call and reflect on our responses to events and emotions which test us. We've seen the holy in Jesus' ministry; we've chosen to become Christ's disciples. Now, as Lent moves us from the mountain to the valley, we start to feel the implications of that decision. What are we being asked to learn? Where is this journey going to lead? What will we have to give up? Whom are we invited to become? The Lenten season is a time of focused contemplation and reflection in light of our faith.

Lent is the 40 days (not counting six Sundays) which fall between Ash Wednesday and Holy Saturday. Sundays are not counted in the 40 days of Lent because every Sunday is considered a "little Easter." In the early church, Lent was a time of final preparation for people who were seeking to be baptized. During this period of baptismal preparation, the church community adopted a 40-day discipline of fasting, almsgiving, and prayer. Prayer was for healing souls, fasting for healing bodies, and almsgiving for sharing – which heals community. People reflected on their own way of life in light of baptismal commitments. Then at dawn on Easter morning, as the rising sun announced the resurrection of Christ, baptism was joyfully celebrated. Church members expressed common faith and commitment by renewing their baptismal promises. And the newly baptized joined the rest of the church in sharing the meal of Communion.

In our day, we're relearning the power and significance of preparing during Lent to celebrate baptism, and renewal of baptism, at Easter.

Many people in the northern hemisphere have believed that the word "Lent" comes from the same root as "length," and refers to the lengthening days of spring. Some now believe, however, that it may actually derive from the Latin word *lentare* which means "to bend." This understanding reinforces a sense of Lent as a time of preparation for personal and collective transformation. Having nurtured ourselves through Advent, Christmas, and Epiphany, Lent becomes the time to look truthfully at ourselves and make changes.

During Lent, the selected scripture readings remind us that God calls us to live humble lives filled with justice and kindness. When we fall short of this vision, scripture assures us that God will forgive us and help us start fresh. When we err because we take over-much upon ourselves, Genesis reminds us that we are made from the dust of the earth. When we fall short because of feelings of fear or desolation, we're reminded we are made in God's image.

The miracle of incarnation, of Holy Spirit in flesh, is that both these reminders are true. And both truths are essential to Lenten learning at different moments in our lives. One reminds us that we are always in need of holy love, and the other that love is ours for the asking.

Finding our true voice through honest self-inquiry is essential to Lenten healing and growth. Naming our destructive responses and behaviors helps us see invitations to change. The authentic confession which comes of inner testing is something we each have to do. It's also something we do together in human community – both because we're linked in a collective kind of bondage, and because when one suffers all suffer. Our failures, temptations, and frailties are our own, and they are also much more than our own. We are persons who participate in families and communities; we live in societies which are dependent on global trade and communication. In today's world, all is interconnected, and the outcome of collective inattention to love is systemic evil.

The biblical theme for Lent is the journey to Jerusalem. As Jesus turned toward Jerusalem, we turn to face our own vulnerability. We come to healing and wholeness by allowing our former self to come apart. Just as Jesus' body was punctured on the cross, our sufferings on the cross of our spiritual unfolding may be painful to body, mind, and spirit. We have to let go of many kinds of illusions which hold our false sense of security together. We have to let go of "false" attachments – anything we attach our souls to instead of to God. We have to open to what's real and face the shadows.

Of course, we can't help feeling we'd rather not face our shadows. We'd much prefer to shield our fragile places. But the pathway keeps opening before us until we finally brave the walk. We need a strong enough self to risk seeing reality for what it is – both shadow and light – and still engage it. To be a resilient self, we have to love and love well without answers that distort what is real. We have to choose, as Jesus chose, to trust the inner leading of God with no other security.

With our Lenten confession, we begin the valley journey to remembering who and whose we really are. Through self-honesty, we remember that we are made from the dust. We remember our human limitations. And we remember, as God's creations, that adult humans are responsible for choosing constructive attitudes and behaviors. We come face to face with the shadows of our lives, with things we dislike about ourselves or can't accept, with places where our love is incomplete, and with loves we have lost. We reach our "Good Friday" when we remember how much we are in need. This is the moment when we renounce our old personas, the moment when our former selves die.

Emptied of ego, our souls learn to bend. In emptiness, we make room for God.

And in the valley of shadows, where the Spirit is hovering, the creative love of God changes us. We remember how Jesus loved us, and how he gave his life to show us what is possible. And mercy breathes into chaos the hope of that love, a love without limit or conditions. We remember love is ours for the asking. And somehow, in the presence of that active, boundless power we find courage to live with our losses. We can choose Easter life. We can accept response-ability as people who can trust in their God. We can choose the integrity of self-revelation, of healthful relationship, and of compassion for the suffering of others. And afterward, strengthened at our most tender places, we're strong enough to serve a shadowed world.

The Easter mystery of Christ reveals the pattern of human transformation – healing comes through sharing with God and with one another the brokenness of living in the world. It is ours to engage with our lessons in loving, and loving well means being willing to suffer. Lent and Holy Week give us language, a story, and symbols to comprehend our mortality, and to turn our experience of pain, abandonment, and failure into possibility and blessing.

Like the prophets of old, we go through our "dark night" to become the whole persons God intends. Risking coming apart, we come together anew in "at-one-ment." To be whole is to be at peace with God. Atonement is the peace of God, a peace the world without God cannot give. Atonement frees us for justice and kindness.

Our personal Lent will not always coincide with a particular season of the Christian Year. But Lent and Holy Week shape us to be people who can deal constructively with suffering when we need to. As God's creations, we will always have Lenten times because we are always "becoming." We are constantly called upon to change. Lent draws us into the faithful persistence of transformation. With Jesus we yield, come apart, and even die – so we can be born anew for God's future.

And time and time again God is present, not just in strength but in weakness. God is working creatively with pain in human history, and working creatively in us. Our changing self is getting ready for our part in building God's peace.

Notes for leaders, prayer partners, parents, and grandparents

Lent marks a difficult season in the Christian story of Jesus' life, death, and resurrection. In our own lives, Lenten prayers and discussions can help us move through pain and challenge toward the blessings of joy and transformation. Each person must freely choose what to do and when to do it.

It is therefore important to outline the intention of each prayer or discussion before you begin, so those present can decide whether they wish to participate. You'll find it helpful to let people know they are always free to "pass." The Lenten process can be difficult, and important issues may emerge with which participants need personal assistance. So please take time when you meet to assure those present you are willing to be available later for personal conversation, or to help locate additional resources if they should ever feel the need.

2. The beauty of Lent – colors, symbols, & art

The color used throughout Lent is violet, the color of repentance. Some faith communities use red for Palm/Passion Sunday and through the poignant days of Holy Week.

Lent is a good time to change the mood of physical surroundings through the tone of decorations. Flowers are generally not used. Candlesticks and crosses can be made of simple wood. Vestments and banners should be stark and simple in design and material.

The symbols for Lent are taken directly from stories about the end of Jesus' life.

- **Palm branches** remind us of Jesus' triumphant entrance into Jerusalem, when joyous crowds waved branches of the palm (John 12:13). In the ancient world, palm leaves were often given to the winners in contests of strength and skill. The Latin saying, "*Palmam qui meruit ferat*" (Let bear the palm who merits it) comes from this custom.
- The **loaf and cup** come from the last supper Jesus shared with his disciples. (Luke 22:19-20)

- The **basin and towel** remind us that Jesus washed the feet of his disciples to show them how to love. (John 13:5)
- The **bag of coins** represents Judas' betrayal of Jesus. (Matthew 26:15)
- The **rooster** reminds us that even Jesus' friend, Peter, denied he knew Jesus at the end. (Luke 22:34)
- The **crown of thorns** was placed on Jesus' head by Roman soldiers, who mocked him as "King of the Jews." (John 19:2)
- **Nails** show us how Jesus was nailed to the cross. (John 20:25)
- And the letters **INRI** represent the first letters of the Latin inscription which Pilate put on Jesus' cross – *Iesus Nazarenum Rex Iudaeorum*, Jesus of Nazareth, King of the Jews (John 19:19).

The cross may be shrouded in black for Good Friday, or stripped of all color during the service of Tenebrae (the liturgy of shadows.)

3. Celebrations during Lent

We move into the Season of Lent through the festivities of Shrove Tuesday and through Ash Wednesday worship.

SHROVE TUESDAY

Shrove Tuesday is the day that anticipates Ash Wednesday, which marks the beginning of Lent. "Shrove" comes from the verb "to shrive," which means to "administer the sacrament of penance." Through the ages, confessing and receiving forgiveness have been associated with the Season of Lent.

In many traditions, Lent follows a carnival time. Shrove Tuesday corresponds to the Mardi Gras (Fat Tuesday) of the French, and to the Pancake Tuesday of the English. In both traditions, Shrove Tuesday celebrates the final feasting before Lenten fasting begins. The word "carnival" means "lifting off of meat."

Shrove Tuesday celebrations give us a rich opportunity to feast and play. The rowdy festivities of carnival come when folks are tired of winter, long for spring, and need to let off some steam. Before we settle down for Lent, carnival lets us live in a reckless, daring, make-believe way. Carnival lifts our shadow side to consciousness. We unmask our usual faces and re-mask to portray our hidden selves.

When you gather for Shrove Tuesday, provide craft materials and invite everyone present to make a mask to show their hidden self. You could even ask them to dress up in costume!

For "Shrovetide" refreshments, pick up the old English custom of sharing a pancake supper. The pancake menu arose from the need to use up the last eggs, cream, and fat before fasting, when neither meat nor meat products would be eaten. Pancakes are also a form of unleavened bread, harkening back to the Israelites' escape from Egypt. You might decide to experiment with pancake-type recipes from various parts of the world (e.g., East Indian chapattis, South American tortillas, etc.)

Some congregations minimize their after supper clean-up without having to resort to disposables by asking everyone to bring their own plates, cups, and cutlery in a bag. At the end of the evening, dirty dishes can be packed back into the bag and taken home to be washed up later. (Remember to set out a few provisions from the kitchen for those who forget to bring their own.)

Through the evening, church leaders can offer some background on Carnival, Shrove Tuesday, Ash Wednesday, and Lent. When they have finished making masks, youth and children can work together crafting a "Hallelujah!" banner. Sing a simple Hallelujah chorus in a round. Then ceremoniously pack the banner away until it comes back out for Easter worship. This action represents our "giving up" Hallelujahs through the pensive and thoughtful days of Lent. Doing this will make Easter still more joyous – we'll sing double Hallelujahs then!

If gathering for two occasions in one week is too much, try moving into your Ash Wednesday worship immediately after Shrove Tuesday supper. Or hold a "Shrove Lunch" after worship the Sunday before Lent begins, and then worship together on Ash Wednesday.

ASH WEDNESDAY

See the *Rituals for Lent and Holy Week* section.

HOLY WEEK

The final week of Lent, culminating in the crucifixion, is known as Holy Week. The lectionary provides readings for each day.

Some congregations sustain a vigil of prayer and readings from Maundy Thursday at sundown through to Easter sunrise, never leaving the church unattended. Everyone – including children – keeps an hour of "Easter Watch," praying, serving others, or reading scripture.

Many faith communities mark the most powerful moments leading up to Easter Sunday with three holistic services of worship. These three services dramatize the events of Jesus' passion, death, and resurrection through a unity of actions, scripture, and prayer.

The historical sequence of the events of Holy Week was first dramatized in 4th century Jerusalem. At no other time in the Christian year do we relive the life and ministry of Jesus in quite so much detail. Participating in the narrative through Maundy Thursday, Good Friday, and Easter Vigil rituals is a way to re-experience the saving events of Christian faith. Outlines for worship services for Maundy Thursday and Good Friday are included in the section *Rituals for Lent and Holy Week*. An outline for an Easter Vigil service is included in *Rituals for Easter and Eastertide*.

Holy Week services are times to share the sacred story in ways which include the whole community – times to learn and grow together through holistic and memorable worship. Louise knows of a farmer in northern Alberta who could imitate a "cock crow" exactly – and did so at precisely the appropriate moment in the scripture reading, from out on the steps of the church. Skin prickled year after year. No one from that congregation would forget how Peter denied that he knew the prisoner just when Jesus needed him most.

Members of faith community can encourage one another to be together as much as possible through these days. You might share in a special Communion meal and foot-washing on Maundy Thursday, in particular remembrance of Jesus' meal with his friends before his death. Note that Good Friday and Holy Saturday are the darkest days of the year, in the "absence" of Jesus, and are traditionally times *not* to share Communion.

4. Rituals for Lent & Holy Week

These rituals and liturgies can be used for large gatherings like Sunday morning worship, for small gatherings, or for families at home. Decide in advance who will lead, who will read, and who will be responsible for actions.

ASH WEDNESDAY

Ash Wednesday marks the beginning of Lent, with roots in the ancient Jewish festival of Yom Kippur, the Day of Atonement. Atonement actually means "at-one-ment." To be at one with God, ourselves, our neighbor, and all creation, we must honestly face who we are. To start afresh, we need to come to terms with our limitations, and open to the transforming power of God. Ash Wednesday is a day of confession, a day to give voice to self-honesty.

The Ash Wednesday service can be held in the evening or early morning. If you choose to worship before school and work, start with breakfast refreshments. While people are eating, have them write their confessions (anything they want to "let go of") on little slips of paper. Gather these slips of paper before the worship service begins.

On the Communion table, have ready an urn or hibachi capable of holding a small fire. (Louise has found that a sheet of asbestos under the urn allays both her own fears and everyone else's. Also make sure you have a fire extinguisher handy!) Fill the baptismal font with water. Participants will also need a leaf of a palm branch – or even better a "palm cross" crafted from last year's Palm Sunday leaves. Palm crosses remind us that many of the same folks who cheered Jesus into Jerusalem soon abandoned

him and yelled, "Crucify him!"

Begin the service at the back of the sanctuary, with a prayer like the following:

Tender God, you hate nothing you have made.
You forgive the sins of all
who turn to you.
We come to you, lamenting
our frailty and error,
so that by the healing power
of your merciful love
our hearts may become
new and honest.
This we pray through the compassion
of Jesus, the beloved. Amen.

Or, read a psalm responsively. The lectionary suggests Psalm 51:1–17, or you might select verses from Psalms 103 or 130.

Move to the communion table, singing something simple. Many worshiping communities avoid singing "Hallelujahs" through Lent. However, if you have not already done so on Shrove Tuesday, you may want to sing one last round of Hallelujahs as you make the shift into the Lenten season. As people reach the communion table, they should place in the urn their palm crosses (or leaves) from the year before.

Read Joel 2:12–17 (either the whole thing or your selection of verses).

Join in an invitation such as the following:

Sisters and brothers, we gather in
faith this Ash Wednesday
to make a new beginning.
With the people of Jerusalem,
we have so often cried "Hosanna,"
reaching out for sacred hope
and guidance.
Then we, too, have turned our backs
on love's way.
And still God is faithful, calling us again
to live with Christ in fullness
and compassion.
With deep sorrow for our failures
and wrongdoings in the past,
and yet confident
of God's unfailing mercy,
let us make our confession.

Read the people's confessions aloud from their slips of paper, ending each confession with, "God have mercy," to which the congregation responds with, "Christ have mercy." Conclude the time of confession with an assurance:

May God have mercy upon us,
and deliver us
from all that hinders love,
confirm us and strengthen us
in the power of compassion,
and bring us into life eternal
in the Spirit of Christ,
who lived and died and rose
to set us free. Amen.

Light a fire of the crosses and leaves in the urn. While singing a hymn, crumple each slip of paper in turn and drop it into the fire. As the fire burns down, sprinkle it with water from the baptismal font until it is completely put out. Invite those present to participate in Lenten observance with words like these:

Beloved in Christ,
let us observe a holy Lent,
waiting and praying with hearts
un-shrouded by deception,
so our brokenness may be changed
into blessing.
To make a right beginning,
and to acknowledge our mortality,
let us wear the sign of the cross,
marked in ashes,
as a reminder of our incomplete loving.
Let us walk with Jesus
the way of the cross,
opening our souls to transformation.

Say a prayer of thanksgiving over the ashes:

God of compassion,
who created us from dust,
grant that these ashes
may be to us a sign
of our human limitation and need.
Grant that the blessing of your love
may change our hearts
so we grow in the image of Christ.
This we pray in Jesus' name. Amen.

Invite those who wish to come forward to receive the mark of the cross. Use a paste of ashes and water to make the sign of the cross on each forehead. (You will need a spoon to transfer ashes from the urn into a dish.) Say to each person:

Know that from dust,
God has created you in love,
a love that is yours for the asking.
Or
Know you are forgiven.
God loves you.
Each person can respond either with "Amen," or by affirming, "I am loved."

Sing a version of Psalm 42 (or another suitable hymn) as people come forward. Remember to ask someone (is there a child who'd like to do this?) to mark the sign of the cross on your own forehead.

Follow with Prayers of the People (Intercessions). Invite participants to pray in silence or aloud:

- for the people of this faith community
- for those who suffer and those who are in trouble
- for the concerns of the local community (the homeless, the unemployed, etc.)
- for the world, its people and its leaders
- for all who seek God and God's purposes.

Close the prayer by praying together as Jesus taught us, "Our Father..." in the version most often used by the faith community.

Invite participants to move about and exchange the peace of Christ (if they are comfortable with this practice.)

One: The peace of Christ be with you.
All: And also with you.

Ask everyone to stand for the gospel: John 3:16–17. Conclude with an assurance and commissioning:

Friends in Christ,
we are beloved and forgiven.
Let us go in peace to love and to serve.

Have warm water and clean cloths ready at the door, for those who wish to wash as they leave.

Table rituals for Lent and Holy Week

Whenever you gather through the Season of Lent, use the ritual which follows to remember the contemplative season. Until the Christ candle is extinguished on Good Friday, turn out electric lights and begin by lighting the candle. As the candle is lighted, share one of the following prayers:

Power of Life,
grant us humility, generosity
and patience.
Help us to see our own errors
as opportunities to change.
Our hope is in you, now and always.
Amen.

Tender Brother,
stretch your wounded hands
across our wills and our spirits,
to heal them
and restore our frail humanity. Amen.

Sacred Heart, teach us
to carry your cross,
so by the power of the Spirit
we can heal the earth,
each other, and our souls. Amen.

If there is closeness and safety among you, invite participants to name the places where they seek healing or change in themselves. Then continue:

Restore to us the joy
of your salvation, O God,
and sustain in our hearts
a willing Spirit. Amen.
(From Psalm 51:12, restated.)

At the end of your time together, close with one of the following:

Precious Friend,
behold your empty vessels
waiting to be filled.
Fill them, we pray. Amen.

Know that from dust,
God has created you in love,
a love that is yours for the asking.
Amen.

Beloved, we are cherished
and forgiven
in the Spirit of Christ.
Let us go in peace to love and serve.
Amen.

A service of prayer for healing

Preparation for faith communities wishing to hold services of healing is very important. A team of leaders may train together in healing touch and in prayer for healing. When both the faith community and worship leaders are ready, the Lenten season is a fine time to start. The following service provides traditional worship forms to help the people feel secure in the power of the Spirit.

It is especially important in any service of prayer for healing that participants know what to expect. Too much reading may not be helpful while the service is unfolding, but it *is* worthwhile to print the full text.

It can also be helpful to print some kind of meditation for private preparation in the worship order. Here is an example:

Holy One, open my heart and my will
to receive your grace,
to receive your love,
to receive to your call,
through the power of your Spirit,
in the love of Christ Jesus. Amen.

Begin the service of prayer for healing in a way that is familiar to those gathered, perhaps with candle-lighting and a hymn. Continue with a greeting which leads into a confession and a period of silence. For example,

One: God be with you.
All: and also with you.
One: Friends in Christ, let us open
to the power of holy love.
And let us share comfort in the presence
of the Spirit,
praying for ourselves, for one another,
and for those in pain or need.
Let us pray together in silence … *(silence)*
One: The love of God revealed in Jesus
sets us free from the past.
Acknowledging our need prepares us
to receive this gift of grace.
Let us confess our need together:
All: Holy God, your desire
is to heal us, not harm us,
to renew us in love
and give us hope.
One: But we have often turned our back
on your love.
And sometimes, our relationship
with you has been disrupted
by experiences we did not want.
All: We all have made choices
that contribute to pain,
choices only you can understand.
We ask that you heal
our relationship with you.
Release us from fear
and from shame.
One: Help us sense you leading
toward the life of joy,
through the boundless compassion
of Christ.
In silence, Holy Presence, we seek you …
(Silence for personal confession and forgiveness of others)

Follow with words of assurance:

One: God is merciful.
All: Christ is merciful.
One: God is merciful. Thanks be to God! (Or use the language of "filled with compassion.")

Continue with a response of praise that is familiar to the people (a Hallelujah or Doxology, perhaps) and exchange the peace of Christ if desired.

Continue with the liturgy of the Word, with readings from scripture, possibly a reflection on scripture, and prayers for the church, the world, and those in need (prayers of intercession).

Follow with the liturgy of the Table, providing opportunities for private prayer, anointing, and the laying on of hands at each communion station. Lead into the liturgy of the Table with words like these:

> **Tender God,**
> we gather to share your gifts of grace,
> trusting in your unfailing love.
> Precious One, grant that we
> may share in your Life,
> so our bodies, minds and souls
> may be restored,
> and our hope and joy in you
> may be strengthened.

After the prayer of Thanksgiving has been completed, invite participants to the table with spoken instructions, and also print them in the worship order. For example:

Friends in Christ, at this table all are welcome and none are turned away. Whether or not you wish personal prayer, you are invited to come forward and be seated as you receive the Bread of Life, dip it in the Cup of Blessing, and eat. You are also welcome to remain if you wish, for prayer, anointing, and the laying on of hands.

Have the healing team come forward to receive Communion first. As they then form separate stations for Communion and prayer, invite the congregation to come to any station that is free.

Prayer after Communion:
One: Grant that we who have yearned
for the voice of your songs,
may be closed to the voices
of clamor and dispute;

that these eyes which have seen
your great love
may behold your blessed hope;
that these lips which have sung your praise
may speak the truth;
that these feet which have walked
your courts,
may walk in regions of light;
and that these bodies which have tasted
your living body,
may be restored to newness of life.
All: Glory be to you for this wondrous gift. Amen.

(Malabar Liturgy, restated.)

Close with a hymn, a blessing and dismissal.

Palm Sunday

Palm Sunday celebrations originated in 4th century Jerusalem. On the Sunday beginning Holy Week, people gathered at the summit of the Mount of Olives to hear the gospel story of Jesus' entry into Jerusalem. Then they proceeded down the Mount and into the city, waving branches of olive and palm trees. As Palm Sunday observance spread, carried back to local churches by those who had been on pilgrimage to Jerusalem, it became customary for each worshiper to receive a piece of palm to take home. A 16th century tradition involved making palm crosses out of palm fronds in remembrance of the way the glad "Hosannas!" of Palm Sunday turned to "Crucify him!" on Good Friday. ("Hosanna" means "Save us now!")

These days, many churches read the whole Palm/Passion story during worship on Palm Sunday, presuming that participants will not be in church again until Easter. We prefer to emphasize the particular days of Holy Week as crucial times to be together as the church. So we like to concentrate on Palm Sunday processions – with palm branches waving in celebrations – without pre-empting the rest of the Holy Week drama. That way the faith community is encouraged to live the rest of the story together through Holy Week services.

Teaching the congregation on Palm Sunday morning how to fold their palm fronds into "crosses" does foreshadow Christ's approaching passion, and turns the community toward its part in later Holy Week events. Participants can then take their palm crosses home to keep for Ash Wednesday next year.

Maundy Thursday

This service includes a foot-washing as well as Communion (or an agape meal). Although there are several parts to this service, there's enough story, symbol, and action to keep children engaged.

Try to have youngsters actively involved in all the movements and symbolic actions. Arrange in advance who will wash their neighbors' feet, and who will provide for fresh towels (or soft paper towels if your numbers are large) and warm water in basins. Warn participants ahead of time to wear socks they can easily remove. Have several stools positioned for participants to be seated as their bared feet are sprinkled with water, and then gently patted dry by a "servant neighbor."

Remember to arrange in advance for communion elements. And if the Tenebrae (the liturgy of shadows) will be included, arrange for people to take on the tasks of stripping the sanctuary of all its decoration and color as worship draws to a close.

The Tenebrae liturgy may either end this evening's worship, or begin the worship service on Good Friday. The word *tenebrae* is Latin for "shadows." Since its origins back in the 8th century church, Tenebrae has been marked by the fading of light, symbolizing both the failing loyalty of the disciples and mounting shadows in the world as Christ departs. Worshipers are encouraged to consider their own behaviors, in light of the failures of Jesus' closest friends in those critical and heart-rending days. We all live with the inner question, "Were you there when they crucified my Lord?" which is often the first hymn sung in the Tenebrae liturgy.

FOOT WASHING

Begin your Maundy Thursday worship with the words of Jesus as recorded in John 8:12. Then continue with a preface like the following:

> **Near the end of his life,**
> Jesus gathered with his friends
> for a meal,
> the last of many they had shared.
> That evening, Jesus gave his friends
> a new commandment.
> Tonight we remember the meal
> known as "Maundy,"
> which means "New Commandment."

Let us pray –
> **Gracious God, through the Christ**
> you command your disciples
> to love one another
> the same way that Jesus loved them.
> By the power of your Spirit,
> write this word upon our hearts,
> that the flame of your love
> may be kindled in us,
> and guide our steps
> to justice and kindness.
> This we pray in the name
> of Christ Jesus, who loves us,
> our brother, teacher, redeemer
> and friend. Amen.

Sing together a hymn such as *Where charity and love prevail,* or something similar. Then set the stage for the unfolding story:

> **Christ was in the world,**
> giving insight, speech and healing
> to those in need.
> Jesus welcomed the stranger,
> found hidden gifts in wrongdoers,
> ate with people no one would touch.
> Jesus showed us how to love
> as God loves.

Read Luke 10:25–28.
Introduce the next reading:

> **Jesus used the language of sacred** friendship to explain what he was doing.

Read John 15:12–15.
Invite those who will be washing their neighbors' feet to take their places at the stools.

Read John 13:3–9, and then continue:

> Friends, I invite you to close your eyes
> and imagine Jesus here in this room.
> See how he cares for you.... Think
> about Jesus washing your feet.....
> Are you reluctant to have Jesus wash
> you? ...
> Can you receive the loving friendship
> Jesus offers? ...
> Can you offer this tenderness to
> others? ...

Read John 13:12–15, and then continue:

> **Sisters and brothers,**
> at Christ's command
> we open to the gift of holy love,
> and with Peter, as we are comfortable,
> to being washed by another friend of God.
> Will you come to your neighbor, who
> awaits you with water and towel?

As each person comes forward, the servant neighbor washes his or her foot, saying, "Receive the love of Christ." (And the one who is washed might say: "Amen.") Write these instructions into your worship order.

During the washing, participants can sing something simple and memorable. *Jesus, remember me* or *Ubi caritas* are very beautiful in these moments, and after the first few repetitions can be sung without relying on printed words.

When the washing is completed, follow with the Prayers of the People (prayers of intercession.) You may want to include a pattern of response to close each separate area of petition. For example:

One: Spirit of holiness,
All: Reveal your love.

Invite people to pray aloud or in silence for
- the people of this congregation
- those who suffer and those who are in trouble
- the concerns of this local community
- the world, its people and its leaders
- those who seek God, and all who seek to be faithful to God's intentions.

Close the Prayers of the People by praying together, "Our Father..." as Jesus taught us, or with a petition to God for empowerment, such as:

> **God, grant us the strength**
> and the courage of Christ,
> that we may be instruments of peace.
> Amen.

Invite participants with words like these to exchange the peace of Christ:

One: Jesus said to his friends, "Peace I leave with you; my peace I give to you; peace which the world cannot give, I give to you." My friends, let us stand and greet one another with words of peace and reconciliation. The peace of Christ be with you always.
All: And also with you.

During the exchange of the peace, you could sing the same piece that was sung through the time of the washing.

THE LAST SUPPER

This liturgy replays the events upon which the Christian ritual meal called Holy Communion (or Lord's Supper, or Eucharist, which means "blessing") is based.

Sharing an intimate Communion on this night is ideal. If there are among you no leaders authorized to transmit this tradition, share an informal agape meal by simply "telling the story" and sharing the bread and the cup.

If practical for the numbers in your gathering, at the close of the peace, invite everyone to gather in a circle around the communion table. Remind them to bring their order of worship with them, if they will need it for prayers or responses. The communion prayer (the "Great Prayer of Thanksgiving") can be brief because so much of the story has been told. Go quickly to the part about Jesus breaking bread with his friends on their last night together. After praying the familiar "Our Father…" together, explain to everyone how to share the meal. For example:

Everyone is welcome to this feast. The loaf of bread will come to you first. Please break off a piece, and then offer the loaf to your neighbor, saying: "The bread of life." Keep your bread until you dip it in the cup. Then pass the cup to your neighbor with the words: "The cup of blessing."

While sharing the meal, sing something simple which people can repeat without relying on printed words. When the meal is completed, the service can end here with a brief commissioning and blessing.

Or, move directly into the liturgy of shadows, the Tenebrae. Ask everyone to be seated. The Tenebrae which follows has been shortened to conclude a full service. (See Good Friday in the *Celebrations for Lent* section for more about the Tenebrae.)

TENEBRAE

The shadow of abandonment

Voice One: As they were at the table, eating, Jesus said,
"Truly, I tell you that
one of you will betray me,
one who is eating with me here."
They began to be sorrowful,
and to say to him,
one after another, "Is it I? Is it I?"

Voice Two: And when they had sung a hymn, they went out to the Mount of Olives.

And Jesus said to them, "You will all fall away; for it is written, 'I will strike the shepherd, and the sheep will be scattered.' But after I am raised up, I will go before you to Galilee."

Peter said, "Though they all fall away, I will not."

Jesus said, "Truly, I say to you, this very night, before the cock crows twice, you will deny me three times."

But Peter argued, "If I must die with you, I will not deny you." And they all said the same.

Voice One: They went to a place called Gethsemane, and he said to his disciples, "Sit here, while I pray." And he took with him Peter and James and John, and he began to be greatly distressed and troubled.

He said to them, "My soul is so deeply grieved, even to death; stay here and keep watch." And going a little farther, he threw himself down on the ground and he prayed that, if it were possible, the hour might pass from him. He said, "Abba, for you all things are possible; remove this cup from me. Yet not what I want, but what you will."

And he came back and found them sleeping, and he said to Peter, "Simon, are you asleep? Could you not keep awake for one hour?"

Have the appointed people remove all plants and most decorations. Extinguish half the candles. If you wish, drape the cross in black cloth. While this is being done, the congregation can sing the first few verses of something appropriate to the gathering shadows of this time.

The shadow of betrayal and violence

Voice Two: And immediately, Judas came, one of the twelve, and with him a crowd with swords and clubs, from the chief priests and the scribes and the elders. Now, the betrayer had given them a sign, saying, "The one I kiss is the man; seize him and take him away under guard."

And when he came, he went up to Jesus at once, and said, "Master!" And he kissed him.

Voice One: And they laid hands on Jesus and seized him.

But one of Jesus' friends drew his sword, and struck the slave of the high priest and cut off his ear.

But Jesus stopped him, and said instead, "Have you come out as against a robber, with swords and clubs to capture me? Day after day I was with you in the temple, teaching, and you didn't seize me. But let the scriptures be fulfilled."

And all his friends forsook him, and fled.

Remove all remaining decorations and extinguish all candles. While this is happening, the congregation sings the closing verses of the hymn.

Send people forth with a simple commissioning and blessing:

My sisters and brothers,
let us go forth to serve.
May Christ Jesus strengthen us, this night and always. Amen.
All depart in silence.

Good Friday

Without the experience of Good Friday, we cannot really comprehend Easter. Encourage one another to gather on Good Friday to remember Christ's suffering and crucifixion. The mood of Good Friday is stark, the service short and dramatic. Have a family or small group construct ahead of time a large cross of thick, rough timbers, at least six feet tall.

An opening prayer like the following may be used:

Look graciously, O God,
upon the people for whom
your beloved child, Jesus,
risked suffering and death on a cross.
Grant us your presence
on this day of his passion,
that we too might pass through death
to resurrection and new life in you.
This we pray in the name
of our crucified Christ,
to whom with you and the Spirit,
one Holy God,
be all honor and praise, now and ever.
Amen.

You could use a variation of the traditional "Reproaches" to meditate on the cross before confession. This one consists of readings (by one or by several people) with each reading being followed by an antiphon, like a chorus or refrain.

Antiphon:
> **Holy God, holy and mighty**
> Holy and immortal one,
> Have mercy on us.

Is it nothing to you, all you who pass by?
See if there is any sorrow
like my sorrow. *(Antiphon)*

O my people, O my church,
in what way have I offended?
I led you out of the land of Egypt,
and delivered you from slavery.
I brought you through tribulation,
and I gave you my body,
the bread of heaven.
But you have prepared for me
a wooden cross instead.
See if there is any sorrow
like my sorrow. *(Antiphon)*

O my people, what more
could I have done?
I went before you in a cloud,
but you have led me
to the judgment hall of Pilate.
I brought you into a land
of milk and honey and freedom,
but you have mocked me
and beaten me and scourged me.
See if there is any sorrow
like my sorrow. *(Antiphon)*

O my people, my peace I gave,
which the world cannot give.
I washed your feet as a sign
of my love.
But you have denied me,
abandoned me and scattered.
See if there is any sorrow like my
sorrow. *(Antiphon)*

O my people, I sent the Spirit of truth
to be your guide,
but you have kept your hearts closed
to the Counselor.
I prayed that all may be as One, but
you have fractured and quarreled.
I grafted you into
my chosen tree of Israel,
but you have turned on them and
made them your scapegoats.
See if there is any sorrow
like my sorrow. *(Antiphon)*

O my people, I came
as the last and least among you.
I was hungry and thirsty, but you
have hoarded your abundance.
I was a stranger
and you have not welcomed me.
I was naked but you have not clothed me,
sick and captive,
but you have not visited.
See if there is any sorrow
like my sorrow. *(Antiphon)*

One: Friends, in sorrow,
let us make our confession:
All: Holy Creator, we turn away
from your unfailing love.
We forsake you. We betray you.
We watch from afar.
We are silent
when your call is most clear.
We are ruled, not by love, but by fear.
Change us, O God,
change our hearts.
This we ask in Jesus' name. Amen.

After a *Kyrie* (if this is your practice), continue with
words of assurance:

Dear people of God,
Christ came not to condemn,
but that through him
the world might be saved,
that all who trust in holy love
might be delivered
from the powers of guilt, fear and rage,
and be transformed in Christ for new life.
Thanks be to God!

If the Tenebrae is used for Good Friday instead of Maundy Thursday, start the story with Jesus warning that someone will betray him, and stop at dramatic points in the narrative to sing, strip the sanctuary, and extinguish candles.

Traditionally the Tenebrae has had seven segments or shadows – the shadows of abandonment, betrayal, violence, denial, injustice, mockery, and death – with a candle extinguished after each segment. (See the Maundy Thursday service of worship.) If the liturgy of shadows was used Maundy Thursday, pick up the Good Friday drama from where the Tenebrae left off.

If your community follows the *Revised Common Lectionary*, the passion narrative in Year A relies on the gospel of Matthew, Year B on Mark, and Year C on Luke. If possible, script the story for several strong readers to speak in the voices of the characters. It helps to rehearse for pacing, audibility, and coherence. Actions should be full and unhurried. When you come to the crucifixion part of the story, have a couple of spikes pounded loudly and harshly into the timbers of the cross. (You might want to have the holes drilled part way through the timbers beforehand.)

Complete the story of Jesus' death. Sing something very tender. Then extinguish the Christ candle. Lead the congregation out in silence.

6. Sharing our story during Lent

The themes of Lenten scriptures include our human freedoms, limitations, and responsibilities, and God's commitment to our spiritual nurture. Lenten scriptures lead us through a reflective time of self-emptying toward openness to divine transformation.

The storytelling exercises which follow have been written for groups with one participant in the role of leader. They can be easily adapted for prayer partners or for personal use. Decide before you start who will read the scripture passages, and who will lead the storytelling for today.

When discussing stories located in a specific city in the ancient world, it will help participants if you can point out these locations on a map, so that they can connect the story's people and their problems with a particular place.

Remember to choose discussions which match the level of comfort and familiarity among those who are present, and remind participants they are always free to "pass." Let the stories and questions unfold as slowly as needed.

Close your session with prayer. You may find it helpful to hold hands in a circle as you pray. The leader can invite the group to offer the hopes and prayers of their hearts, and start the prayer with his/her own words. As the leader finishes, he/she squeezes the hand of the next person in the circle who either prays or passes the "squeeze" on to the next person.

GOD'S PROMISES

Genesis 9:8–17 (God's covenant with Noah), Genesis 17:1–7 and 15–16 (God promises children to Abraham and Sarah)

Read aloud the scripture passages. Reflect on each question and share responses.

- Describe God's promises to Noah, Abraham, and Sarah. Why is it significant that these foundational covenants bind God to caring for humanity – no matter how humanity behaves? What does this say about the way that God loves us?
- What's the most important implication for you of God's promises? How can you respond?

MAKING CHOICES

Genesis 2:15–17 and Genesis 3:1–13 (Adam and Eve disobey God)

Read aloud the scripture passages. Reflect on each question and share responses.

- In this part of the creation story, how were human beings to use their freedom? What were they meant to avoid? How is freedom to live as God desires us to live different from behaving "like God"?
- What is the significance in Adam and Eve both blaming someone else for their choices? What does this story tell us about our human responsibilities?
- Name some way you have chosen to "act like God" instead of living as God desires. Name some way you have not accepted the personal responsibility that comes with your freedom to choose. In each case, what have the consequences been? How does your freedom empower you to live as God intends? How can you respond?

THE GREAT COMMANDMENTS

Exodus 20:1–20, Deuteronomy 6:4–5, and Matthew 22:36–40 (the great commandments); also Isaiah 61:1–3 and Luke 4:16–21 ("the spirit of the Lord is upon me)

Read aloud the scripture passages and the following summary. Reflect on each question and share responses.

The Ten Commandments name the ways by which we violate relationship with God. Jesus' statement of ministry describes how Christ wants us to live the law of love. Together, these passages frame the ethics of Christian community and discipline our lives.

- How is it different to obey out of thankfulness for love which God has given so freely, rather than to obey out of fear? How does thankfulness affect our attitudes and behaviors?
- Reflect in silence for one minute on which aspect of Judaeo-Christian ethics you find most challenging in your everyday life. To what changes does the spiritual discipline of faithfulness invite you? How might changing affect your life and your community? What steps can you take toward change? Where is God in this work?

INTO THE UNKNOWN

Genesis 12:1–5 and Romans 4:1–5 (Abraham as believer)

Read aloud the scripture passages and the following summary. Reflect on each question and share responses.

Both these readings focus on Abraham's journey of faith. Those of us whose ancestors came from far away can imagine the challenge our fore-parents faced, leaving home and traveling to unknown places – although it is not necessary to leave home to commence a faith journey.

- What "journeys" have you embarked on in your lifetime? In an era of continuous transition and uncertainty, what lessons can we learn from the choices of Abraham and Sarah? Where did Abraham and Sarah place their trust?
- Can you describe a moment in your life when you chose to act on faith – trusting God, with no other security? How has that journey unfolded? In what ways have you experienced encouragement and support along the way? How has God been part of your journey?

THE EFFECTS OF SIN

Psalm 51:1–17 ("Have mercy on me") and Exodus 34:6–7 (God punishes the third or fourth generation) Read aloud the scripture passages and the following summary. Reflect on each question and share responses.

The effects of sins can affect more than one generation. Some earlier translations of scripture suggested children were "conceived in sin," that is, through sex. More recent translations prefer the sense that the infant is "born guilty," that is, affected by the sins of its predecessors.

- That an infant could be guilty or sinful sounds strange to us – except perhaps in the context of predispositions or patterns passed on by earlier generations. Describe some family patterns you have seen passed on from one generation to the next.
- Describe a destructive attitude you have observed in other social institutions (hospital, school, corporation, nation-state,) that is passed on to future participants. What consequences have you observed? What makes it possible to change this "systemic evil"?
- Reflect for one minute in silence on any consequence of systemic evil you yourself may have experienced. In what ways does

the concept of "born guilty" limit children's responsibility for unhelpful attitudes and behaviors? What are the freedoms and responsibilities of adults in dealing with destructive attitudes and behaviors?
- Can you think of a situation where you experienced forgiveness, and still had to grapple with consequences? What helps you to change? How is God present in this?

TEMPTATION

Matthew 4:1–11 or Luke 4:1–13 (Jesus' temptations in the wilderness) Read aloud the scripture passages. Reflect on each question and share responses.

- What might the temptations that Jesus experienced be like in the life of an ordinary person in our everyday world? Describe an incident in history where a political or religious leader surrendered to one or more of these temptations. What were the consequences for other people?
- Reflect for a minute in silence on the temptations which can emerge in your life. What might the consequences be for you and others? In what ways do temptations invite you to grow? Where is God in this work?

LIVING JESUS' WAY

John 13:33–38 (a new commandment), John 18:12–18a and 25–27 (Peter denies Jesus) Read aloud the scripture passages and the following summary. Reflect on each question and share responses.

These readings contrast Jesus' instructions to his disciples on how they are to act in following his example with what one of them actually does.
- How does Jesus define the central task of discipleship? How is Peter's grandiose self-image shattered? What will Peter need to

acknowledge about himself so he can change? How is God inviting him to grow?

- Reflect for one minute in silence on some way your loving has been incomplete. Is your sense of self free of false pride? Of false modesty? Has your self-image ever been shattered? What do you need to acknowledge about yourself so you can change? How is God inviting you to grow?

A NEW WAY

Jeremiah 31:31–34 (a new covenant) and Isaiah 43:16–21 (a new way of living)
Read aloud the scripture passages. Reflect on each question and share responses.

- How do these passages encourage us to feel about change? How do the prophets suggest things will be different after the "new" has emerged? In what ways is it already present?
- Do you experience the law of love as something external, or as something that is written in your heart? When in your life have you known holy presence as forgiveness? When do you know holy presence as possibility?

MAKING CHOICES

John 12:20–33 (Greeks come to Jesus), Luke 13:31–35 (Pharisees warn Jesus), and Romans 5:1–17 (reconciled through Jesus)
Read aloud the scripture passages. Reflect on each question and share responses.

- What does Jesus model for us as he anticipates Jerusalem? If Christ is the firstborn of God's new creation, what does Jesus' trust and commitment suggest is possible for us?
- What does Paul's letter to the church at Rome tell us about the process of human transformation? Where is God in this unfolding?

- How do you go about deciding what God wants you to do? What is the most difficult choice you have ever had to make? In what ways have you grown through that experience? What has made this possible for you?
- How does seeking to be faithful strengthen your relationship with God?

SEEKING JUSTICE

John 2:13–22 (Jesus clears the temple)
Read aloud the scripture passage and the following summary. Reflect on each question and share responses.

For Jesus, faithfulness to God meant creating just and healing community. The temple in Jerusalem was the center of a "purity system" which not only excluded the sick and the maimed, but exploited the poor in particular.

- What evidence are we given that Jesus somehow sealed his political fate by trying to cleanse temple culture of perversions?
- Where in the world today are political killings used to suppress protest?
- What kinds of situations in the world could prompt you to risk your life for the sake of building a just and healing community?

LEARNING OBEDIENCE

John 11:1–44 (the raising of Lazarus) and Hebrews 5:7–10 (Jesus the high priest)
Read aloud the scripture passages and the following summary. Reflect on each question and share responses.

Jesus was very moved and very grieved that his beloved friends should suffer. He also recognized the death of Lazarus as an opportunity to reveal the power of God. As the model of Spirit-filled humanity in the world, Jesus himself suffered, revealing the pain and love of God. Through his experience of suffering, Hebrews suggests, Jesus learned obedience.

In both Latin and Greek, the word "obey" means "to listen beneath."

- What does the way Jesus relates to death and suffering suggest about the way God related to Jesus' own death and suffering?
- Describe some ways meaning, compassion, and insight can emerge through the reality of human suffering. How do these changes reveal the power of God?
- Can you describe an experience of suffering through which you learned to "listen beneath" for holy wisdom? Is there some kind of pain in your life at this time, through which you could open your heart to God?

A FRESH START

Numbers 21:4–9 (the bronze serpent) and John 3:14–16 (Jesus compares himself with the bronze serpent); or Exodus 17:1–7 (the Hebrews demand water) and John 4:5–26 (Jesus at the well). Also John John 3:1–10 (Jesus visits Nicodemus) Read aloud either the Numbers 21 and John 3 passages, or the Exodus 17 and John 4 passages. Read the story of Nicodemus from John 3. Reflect on each question and share responses.

- All these stories suggest that people can make a fresh start, a new beginning. How can stories of personal and collective transformation keep hope alive in dangerous times? What signs of holy presence and possibility can we share in our time? What steps can we begin to take?
- Which of these images of transformation speaks most closely to your heart? What does it invite you to do or be? Who is Christ for you in this?

Sharing our stories during Holy Week

We encourage you to experience the Holy Week scriptures read aloud, together in worship if possible. Depending on the year, in the three-year cycle of the *Revised Common Lectionary,* you may hear the story of Jesus' arrest, trial, and crucifixion in Matthew 26:14–27:66, Mark 14:1–15:47, or Luke 22:14–23:56.

You will also find it moving to read these stories in a group, with different people taking on the voices of various characters.

If you are reading on your own, give yourself time to absorb the full story, and read in a quiet, comfortable place.

Reflect on each question and share responses with others.

- Where do we experience Christ living and dying in our world today, to open possibilities for others? How is God present in this?
- How does Christ lead us through the shadows of our own guilt and death?

6. Embodied prayers
for Lent

In Lent, we empty ourselves of false attachments to make room for God. In this contemplative time, our body prayers can help us integrate the power of love which breathes in bodies, minds and spirits.

We long to feel the breath of Spirit in our bodies. The Hebrew word for Spirit also means "breath." The Bible tells us God breathed into the first human's nostrils and the creature became a living being. (Genesis 2:7) When we breathe *in* strength and courage, and breathe *out* fear and pain, God breathes new life into us.

Since all our life systems are interlinked in subtle ways, changing our breathing affects our whole self. Deep, slow breathing is the body's natural way of moving into relaxation, which in turn helps us attend to our experience. Combining breathing and prayer can help us focus and center on the presence of the Spirit, and deepen our awareness of that Spirit in our physical being.

INSTRUCTIONS

These prayers can be part of daily spiritual disciplines. They are written for groups, for prayer partners, or for personal use.

When used by a group, one participant will need to assume the role of guide. Decide in advance who will lead the prayers today, letting each prayer unfold slowly and gently.

For an effective pace, we suggest you take two full breaths whenever you see "…" before you start the next phrase. If a time frame is suggested, remember that one minute equals about eight full breaths. Give your group permission to breathe normally at any time, especially if they feel distressed or anxious. Tell the group never to strain or hold the breath. A deep breath is gentle and relaxed.

PREPARATION

Always begin embodied prayer sessions with this exercise. If you are practicing embodied prayers alone, read through the following instructions carefully before starting. If you are leading a group, read the following slowly and calmly aloud, with appropriate pauses.

Sit comfortably, with your spine fairly straight. Close your eyes. Without changing how you breathe, pay attention to the sensations of breathing … Pay attention to the sensation of breath moving in and out of your nose or your mouth … Can you feel the path of breath as it moves through your body into your lungs? … Can you feel the breath move your chest and rib cage, and then release again as you breathe out? … Continue to follow the flow of your breathing, without straining to do anything …

Now breathe in and send the breath into your abdomen as though you are filling your stomach. Exhale, letting the stomach fall back to normal. Breathing in, your belly rises; breathing out, it falls back. Breathe this relaxed "belly breath" for one minute … Don't strain or force your breath … Relax as you breathe in and your belly rises, and relax as you breathe out …

As you breathe quietly, begin to listen to the sounds in the room … Move your fingers and your toes. Open your eyes when you are ready.

THE SILENCE OF PRESENCE
1 Kings 19:12b (a sound of sheer silence)

In the first book of Kings, the prophet Elijah flees to a mountain cave. He experiences mighty disruptions, but only hears God's voice in the silence. Let us begin.

Sit comfortably with your eyes closed and pay attention to the sensations of breathing … Feel the Spirit breath flowing into your body … For a minute, feel how God breathes you …

As you follow the flow of your breathing, listen for sounds inside or outside the room … Invite these distractions one at a time, releasing each one to God as you exhale your breath. Then bring your focus back to the sensations of your breath … Each time a distraction enters your mind, release it to God and bring your focus back to your breath …

Now listen to the thoughts in your mind that are trying to distract you … Invite these thoughts one at a time, then release each one to God as a prayer when you exhale your breath … Bring your focus back to the sensations of your breath … Invite each thought when it arises, graciously release it to God, then bring your focus back to your breath … Feel the stillness of your being rising fully within you as you attend to your breath …

For about two minutes, listen for "a sound of sheer silence" in your stillness … Listen …

As you breathe quietly, begin to listen to the sounds in the room … Move your fingers and your toes. Open your eyes when you are ready.

Encourage participants to try to keep at least five minutes of your their regular prayer time in silence, listening for the presence of God.

A LENTEN JOURNEY

Sit comfortably with your eyes closed, and pay attention to the sensations of breathing … Allow your body to relax as you breathe for about one minute …

The Lenten journey is an invitation to seek the dry places of our souls and let the Spirit transform them. As we begin, can you find a place within yourself where you know you fall short of God's vision? … a place where love feels wilted and faded? … Perhaps there is a place where your spiritual landscape feels barren … where you stand in the dust of a desert … Feel the dust … Feel the dryness in your breath …

Now, for a moment, imagine you are a tree, withered and wasting in a desert. Can you reach deep down within yourself to find your will? … To find strength to send your roots through the parched earth? … Can you find the strength to search for God? … Send your roots out … Seek the living water … Persist … Look for the love that is yours for the asking … Ask God to pour the waters for your soul into the dryness of the ground …

Feel God's love flooding through you … Feel the nourishment you draw through your roots in moist earth … Feel your self changing, from dry and withered to vibrant and full … Feel holy love transforming your roots, your trunk, and your limbs … Feel your color returning … Feel your leaves, green and breathing …

Return your attention to your roots in the earth, and feel the depth and solidity of divine connection … Feel how rooted you are in God's love … You are solid yet yielding, a supple tree in the wind … Feel air moving around your body, as a gentle breeze would move about a tree … Let your body sway slightly from side to side … Feel how your rootedness allows you to bend and move … Feel how your rootedness allows you to bend to God's intention …

As you breathe quietly, begin to listen to the sounds in the room … Move your fingers and your toes. Open your eyes when you are ready.

CLEARING THE TEMPLE OF YOUR HEART
John 2:13-22 (Jesus purifies the temple)

In the second chapter of the gospel of John, Jesus purifies the temple at the heart of Jewish religious life. Let us begin.

Sit comfortably with your eyes closed. Breathe naturally and allow your body to relax …

Christ is a name we use to describe a Spirit-filled life, which was lived long ago in the ancient land of Galilee and is still lived here among us now. This prayer is meant to help us find the quiet center of our Christ-life, the temple of our heart.

To find the quiet of our hearts where the Spirit is indwelling, we will need to let go of clutter in our minds and tension in our bodies. Do this by focusing on the simplest of motions, the motion of your breath … Pay attention to the natural rhythm of your breath … Let the breath flow in and flow out with ease … Let the motion of your breath rock you gently from inside … Let it help you to relax … Breathe and rock gently … Let go of tension … Let go …

Now allow your mind to settle as you focus on your breath … As you exhale, say in silence the word, *Alaha* … Alaha is an Aramaic word for holy presence, possibly a word that Jesus and his people would have used … As you exhale, repeat the word Alaha … Let the word Alaha lead you to stillness … For a couple of minutes, repeat Alaha in your mind each time you exhale …

As you repeat Alaha, you are clearing the place where Alaha breathes in you … where you commune with the eternal … where the Spirit is within you, and among us, and beyond us … This is the oneness of God, where the creative mind of God lives in you and you are part of Christ's body … This is the center, where holy wisdom is embodied and available to you …

Let the feeling of peace lead you into awareness of the beating of your heart. Focus on your heart … Can you feel your heartbeat? … In your chest, or pulsing in your veins? … Feel the rhythm of your heartbeat if you can, and feel the breath continue … Feel the heartbeat and the breath work together, giving life to Christ indwelling in the temple of your heart … creating a place of silence and peace … Alaha … The silence is the temple at the heart of the Christ-life … The peace is the Spirit of God …

As you breathe quietly, begin to listen to the sounds in the room … Move your fingers and your toes. Open your eyes when you are ready.

Other opportunities
Leaders may want to offer these further opportunities to group participants.

Here are some additional ways to applying your discoveries in this embodied prayer:

When you feel overly busy with work or daily tasks, and you need to connect to the peace of Christ, take a few breaths and silently repeat the word "Alaha" to yourself. Allow your tension and anxiety to fall away. Clear the silent space inside your self where the peace of Christ breathes. Clear the sacred temple of your heart anytime you feel the need.

When you feel overwhelmed with emotional turmoil, go to your inner temple of the heart. Take a few breaths and say silently to yourself, "Alaha." Allow the sound of Alaha to resonate through your thoughts and through your body. Allow the sound of Alaha to clear the space inside your self where Christ lives as God's peace. Listen to the motion of your heartbeat. Does the creative rhythm of your heartbeat and your breath help you feel the action or non-action that is appropriate for you now?

When you feel trapped in a habitual response that you know is not healthy for you or for others, take a moment to clear the temple of your heart. Use the prayer above to help you find peace and silence. Let a vision of a new way to respond emerge out of this space. Rehearse it in your mind a few times. See it clearly. Feel it in your body. The next time a similar situation arises, act from the inner temple of your heart.

LETTING GO OF ILLUSION

For this prayer, remember to allow two full breaths (about ten seconds) when you see "..." Remind your group that they can wiggle their fingers and toes if they feel uncomfortable.

Sit comfortably with your eyes closed and focus on how you are breathing ... Allow your body to relax with your breathing ... Let go ... Feel the Spirit breath flowing into your body ... Feel how God breathes you ...

Now, bring your focus to your thumbs ... Try to imagine that your thumbs are filled with space ... Focus on the space inside your thumbs ...

Now, move your focus to your fingers. Imagine that all your fingers are filled with space ... Focus on the space inside your fingers ...

Move your focus to your hands and lower arms. Imagine that your hands and lower arms are filled with space ... Focus on the space inside your hands and arms ...

Now move your focus to the region between your elbows and shoulders ... Imagine the region between your elbows and shoulders is filled with space ...

Move to the region between your shoulders ... Imagine that the region between your shoulders is filled with space ... Now to your chest. Imagine that your chest is filled with space ... Move your focus on to your throat and your neck. Imagine your throat and neck are filled with space ...

Now, move your focus to your head. Imagine that your head is filled with space ... Focus on the space inside your head ... Imagine that your whole head, neck, upper torso, and your arms and hands are all filled with space ... Feel your whole head, neck, upper torso, and your arms and hands filled with space ...

While still imagining space inside your body, can you also imagine the space that surrounds your body? ... Imagine the space between your fingers ... the space around your arms ... in front of your chest ... behind your back ... Imagine the space around your neck and head ... and the space above your head ...

Now imagine that the boundaries between the space inside your body and the space outside your body are dissolving. The space inside and the space outside become one continuous and unified space ... Imagine the boundaries between inside and outside dissolving ... All the space is of God, inside of you and outside of you ... Can you let go of the illusion of boundaries between yourself and God? ... Let go of any limits you may have set between God's love and your love ... Ask God to surround you and fill you with healing and love ... Feel the fullness and strength of your love ...

As you breathe quietly, begin to listen to the sounds in the room ... Move your fingers and your toes. Open your eyes when you are ready.

7. Written prayers
for Lent and Holy Week

These written prayers can be a starting point for collective or personal devotions through the Season of Lent.

Prayers for delighting in God

Taking courage,
facing darkness,
we re-focus, and behold
the light of Christ. Amen.

Although I have often abandoned
you, O Lord,
you have never abandoned me.
Your hand of love is always out-
stretched towards me,
even when I stubbornly
look the other way.
And your gentle voice constantly calls me,
even when I obstinately
refuse to listen. Amen.
(Teresa of Avila, 1515–1582)

Friends in Christ,
this is God's gracious promise:
God seeks to create in us
new heart and spirit.
In Christ's love, we are cleansed
and renewed to speak truth.
Thanks be to God –
Creator, Christ and Spirit! Amen.

The soul is kissed by God
in its innermost regions.
With interior yearning,
grace and blessing are bestowed.
It is a yearning to take on
God's gentle yoke,
It is a yearning to give one's self
to God's way.
The marvels of God are not
brought forth from one's self.
Rather, it is more like a chord,
a sound that is played.
The tone does not come out
of the chord itself, but rather,
through the touch of the musician.
I am, of course, the lyre and harp of
God's kindness! Amen.
(Hildegard of Bingen, 1098-1179)

Dearly beloved,
in the love of Jesus Christ,
God grants healing of heart
and the fullness of grace,
courage in the struggle
for justice and peace,
and the empowering presence
of the Spirit.
Sisters and brothers in Christ,
receive the message of the gospel!
Amen.

Christ is our journey.
Christ is our task.
Christ is our life. Amen.

Sisters and brothers,
Christ dies so we can live
in the confidence and hope God intends.
Believe the good news of the gospel!
Let us offer our lives from this day.
Amen.

May the gospel awaken us,
the grace of Christ free us,
the love of God heal us,
 and the Spirit empower us,
this day and forever. Amen.

The work of love is small.
It moves slowly.
But like water on a rock,
it makes for change. Amen.

There is no distance
that God cannot span,
no separateness God cannot bridge.
God always welcomes us home. Amen.

Save us while waking,
and defend us while sleeping,
that when we wake
we watch with the Christ,
and when we sleep,
we rest in your peace. Amen.

(Compline antiphon, restated)

Prayers for transformation and renewal

Merciful God, who loves us
more than we deserve,
who for us has borne the suffering
of the cross,
give us courage to examine
who we are and what we do,
that we might share the bread of life
with a broken, hungry world,
and meet the risen Christ with joy
on Easter morning. Amen.

Holy One, renew our hearts,
Power of Love, refresh our minds,
Child of Earth, O Child of Earth,
bring us peace. Amen.

Holy lover of the poor
and the yearning,
as the mist scatters
from the crest of the hills,
may all dimness be cleared
from our vision.
O keeper of the least
and the lost and betrayed,
open now our eyes
to your dream of peace.
Awaken us. In silence, we seek you ...
Amen.

God of liberation,
who bids us follow Christ,
we remember Jesus entering
Jerusalem in triumph,
welcomed with palms
and shouts of praise.
Today we greet him with joy
as the sovereign of our souls,
knowing that his power is compassion,
and its cost is the cross.
Guide us through this holy week,
that we may empty our hearts
to live for the coming
of your new community,
committed to new life for all. Amen.

Gracious God, forgive us.
Our branches of welcome
turn to palm crosses so quickly.
How often we welcome you
with our lips and our worship,
and then reject you
with our attitudes and actions.
Change our hearts, we pray,
so we will not abandon you again.
Amen.

So teach us to count our days
that we may gain a heart of wisdom.
Amen.

(Psalm 90:12 restated)

From moment to moment

one can bear much. Amen.

(Teresa of Avila, 1515–1582)

O my God how does it happen

in this poor old world
that you are so great
and yet nobody finds you,
that you call so loudly
and yet nobody hears you,
that you are so near
and yet nobody feels you,
that you give yourself to everybody,
and yet no one knows your name?
We flee from you and say
we cannot find you;
we turn our backs and say
we cannot see you;
we stop our ears and say
we cannot hear you.

(Hans Denck, 16ᵗʰ century, restated.)

Gracious God,

whose self-emptying love
is shown in Christ,
teach us how to love as you love,
in word and deed,
that we too may be instruments
of peace, bringing hope
to the hopeless. Amen.

Power of Life, take from me

the spirit of sloth and faint-
heartedness,
lust for power and pleasure in idle talk.
Give rather a spirit of charity, humility,
generosity, and patience to your servant.
Help me to see my own errors
and frailties,
and not to judge my brother
or my sister,
for in you I trust, now and forever.
Amen.

(Orthodox prayer, restated)

Renew my will from day to day,

Blend it with thine, and take away
All that now makes it hard to say,
"Thy will be done!" Amen.

(Charlotte Elliot, 1789–1871)

How rigid and inflexible I am!

I can overcome my own stubbornness
only with the greatest difficulty.
And yet, when I beg you for help,
you seem to do nothing.
Are you ignoring me on purpose?
Are you waiting for me to take
the thorns of sin from my flesh
before you will assist me?
Yes, I know I must dig out these thorns
before they poison and destroy me
completely.
But I cannot do it without you. Amen.

(Hildegard of Bingen, 1098–1179)

God Almighty, I pray

for your great mercy
and by the token of the holy rood,
guide me to your will, to my soul's
need, better than I can myself;
and shield me against my foes,
seen and unseen;
and teach me to do your will
that I may inwardly love you
before all things
with a clean mind and clean body.
For you are my maker and my redeemer,
my help, my comfort, my trust,
and my hope.
Praise and glory be to you,
now, and ever and ever,
world without end. Amen.

(King Alfred, 849–899, restated)

Penetrate these murky corners
where we hide memories,
and tendencies on which we do not
care to look,
but which we will not yield up freely
to you, that you may purify
and transmute them.
The persistent buried grudge,
the half-acknowledged enmity
which is still smoldering,
the bitterness of that loss
we have not turned into sacrifice,
the private comfort we cling to,
the secret fear of failure
which saps our initiative
and is really inverted pride,
the pessimism which is an insult
to your joy.
Lord, we bring all these to you,
and we review them with shame
and penitence in your steadfast light.
Amen.

(Evelyn Underhill, 1875–1941)

You wake us to delight
in your praises;
for you made us for yourself,
and our heart is restless
until it rests in you. Amen.

(St. Augustine, 354–430)

I have gone astray
like a lost sheep:
seek out your servant. Amen.

(Psalm 119:176)

O Heart of Love,
I place all my trust in You.
I fear all things from my own weakness,
but I hope for all things
from Your goodness. Amen.

(Marguerite-Marie Alacoque, 1647–1690)

As a hart longs
for flowing streams,
so my soul longs for you.
My soul thirsts for you,
the living God. Amen.

(From Psalm 42, restated)

Help me, O Lord, to make a true use
of all disappointments and calamities
in this life,
in such a way that they may unite
my heart more closely with you.
Cause them to separate my affections
from worldly things
and inspire my soul with more vigor
in the pursuit of true happiness.
Amen.

(Susanna Wesley, 1669–1742)

I know that at times
I will be troubled,
I know that at times I will be belabored,
I know that at times I will be disquieted,
but I believe that I will not
be overcome. Amen.

(Julian of Norwich, 1342–1419)

God of shadows and light,
when devastations threaten
to overwhelm us,
help us remember the courage
of Christ
and trust in your unfailing presence.
Help us see your reflection
in the shadows and light
of our own hearts
and those of our neighbors.
Help us walk the path of Christ
through the shadows into light,
empty of self-pride, willing to learn,
and patient in the work of transformation.
Holy Presence, we seek you. Amen.

Most Beloved,
you come among us like a lover –
persistent, and longing to be received.
No sacrifice is too much for you.
Awaken within us
the stirrings of hope,
that trusting in your faithfulness
we may be healed and transformed,
daring to love in your name. Amen.

Now may Jesus Christ himself,
and God our Father,
who loved us and gave us eternal
comfort
and good hope through grace,
comfort your hearts
and establish them in every
good work and word. Amen.

(2 Thessalonians 2:16–17 restated)

Restore to me the joy
of your salvation,
and sustain in me a willing spirit.
Amen.

(Psalm 51:12)

Precious Love,
you call us from the life of self-serving
into the life of self-giving.
Free our hearts, we pray,
from the bondage of fear,
that the world may become your new
community. Amen.

Behold, Lord, an empty vessel
that needs to be filled.
My Lord, fill it.
I am weak in the faith;
strengthen thou me.
I am cold in love;
warm me and make me fervent
that my love may go out to my neighbor.
I do not have a strong and firm faith;

at times I doubt and am unable
to trust thee altogether.
O Lord, help me.
Strengthen my faith and trust in thee.
In thee I have sealed
the treasures of all I have.
I am poor; thou art rich and
didst come to be merciful to the poor.
I am a sinner; thou art upright.
With me there is an abundance of sin;
in thee is the fullness of righteousness.
There, I will remain with thee
of whom I can receive
but to whom I may not give. Amen.

(Martin Luther, 1483–1546)

We give back to you, O God,
those whom you gave to us.
You did not lose them
when you gave them to us,
and we do not lose them
by their return to you.
Your dear Son has taught us that life
is eternal and love cannot die.
So death is only a horizon, and an
horizon is only the limit of our sight.
Open our eyes to see more clearly,
and draw us closer to you
that we may know that we are nearer
to our loved ones, who are with you.
You have told us that
you are preparing a place for us:
prepare us also for that happy place,
that where you are we may also be
always,
O dear God of life and death. Amen.

(William Penn, 1644–1718, restated)

Bring us, O God,
at our last awakening
into the house and gate of heaven,
to enter into that gate
and dwell in that house,
where there shall be no darkness
nor dazzling,
but one equal light;
no noise nor silence,
but one equal music;
no fears nor hopes,
but one equal possession;
no ends nor beginnings,
but one equal eternity;
in the dwellings of your glory
and dominion
world without end. Amen.

(John Donne, 1572–1631, restated)

Holy Presence, you call us
into life as your people,
bound by water and the spirit
to one another.
From the shadows of our past,
draw us into new community
with hearts and minds
open to the future.
Living Spirit of Light, fall afresh upon us.
Renew us as instruments of hope.
This we ask in Jesus' name. Amen.

Where can I go from your spirit?
Or where can I flee from your presence?
Search me, O God,
and know my heart;
test me and know my thoughts.
See if there is any wicked way in me,
and lead me in the way everlasting.
Amen.

(from Psalm 139)

In this prayer, remember to allow a pause of about two breaths each time you see "…"

Spirit of Healing, lead us back
to a moment
when pride filled us,
so we didn't hear you …
Holy One, renew us …
Spirit of Healing, lead us back
to a moment
when fear closed our eyes,
so we didn't see you …
Power of Love, refresh us …
Spirit of Healing, lead us back
to a moment
when some wound overwhelmed us,
so we wouldn't trust you …
Child of the Earth, bring us peace …
Spirit of Healing, you promised
never again
would you destroy your creation
when we fail you.
In Jesus, you were faithful unto death
for love of those who fear and falter.
In such a love, O God, we hear your
call and know what is possible …
In silence, Holy Presence, we seek you
… Amen.

Friends, let us remember
the saints of the church
who blessed one another
with the kiss of peace.
And let us remember that Christ
comes to us now
and walks with us
as the neighbor and the stranger.
As angels ministered to Jesus,
let us minister to one another,
with signs of reconciliation and love.
The Peace of Christ be with you.
All: And also with you.
Amen.

Prayers of thanks and dedication

Blessed be the God and Father
of our Lord Jesus Christ,
the Father of mercies
and God of all comfort,
who comforts us in all our affliction,
so that we may be able to comfort
those who are in any affliction,
with the comfort with which
we ourselves are comforted by God.
For as we share abundantly
in Christ's sufferings,
so through Christ we share
abundantly in comfort too. Amen.

(2 Corinthians 1:3–5 restated)

Blessed is the one
who leads us into Jerusalem
to celebrate the hope of salvation.
Blessed is the one who leads us into
holy darkness, through the cross,
to new life in the Spirit.
Blessed is the one
who comes to us as a healer,
that we and all creation might be whole.
Hosanna! Hosanna in the highest!
Amen.

We offer you now
our crosses and gifts,
our shadows and light,
as symbols of the Christ
who has loved us completely,
even unto death on a cross. Amen.

Perfect Love,
we give thanks
for the emptiness of humility,
for the emptiness of trust,
for the emptiness of silence,
for the emptiness of hearts broken open,
to be filled with compassion. Amen.

Gracious God, we thank you
for your power of redemption,
for your spirit of transformation,
and for your persistence in love.
We thank you, O God,
for the saints of all ages;
for those who in times of darkness
kept the lamp of faith burning;
for the souls who saw visions of larger
truth and dared to declare it;
for the multitude of quiet
and gracious souls
whose presence has purified and
sanctified the world;
and for those known and loved by us,
who have passed
from this earthly fellowship
into the fuller light of life with you.
Amen.

(Source unknown)

Holy One, we thank you
for your presence in the silence
in the valley of shadows. Amen.

We give you thanks, gracious God,
for your holy gifts and ways,
which turn us ever outward to share.
We give you thanks for faith community
which teaches us to love
and empowers us
to walk the sacred path.
We give you thanks for the presence
of Christ in our midst,
drawing all suffering
into your heart,
and changing our brokenness
to blessing.
Receive the gifts and symbols
we return to you now,
and make our lives your work
of compassion.
Through Christ, with Christ,

and in Christ,
in the unity of the Spirit
all power and radiance is yours,
God most holy, now and forever. Amen.

God, whose holy word
holds the promise of life,
we give thanks for the law of love
written on our hearts,
for love shared through the prophets,
for love's presence in this community,
and for the love revealed
in sacred friendship.
Accept our gifts of love
and bless our service in your name,
through Christ, with Christ,
and in Christ,
in the unity of the Spirit. Amen.

Jesus will be in agony until
the end of the world
and we must not sleep until that time.

(Blaise Pascal, 1623–1662)

I give you thanks, O God,
with my whole heart.
On the day I called, you answered me,
you increased my strength of soul.

(from Psalm 138)

Prayers for the world, ourselves, and others

Long have I loved you,
O Beauty so ancient and new;
long have I loved you: for behold you
were within me, and I outside;
and I sought you outside,
and in my unloveliness
fell upon those lovely things
that you have made.
You were with me, and I was not with you.
I was kept from you by those things,

yet had they not been in you,
they would not have been at all.
You called and cried to me
to break open my deafness;
You sent your beams and shone on me
to chase away my blindness;
You breathed fragrance upon me,
and I drew in my breath,
and now I pant for you;
I tasted you, and now I hunger
and thirst for you;
You touched me, and I have burned
for your peace. Amen.

(St. Augustine, 354–430, restated)

Jesus, remember me, when you
come into your Kingdom. Amen.

(Luke 23:42)

May the love of God empower us,
the love of Christ beckon,
and the Spirit of love grant us courage,
this day and forever. Amen.

We beg you, God,
to help us and defend us.
Deliver the oppressed,
pity the insignificant,
raise the fallen,
show yourself to the needy,
heal the sick,
bring back those of your people
who have gone astray,
feed the hungry,
lift up the weak,
take off the prisoners' chains.
May all the nations come to know
that you are God,
that Jesus Christ is your Child,
and that we are your people,
the sheep that you pasture. Amen.

(St. Clement of Rome, c. 100)

Now my soul is troubled. And what should I say – "Father, save me from this hour"? No, it is for this reason that I have come to this hour. Father, glorify your name. Amen.

(John 12:27)

Almighty and eternal God,
who drew out a fountain of living
water in the desert for the people...
draw from the hardness of our hearts
tears of compunction,
that we may be able
to lament our wrong-doing,
and may merit to receive you
in your mercy. Amen.

(Latin, late 14th century, restated)

O Perfect Truth
be shelter for those without refuge.
We pray for the coming of day. Amen.

Take, Lord, all my liberty.
Receive my memory,
my understanding and my whole will.
Whatever I have and possess
you have given to me;
To you I restore it completely,
and to your will I surrender it
for your direction.
Give me only your love,
with your grace,
that is enough for me;
I ask nothing else. Amen.

(St. Ignatius of Loyola, 1491–1556, restated.)

I am yours, O save me:
for I have sought
your commandments. Amen.

(Psalm 119:94 restated)

O Lord, remember not only
the men and women of goodwill,
but also those of ill will.
But do not only remember
the suffering they have inflicted on us,
remember the fruits we bore,
thanks to this suffering:
our comradeship, our loyalty, our
humility,
the courage, the generosity,
the greatness of heart which has
grown out of all this.
And when they come to judgment
let all the fruits that we have borne
be their forgiveness.
Amen. Amen. Amen.

(Written by an unknown holocaust victim, found on a piece of paper near the body of a dead child in Ravensbruck, where 92,000 women and children died, 1945)

Dearest Jesus, teach me
to be generous;
Teach me to serve you as you deserve;
To give and not to count the cost,
To fight and not to heed the wounds,
To toil and not to seek for rest,
To labor and not to seek reward,
Save that of knowing
that I do your will. Amen.

(St. Ignatius of Loyola, 1491–1556, restated.)

Grant unto your servants
To our God – a heart of flame,
To our brothers and sisters –
a heart of love,
To ourselves – a heart of steel. Amen.

(St. Augustine of Hippo, 354–430, restated.)

O Lord, I know not what to ask of you.
You alone know
what are my true needs.
You love me more than I myself
know how to love.
Help me to see my real needs
which are concealed from me.
I dare not ask either a cross or
consolation.
I can only wait on you.
My heart is open to you.
Visit and help me,
for your great mercy's sake.
Strike me and heal me,
cast me down and raise me up.
I worship in silence your holy will
and your inscrutable ways.
I offer myself as a sacrifice to you.
I put all my trust in you.
I have no other desire
than to fulfill your will.
Teach me how to pray.
Pray you yourself in me. Amen.

(Metropolitan Philaret of Moscow, 1553–1633, restated)

For God, my soul waits in silence;
from God alone comes my rescue.
Amen.

(Psalm 62:1–2a restated)

Lord, make me according
to your heart. Amen.

(Brother Lawrence, 1605–1691)

Be present, O God,
and protect us
through the hours of the night,
so that we who are wearied
by the changes and the chances
of this fleeting world,
may rest in the arms of your peace.
Amen.

My God, look upon their threats,
and grant that your servants may
speak your word with all boldness,
while you stretch out your hand to
heal, and signs and wonders are
performed through the name of your
holy servant Jesus. Amen.

(Acts 4:29–30)

Lord Jesus, receive my spirit.
Lord, do not hold this sin
against them. Amen.

(From Acts 7:59, 60)

Abba, Father, all things are possible
for you: remove this cup from me;
yet not what I will, but what you will.
Amen.

(Mark 14:36 restated)

O God, be with all
who face death today
in fear or loneliness. Amen.

Father, the hour has come; glorify
your Son that the Son may glorify you.
I have manifested your name to those
you have given me out of the world.
I am praying for them.
Father, keep them in your name,
which you have given me,
that they may be one, even as we are one.
I do not pray that you should take
them out of the world,
but that you should keep them
from the evil one.
Sanctify them in the truth;
thy world is truth.
For their sake I consecrate myself,
that they also may be consecrated
in truth.
I do not pray for these only,

but also for those who believe in me
through their word,
that they may all be one, even as you,
Father are in me, and I in you,
that they also may be in us,
so that the world may believe
that you have sent me,
and have loved them
even as you have loved me.
Father, I desire that they may be
with me where I am,
to behold my glory, which you
have given me.
I have made known your name,
and I will make it known,
that the love with which you
have loved me may be in them,
and I in them. Amen.

(John 17, selected excerpts, restated)

Father, forgive them;
for they do not know
what they do. Amen.

(Luke 23:34).

Abide with us, Holy Presence,
for the day is far spent, and night is near.
Abide with us,
and with the little ones who seek you.
Abide with us,
in the shadows of the evening.
Abide with us, in the shadows of our life.
Abide with us, in the shadows of the
world. Amen.

"My God, my God,
why have you forsaken me?"

(Mark 15:34)

O Jesus, my feet are dirty.
Come even as a slave to me,
pour water into your bowl,
come and wash my feet.
In asking such a thing
I know I am overbold
but I dread what was threatened
when you said to me,
"If I do not wash your feet
I have no fellowship with you."
Wash my feet then, because
I long for your companionship.

(Origen, 185–254)

8. Guided prayers and meditations for Lent

These prayer suggestions for Lent and Holy Week have been written for groups with one participant in the role of guide. They can easily be adapted for prayer partners and for personal use. Decide in advance who will read scripture and who will lead the prayers. Let each prayer unfold slowly and gently.

Remember to choose prayer-styles which match the level of comfort and familiarity among those who are present, and to remind them they are always free to pass. Encourage participants to keep a prayer journal, and to spend ten minutes or so reflecting on each prayer time on paper, letting God speak through their writing or drawing.

DIVINE READING

Gospel of Mark

Read prayerfully through the whole gospel of Mark, pausing often to close your eyes and imagine yourself present in the scenes of the story. It will probably take you a couple of hours. Don't rush it. Take your time.

DIVINE DRAMA

Ezekiel 37:1–14 (the valley of dry bones)

Read aloud the drama of Ezekiel, thinking about it as a quest for life out of struggle and death. Read the passage through a second time aloud, to get familiar with it. Then invite participants to enact the story with their bodies as the passage is read slowly again. This is especially wonderful for children or youth, and very powerful during worship.

A MEDITATION ON EMPTINESS

Based on Luke 23:46 ("Into your hands I commend my spirit.")

Contemporary prayers combine sensing, thinking, feeling, and intuition in many different ways. By helping us name empty places inside, the following prayer can help us change fears and burdens into opportunities and blessings.

Take a few moments to prepare. Sit or lie comfortably, eyes closed. Focus on your regular breathing pattern, to come fully into the present … Relax with your breathing …

As you breathe, become aware of some emptiness in your life. Perhaps this emptiness is the result of a loss or an unfulfilled need. Name the emptiness inside you …

Consider ways you may be keeping that empty space filled … Some ways may be helpful. Other ways may be harmful … To whom or what have you given your Spirit? … Be gentle with yourself, but be honest …

Open yourself to this new opportunity. Open the empty space inside you to God, asking God to fill it …

Repeat to yourself Jesus' homecoming prayer to God, "Into your hands I commend my Spirit." (Luke 23:46)

Rest quietly in the presence of God … Feel the Spirit breath flowing into your body … Feel how God breathes you … Pray in silence, giving thanks for the fullness of the Spirit …

As you breathe quietly, begin to listen to the sounds in the room … Outside the room … Move your fingers and your toes. Open your eyes when you are ready.

A REFLECTION FOR THE CLOSE OF DAY

This prayer, based on an Ignatian exercise, can help us notice and be thankful for our experience of love. It can also help us notice where we can change – and know that we are loved and empowered to become all that God invites us to be.

Take a few moments to prepare. Sit or lie comfortably, eyes closed. Focus on your regular breathing pattern, to come fully into the present ... Relax with your breathing ... Feel the Spirit breath flowing into your body ... Feel how God breathes you ...

As you breathe, ask yourself, "Where was love today?" ... See and hear the places, events and persons in your day ... Let the day pass before you in your mind ... Focus on each moment of love, either expressed or implicit ... Welcome each moment of love to your memory ... Give thanks for each one ...

Now ask yourself, "Where has my loving been incomplete?" See and hear the places, events and persons in your day, where your attitude or behavior may have been unloving ...

Hear Jesus say to you, "I know you ... I love you ... I will help you" ... Now, replay each moment in your mind as you would wish it to be, extending empathy ... acceptance ... generosity ... humor ... and joy ...

What is God inviting you to do or to be tomorrow? ... Hear Jesus say to you, "My grace is sufficient for you" ... See yourself as God sees you could be ...

Rest quietly in the presence of God ... Pray in silence, giving thanks for the power of the Spirit in your life ... Sleep well.

A MEDITATION ON GENEROSITY
Matthew 25:31–40 (the parable of the sheep and the goats), Isaiah 58:6–11 (to care for the poor and the hungry), and James 2:14–26)

Take a few moments to prepare. Sit or lie comfortably, eyes closed. Focus on your regular breathing pattern, to come fully into the present ... Relax with your breathing ... Feel the Spirit breath flowing into your body ... Feel how God breathes you ... Listen for the word of God ...

Read aloud the passages. Leave a minute or two of silence after the readings. Then continue:

As you breathe the Spirit breath, reflect on the virtue of generosity. What does generosity mean to you? ... How could generosity help you to integrate your body, your mind, and your soul? ...

Who have you known who was authentically generous, and acted in the spirit of generosity? How did that person affect your life? ... When and how have you yourself been generous? ...

When you are not generous, what feeling holds you back? ... What would help you let go of this feeling? ...

What changes could you make in your life to help you grow in generosity? ... What could you do today to practice the spirit of generosity? ...

Rest quietly in the presence of God ... Pray in silence for yourself, that God will free your heart for generosity ...

Ask someone near you to pray for you, silently or aloud, that you may grow in generosity ... Pray for others as you are asked, and for those who are in special need today ... Finish with a prayer or a blessing you know by heart ... Open your eyes when you are ready.

A MEDITATION ON HUMILITY
Matthew 11:29–30 ("Take my yoke"), Luke 14:7–11 ("Take the lowest place"), and 1 Corinthians 4:7 (gift from God)

Take a few moments to prepare. Sit or lie comfortably, eyes closed. Focus on your regular breathing pattern, to come fully into the present ... Relax with your breathing ... Feel the Spirit breath flowing into your body ... Feel how God breathes you ... Listen for the word of God ...

Read aloud the biblical passages. Leave a minute of silence after the readings.

Reflect on the virtue of humility. What does humility mean to you? … How could humility help you to integrate your body, your mind, and your spirit?

Who have you known who was authentically humble? … How did this person affect your life? … And other lives? …

What does Jesus mean when he says, "Learn from me; for I am gentle and humble in heart"? How could humility help you "find rest" for your soul? … How have you been humbled in the past? … What gift did you receive in that humbling? …

What changes could you make in your life to help you deepen in humility? … What could you do today to practice humility? …

Rest quietly in the presence of God …

Pray in silence for yourself, that God will free your heart for humility …

Ask someone near you to pray for you, either silently or aloud, that you may grow in humility … Pray for others as you are asked, and for those who are in special need today … Finish with a prayer or a blessing you know by heart … Open your eyes when you are ready.

A MEDITATION ON GRACE
Based on Luke 15:11–32 (the prodigal son)

Take a few moments to prepare. Sit or lie comfortably, eyes closed. Focus on your regular breathing pattern, to come fully into the present … Feel the Spirit breath flowing into your body … Relax with your breathing …

Some of us long for peace. Some of us long for potency. Or maybe we long for both at once. Let us open our hearts to what God may say to each of us through this parable:

Read the story of the prodigal son through twice, aloud. Leave a minute of silence when you finish reading.

Picture the family in their home together … the father and the mother, two brothers. Picture the room where they gather … See the younger brother, falling in love with all the pleasures of the world … See him asking for his inheritance … See him leaving home … See him rushing to the world, wildly wasting his gifts … See him endangering himself … impoverishing himself … very far from home … See his willfulness, his pride …

Go back to the family's home, and picture the other brother, the perfectionist one, still at home … working dutifully … See him following the path of self-denial … See him shutting down his feelings, moving away emotionally and spiritually … See his passivity, see the lack of engagement … See how he fails to claim his gifts … See his fear …

Feel how alienated both brothers are from their parents … how they distance themselves from the goodness of those who love them … Picture the father and the mother, grieving …

Now, picture the prodigal son "coming to himself"… See him weeping … Let him tell you how much he has lost, how much harm he has done … how deeply sorry he is … See him turning inward, recovering himself, moving away from his obsessions with worldly pleasures … See how he turns his gaze homeward … Feel him yearn for wholeness … Feel him choose … See his parents waiting, see them embrace their dear child … Hear the sounds of a party. Smell the wonderful foods. Hear the wonderful words, "You are forgiven! You are beloved! You are home!" …

Now, see the perfectionist brother leave his work … See him turn from his addiction, still locked in his anger … Hear him explode at his parents … Let him tell you how he feels, how he just can't do it anymore … Feel the healing begin as he experiences his own yearning for life and for pleasure … Feel how God seeks him … See his parents pleading …

Hear, "Claim your inheritance! You are beloved! This is for you!"

Consider which of the brothers is most like you ... Have the conversation you need to have with your parent ... Hear God's word of grace to you: "You are forgiven!" Or, "Claim your inheritance!" Hear: "You are beloved ... You are home ... This is for you" ... Repeat these words as you breathe in and out ...

Rest quietly in the presence of God ...

Pray in silence, giving thanks for God's grace ...

Ask someone near you to pray for you, either silently or aloud, that you may know you are beloved. Pray for others as you are asked, and for those who are in special need today ... Finish with a prayer or a blessing you know by heart ... Open your eyes when you are ready.

A MEDITATION ON SELF-EMPTYING
Philippians 2:4–8 (having the mind of Christ)

Take a few moments to prepare. Sit or lie comfortably, eyes closed. Focus on your regular breathing pattern, to come fully into the present. Relax with your breathing ... Feel the Spirit breath flowing into your body ... Feel how God breathes you ... Listen for the word of God ...

Read the biblical passage through three times slowly, aloud. Leave a minute of silence.

Reflect on the attitude of Christ we are to take as our own. What is there within you which needs to be emptied? ...

How could taking the attitude of "a slave" be creative (and not abusive) in your life? ... What would this mean in your way of relating to those with whom you live, or work, or share your faith? ...

What changes could you make to help you live with a more Christ-like attitude toward God, yourself, and others? ... What could you do today to practice self-emptying? ...

Rest quietly in the presence of God ... Pray in silence for yourself, that God will open the space within you ...

Ask someone near you to pray for you either silently or aloud, that you may be enabled to empty yourself. Pray for others as you are asked, and for those who are in special need today ... Finish with a prayer or a blessing you know by heart ... Open your eyes when you are ready.

A MEDITATION ON ENVY
Mark 15:10 (jealousy of the priests)

Take a few moments to prepare. Sit or lie comfortably, eyes closed. Focus on your regular breathing pattern, to come fully into the present. Relax with your breathing ... Feel the Spirit breath flowing into your body ... Feel how God breathes you ... Listen for the word of God ...

Read the biblical passage through three times slowly, aloud. Leave a minute of silence.

Reflect on the fault of envy. What does envy mean to you? ... Why do people feel envious? ...

How was envy a cause of Jesus' death? ... How is love the opposite of envy? ...

Have you ever suffered because someone else envied you? ... What did you do with your feelings? ...

Have you ever felt sad or angry at another's success? Have you been aware of feeling envious? ... What have you done about this feeling? ... How might you recognize whether or not you still feel envy towards another? ... What could you do to avoid being envious? ... How can you begin? ...

Rest quietly in the presence of God ... Pray in silence for yourself, that God will strengthen you to release the hold of envy ...

Ask someone near you to pray for you either silently or aloud, that you may be strengthened in personal confidence, and blessed with joy in the achievements of others. Pray for others as you are asked, and for those who are in special need today ... Finish with a prayer or a blessing you know by heart ... Open your eyes when you are ready.

A MEDITATION ON THE BEATITUDES
Matthew 5:1–12 (the Beatitudes)

Take a few moments to prepare ... Sit or lie comfortably, eyes closed ... Focus on your regular breathing pattern, to come fully into the present ... Relax with your breathing ... Feel the Spirit breath flowing into your body ... Feel how God breathes you ... Listen for the word of God ...

Read through the biblical passage twice slowly, aloud.

Reflect in the silence on the teachings of Christ. Consider how they speak to the violence within us and among us ... to our cynicism ... to the temptation to ignore violence ... to the way we "want it all" ... Consider how these teachings speak to our omissions in concern for those in need ... to our self-involvement ... our withdrawal ... and our blaming ...

Read through the passage once again, aloud.

Reflect in silence on the teachings of Christ. Consider how these teachings could increase within us the power of compassion ... our capacity to feel ... our attentiveness to dialogue ... our simplicity of need ...

What are the implications for prayer? ... for practical assistance to others? ... for commitment to relationship? ...

Now consider what changes in your life would draw you closer to Christ. What might you have to let go? ... What dangers might you face? ... Where will you place your trust? ... Are you willing to commit to these changes? ... How can you begin? ...

Rest quietly in the presence of God ... Pray in silence for yourself, that God will strengthen you and guide you in discipleship ...

Ask someone near you to pray for you either silently or aloud, that you may be empowered and encouraged to seek the holy. Pray for others as you are asked, and for those who are in special need today ... Finish with a prayer or a blessing you know by heart ... Open your eyes when you are ready.

A MEDITATION ON HEALING THROUGH OBEDIENCE
1 Samuel 3:1–10 (young Samuel hears God)
Exodus 15:22–26 (God protects God's people)

Our English word "obey" comes from the Latin *ob-edire* meaning "to listen beneath." The Greek word for obey also means "to listen beneath." This prayer can help us grow in our capacity to "listen beneath," to be attentive to what's beneath the surface of things and to empty our self-concerned agenda.

Take a few moments to prepare. Sit or lie comfortably, eyes closed. Focus on your regular breathing pattern, to come fully into the present. Relax with your breathing ... Feel the Spirit breath flowing into your body ... Feel how God breathes you ... Listen for the word of God ...

Read the passage from Samuel through twice, aloud. After reading, leave a minute of silence.

Take a few minutes to recollect the people with whom you interacted today. See each of them in your mind, one after another ... Notice what each one is wearing ... the way each one carries his or her body ... the set of their shoulders ... Notice the eyes of each person speaking to you ... Notice the feeling in the voice ...

Once you have noticed, pray the prayer of young Samuel, "Speak, my God, for your servant is listening" ... Say, "God, if there's something you want to say to me in this, I am listening" ...

Read the passage from Exodus through two times, aloud. Follow the reading with a minute of silence.

Take a few minutes to remember yourself interacting with others today. In each interaction when your attitude was less than loving, notice where there is tension in your body ... Notice the sensation in your shoulders ... Notice your feelings, and the memories which are held in those feelings ... Allow each recollection to come before you, and as it comes before you, repeat in your heart: "For I am the God who heals you ... For I am the God who heals you" ...

Consider what God may be inviting you to do or to become ... How could you begin tomorrow? ...

Rest quietly in God's presence, focusing only on the flow of your breathing, in and out ... Stay open to God's possibilities ...

Pray for yourself, for wisdom and courage and strength ...

Now ask someone near you to pray for you, either silently or aloud, that you may be healed and strengthened in love through "listening beneath" to the voice of God ... Pray for others as you are asked, and for those who are in special need today ... Finish with a prayer or a blessing you know by heart ... Open your eyes when you are ready.

A MEDITATION ON FORGIVENESS
Colossians 3:15 (the peace of Christ)

Take a few moments to prepare. Sit or lie comfortably, eyes closed. Focus on your regular breathing pattern, to come fully into the present. Relax with your breathing ... Feel the Spirit breath flowing into your body ... Feel how God breathes you ... Listen for the word of God ...

Read the biblical passage through two times, aloud. Follow the reading with a minute of silence.

Reflect on your need to be forgiven. What have you done that needs forgiving? ... In your heart, name the persons you are hoping will forgive you ...

Can you accept that you have limitations? ... Can you empty your soul of false pride? ...

Reflect on your need to forgive. Are there people you have not yet forgiven? ... What feeling holds you in the past? ... If you forgave, what would you have to give up? ... A need for vengeance? An illusion? Familiar wounds? ... How could you empty your soul of un-love? ...

Reflect on how and where your heart is broken. Can you begin to see your heart as broken "open"? ... Can you let holy love flow right through you, like fire and wind? ... Can you empty your soul of past pain? ...

With your heart broken "open," how could you turn your past into blessing for the future? ...

Rest quietly in God's presence, focusing only on the flow of your breathing, in and out ...

Ask someone near you to pray for you, either silently or aloud, that your soul may be emptied and re-filled ... Pray for others as you are asked, and for yourself that God will help you ... Pray for those who are in special need today ... Finish with a prayer or a blessing you know by heart ... Open your eyes when you are ready.

A MEDITATION ON HEALING RELATIONSHIPS

Hebrews 13:8 (Jesus the same yesterday, today, and forever)

Because this prayer is meant to help us work with things in the past, it asks us to visit a shadowed moment in a relationship and open this moment to healing. Every person should feel free to pass.

Re-interpreting our past can be profoundly freeing; it can also lead us into painful areas of self-discovery where we find ourselves in need of assistance. Just in case any participant in prayer finds him- or herself moving into this place, it is important to assure everyone in advance that you (and other group leaders and/or friends) will be willing to spend time with them after, or to refer them to other resources.

Take a few moments to prepare. Sit or lie comfortably, eyes closed. Focus on your regular breathing pattern, to come fully into the present. Relax with your breathing ... Feel the breath of the Spirit flowing into your body ... Feel how God breathes you ... Listen for the word of God ...

Read the Hebrews passage through three times slowly, aloud.

As you breathe in and out, repeat these words silently within yourself: "Jesus Christ is the same, yesterday and today and forever." ... What do these words promise to you? ... How do they relate to your life? ...

As you breathe in and out, become aware of what God may be saying to you through these words: "Jesus Christ is the same, yesterday and today and forever." ... What expression of constant love is God imprinting in us through the Christ? ... Can you receive this love into your present? ... Can you receive this love into your past? ...

As you breathe in and out, let your attention come to a relationship in your life where there is unresolved grief or anger or fear ... Focus on a particular interaction or incident, perhaps the first experience of distress you can remember in the relationship ... or simply an incident which disrupts your peace today ... Remember how you felt about what happened ...

As you breathe in and out, become aware of Jesus with you in the place where you were when this incident occurred ... See how his presence releases each person present to be the finest self he or she can be ... Imagine how each one, finally freed to be their best, would want things to unfold a different way ... Now, replay the moment as you wish it could have been, the way that Christ would wish it to be ...

As you breathe in and out, know the love around you now, as you live the scene afresh, is the same love which surrounded you back then ... Hear the healing Spirit speak these words into your heart: "Jesus Christ is the same, yesterday and today and forever" ... You were beloved then ... You are beloved now ... Receive this love ... You were beloved then ... You are beloved now ... Receive this love ...

As you breathe in and out, imagine you have opened the door to your heart, and feel the loving Spirit flowing in ... Feel the healing Spirit flowing into your center, releasing your distress ... bringing peace ...

Continue with your breathing, in and out ... Breathe in strength and courage ... Breathe out fear and pain ... Breathe the healing Spirit through your body ... Breathe the words, "Jesus Christ is the same, yesterday and today and forever" ...

As you breathe in and out, rest quietly in the presence of God ... Stay open to God's possibilities ...

Pray for yourself, for wisdom and courage and strength ...

Ask someone near you to pray for you, either silently or aloud, that God will bless you with the strength and courage you need. Pray for others as you are asked and for those who are in special need today ... Finish with a prayer or a blessing you know by heart ... Open your eyes when you are ready.

Another option
Mark 14:32–42 (the garden of Gethsemane)
Read Mark 14:32–42 (the garden of Gethsemane) through twice, aloud. Invite participants to imagine the shadows in the Garden of Gethsemane, its colors, its sounds, and its smells. Ask them to hear Jesus struggling with his destiny: "Abba, Father, for you all things are possible; remove this cup (of suffering) from me." Remind them Jesus looks for comfort to Peter, James, and John, but finds them sleeping. Ask them to remember a moment in their lives when they too felt abandoned and alone, perhaps when they were doing what they felt was right to do. Pray with them for strength and courage, to trust in God through dark nights of the soul.

PRAYING LENTEN PSALMS
- Psalm 32:1–7 (joy in confession and forgiveness)
- Psalm 51:10–12 (prayer for cleansing and renewal)
- Psalm 91:1–2, 9–16, or Psalm 23, or Psalm 121 (assurance of loving protection)
- Psalm 130 (hope in God's love)
- Psalm 25:1–10 (prayer for mercy and guidance)
- Psalm 107:1–3, 17–22 (thanks for deliverance and healing)
- Psalm 27:1, 7–14 (confidence in God)
- Psalm 63: 1–8 (confidence in God's presence)
- Psalm 36: 1–9 (human evil and divine goodness)
- Psalm 116: 1–9 (thanksgiving for recovery)
- Psalm 77:1–15 (remembering God's mercy)
- Psalm 22: 1–2, 9–24 (remembering God's deliverance).

You can use this prayer meditation over and over, by changing the psalm you choose each time.

The Psalms mirror the full range of our human emotions. Praying the psalms helps us keep our souls cleansed of pent-up feelings. Remember, Jesus prayed these same psalms.

Take a few moments to prepare ... Sit or lie comfortably, eyes closed ... Focus on your regular breathing pattern, to come fully into the present ... Relax with your breathing ... Feel the Spirit breath flowing into your body ... Feel how God breathes you ... Listen for the word of God ...

Read one of the psalm selections through two times slowly, aloud:

Reflect in the silence on the feeling in this psalm. How does it speak to you now? ... How does it relate to your life? ...

Read through the chosen psalm selection once again, aloud.

Is there a turning point in this psalm? ... What helps you remember God's steadfast presence and love? ... How might God be trying to speak to you through this psalm? ...

Rest quietly in God's presence, focusing only on the flow of your breathing, in and out ... Stay open to God's possibilities ...

Pray for yourself, for wisdom and courage and strength ...

Ask someone near you to pray for you, either silently or aloud, that you may be comforted and encouraged by the Spirit of God ... Pray for others as you are asked and for those who are in special need today ... Finish with a prayer or a blessing you know by heart ... Open your eyes when you are ready.

A MEDITATION ON MORTALITY
Isaiah 40:6–8 (on the mortality of all things)

All healing and health in the physical body is temporary. Eventually, everyone dies. Genesis 6:3 tells us that God said, "My spirit shall not abide in mortals forever; for they are flesh; their days shall be one hundred twenty years." The human body is not created to last forever. This prayer is meant to help us find our peace in God as we grapple with the reality that physical death will come to us all.

Take a few moments to prepare. Sit or lie comfortably, eyes closed. Focus on your regular breathing pattern, to come fully into the present. Relax with your breathing … Feel the Spirit breath flowing into your body … Feel how God breathes you …

Listen for the word of God … Listen for words or phrases that attract you strongly …

Read the following passage from Isaiah through slowly two times, aloud.

Take a minute of silence for reflection. If your life on the earth were to end tomorrow, what would be your greatest loss? … What would you most regret? …. Are you able to accept that you will die? If not, why is this difficult? Is there something in particular you fear? …

Listen again for the word of God … Choose a word or a phrase that attracts you strongly …

Read the passage from Isaiah through again.

As you breathe, repeat within you the word or phrase you have chosen, in rhythm with your breathing …

Become aware of the feelings that your chosen word or phrase arouses. Listen for what God may be saying to you through your feelings … Is there something that you need to let go? … Is there something calling for your attention? … What would help you release your fear? …

Now become aware of what God may be inviting you to do or to be in the present … How can you live more creatively within your human limitations? … How can the way you live be a gift for other people? …

Rest quietly in God's presence, focusing only on the flow of your breathing, in and out … Stay open to God's possibilities …

Pray for yourself, for wisdom and courage and strength …

Ask someone near you to pray for you, either silently or aloud, that you may be enabled to respond to God's invitation … Pray for others as you are asked … and for those who are in special need today … Finish with a prayer or a blessing you know by heart … Open your eyes when you are ready.

9. Inner reflections for Lent & Holy Week

Ah, the light is so warm –
can I not just bask
in this glory
on this mountaintop
and stay – a little longer
just to linger in this loveliness?

But the valley shadows
hold their own beauty and gifts
and I will not ignore their call.
I pause at the pathway
to those deepest places,
and I go down
down to the pools of pain.
I see my own reflection.

And though I cannot see you
I cannot hear you
I know.
From a faint echoed melody
from a vague remembered dream,
I know you have not left me alone.

In Lent, we go to Ezekiel's valley of dry bones to empty ourselves, to acknowledge our human frailty. We break our hearts open to prepare for the life-breath of God's grace.

Again, find your quiet spot, your candle, paper, pen, and pencil. During this Lenten retreat time, we invite you to explore your own deepest places of shadow.

THE MOUNTAINTOP

Six days later, Jesus took with him
Peter, and James and John,
and led them up a high mountain
apart, by themselves.

And he was transfigured before them,
and his clothes became dazzling white.
(Mark 9:2–3a)

Light your candle and think of some mountaintop "glory" moments in your experience.

• How was your identity revealed to you? How was your sense of purpose clarified?
• Was it difficult for you to leave your mountaintop?

In closure, find words to give thanks for the learnings of the mountaintop.

THE SHADOWED PATHWAY

Even though I walk through the darkest valley, I fear no evil; for you are with me

(Psalm 23:4)

Light your candle and be aware of shadows in the room.

- Where have the shadows in your life experience been frightening? What fears do these shadows represent?
- Did fear stop you from moving along the pathway? How did you deal with your fear?

In closure, find words to give thanks for the learnings of the shadowed pathway.

THE POOLS OF PAIN

"I establish my covenant with you, that never again shall all flesh be cut off by the waters of flood, and never again shall there be a flood to destroy the earth." God said, "This is the sign of the covenant that I make between me and you and every living creature that is with you, for all future generations: I have set my bow in the clouds, and it shall be a sign of the covenant between me and the earth."

(Genesis 9:11–13).

Light your candle and think of pools of pain in your life.

- What is in those pain-filled pools? How is your own reflection part of the pain?
- Have you ever felt you were being punished?
- Have you been frightened that pain could destroy you?
- How can the rainbow covenant give you courage to work with your pain?

In closure, find words to give thanks for the learnings of the pools of pain.

HOLY SILENCE

...and after the fire a sound of sheer silence. When Elijah heard it, he wrapped his face in his mantle and went out and stood at the entrance to the cave. Then there came a voice to him that said, " What are you doing here, Elijah?"

(1 Kings 19:12b–13)

Light your candle and listen to the silence.

- What enables you to "hear" holy presence, when the only sound you hear is "sheer silence"? What helps you to stand in God's presence?
- Where do the faint echoed melodies of holy love come from? What vague dreams invite you to hope?
- What helps you with the question, "What are you doing here?"

In closure, find words to give thanks for the learnings of holy silence.

FINDING HOME

May those who sow in tears reap with shouts of joy. Those who go out weeping, bearing the seed for sowing, shall come home with shouts of joy carrying their sheaves.

(Psalm 126:5–6).

We know the rhythm of moving from the mountain through the valley. We know that neither place is home, but we can dare to travel through both places because our home is in God. On one half of your paper, write words to describe the exhilaration of the mountaintop; on the other half, write words to describe the depths of the valley.

- How is God "home" on both the mountaintop *and* in the valley?

To close, find words to give thanks for God as home.

10. Activities for Lent & Holy Week

The activities of this season have a pensive and meditative feel. As we engage our self-inquiry, we clarify our intention to fulfill our baptismal commitments as disciples of Christ. Our activities therefore reflect our intention, as communities and individuals, to be signs of God's reign of love in this world. Our signs will not come through our joy in this season; but through our contemplation, self-honesty, and action.

A LENTEN ALTAR

Collect a variety of items from the winter landscape such as twigs, stones, seed-pods, and dead leaves.

Choose a special container and fill it with soil.

On a standing card write the words "You are dust; and to dust you shall return" (Genesis 3:19b). Decorate the card with winter colors. Using your collected items, the soil and the Genesis passage, create an altar on a shelf or a table – any small space that can be left undisturbed for the duration of the season of Lent. As the days of Lent pass and spring begins, add symbols of growth to your altar.

A COLLECTING JAR

There are many places of pain in our world; places where our awareness and our sharing can lighten others' burdens. List places of pain in our world, and choose one place for intentional sharing. This can be done by a church group, a family or an individual. (Try to pick a development or relief project with which your denomination is already involved.)

Choose a jar and wrap it with burlap and twine. Decorate a paper strip with Lenten symbols, and tape it around the jar. Place the collecting jar on your Lenten altar, or someplace where you will remember it daily.

Decide on your method of money collection: for example, coins linked to items and activities in your life *(see A Lenten calendar below)*. Or have each person contribute their "least coin" to the box each day before going to bed. You'll be amazed at how much you will gather! At Lent's end, share your gift anonymously.

A LENTEN CALENDAR

Before the start of Lent, draw a calendar grid that contains 40 spaces (six days a week, excluding Sundays). Clearly define the days of the week and the change in months, but keep the 40 spaces as one unit. Your calendar grid might be large enough for a wall or it could be one small sheet of paper. Decorate the edges of the calendar with designs in winter colors.

Create these lists:

- Ways we hurt creation
- Ways we hurt others (in our own communities, in our global community)
- Ways we hurt ourselves
- Ways we hurt our relationship with God.

Brainstorm and record ideas for each list. For each idea on each list, come up with a positive suggestion toward healing the hurt – some way to reconcile and make new!

Begin entering healing suggestions in the spaces on your calendar grid. Try not to overload your grid. (Remember the parable of the Advent mural!) Some of your healing can come in the form of coins for your collecting jar. Not using the car today could mean a dollar for the collecting jar, for example. Or you could write a letter to the editor of your newspaper, thanking food bank volunteers, and contribute a quarter for the collecting jar.

In a larger group, make sure leadership and organizational flow are very clear. Use calendar-making as your gathering activity, with materials ready on the tables as people enter. Have people work on each list in small groups, or have people move from list to list and record ideas.

When brainstorming ways to heal the hurt, ask each small group to work on one list, then invite the whole group to discuss and augment the healing suggestions before entering them on the calendar.

LENTEN RECIPES

Collect recipes that invite you to eat less meat. Go to the library and choose one or two vegetarian recipes to test on friends or family, or at a potluck at your church. Create a booklet of your favorite vegetarian recipes.

You might even consider a healthful fast. Where self-indulgence and affluence lure us into excess, the discipline of a fast can help us recover simplicity, moderation, and balance. However, it's important not to see fasting as "punishing" ourselves or our bodies, as that can launch us into negative cycles. Our bodies are worthy of love and respect, and nourishment is God's gracious gift. We should fast *for* our bodies, not against them.

Lent might also be the time to start walking to work, and cycling every week around the park.

But remember, "Whenever you fast, do not look dismal as the hypocrites do; when you fast,

put oil on your head and wash your face" (Matthew 6:16–17). Enjoy!

LENTEN SERVICE

Just as our monetary gifts from our collecting jars can lighten others' burdens, so too can the gift of our time. Be clear with yourself about the amount of time you have to give, and make a commitment to a specific duration of volunteer service.

Choose a place of need in your community. You might check with the hospital, a food bank, or a seniors' facility. Record your commitment to service on your Lenten calendar.

WAYS TO CARE

Always, Christ showed compassion for the most vulnerable ones in his world: the lonely, the ill, and the rejected. Who are the most vulnerable in our community?

God's creation is also vulnerable. How can we show our caring concern for creation in this season? Plan all intentional activities for Lent as expressions of the compassion of Christ.

V

THE
Easter Season

I. The spirit of Easter –
an overview

Easter is the joy and celebration of the Christ-life. The stone is rolled away – the tomb is empty and hearts are full. Jesus lives! Easter ushers in the end-time, when love reigns supreme. It's the day of acclamation, the day we say "yes!" to never-ending life in the Spirit.

The Easter season is "The Great Fifty Days" of revelation when all creation sings for joy, and the whole panorama of salvation through Christ unfolds before our wondering eyes. The Easter season prepares us for the great synchronicity of life in the Spirit, culminating in the fiery, windy festival of Pentecost, when the Spirit breathes new life into us. During the seven weeks of the Season of Easter, we rejoice in the victory of love which is revealed in the resurrection of Jesus, in the transformation of Jesus' followers, and in the biblical vision of Christ as harmony for all of creation.

Through the Season of Easter, we're transformed for sacred friendship with Christ and one another in community. The power of resurrection in peoples' lives and in communities is shown in scripture by the transformation of Christ's disciples. Week by week in Sunday worship we hear how the risen Christ came to the disciples, to help them understand how God was making things new, and to help them see the holy in new ways. We hear how the disciples received the gifts of the Spirit, and how the Spirit sent them out as "apostles" speaking languages of love. And we hear how the apostles became a close-knit community, continuing Jesus' ministry as channels of healing and as witnesses to holy love and presence.

Easter offers us a vision of joy that inspires us to get on with the work of becoming whole and holy human beings. Our Lenten contemplations helped us see the fears and wounds which have blocked us from growing in love. Now at Easter, in the continuing light of Christ's presence, we release our self-deceptions to seek the truth. The risen Christ shows us the wounds that brought him death, and our wounds are transformed into strengths by the power of resurrection. Our fears are turned to trust in holy love, and all our struggles into learning.

At Easter, we know that the limitations of humanness – the fears and wounds of the world which lead to crucifixions – can open up the way to "new life." God will help us turn our tragedies into blessings. As Easter people, we know the Spirit makes things new. This is what redemption means.

The joy of intimacy with God comes to us through the experience of inner death and resurrection in the Spirit. The oppressed find integrity sustained through their endurance. Fugitives find forgiveness and reprieve from guilt's bondage. Outcasts are fulfilled by the embrace of belonging. Aliens come home to God in harmony and peace. And those who battle evil see that powers of death are vanquished as a new earth and heaven are born.

Those who live the Christ-life through inner death to resurrection find release from their fear, and new hope for the future, in the truth of holy love without limit. Having centered our lives in ourselves or in the world, now we center our new life in God. We grow in wisdom, intuition, and insight as we seek holy guidance. Freed from fear, we are released from the fear-driven needs which once distorted our vision of the holy.

So our Easter spirituality is characterized by attentiveness to seeking God's truth in all things. We learn to trust that holy blessing will come, and we learn how to see it. Then we live in constant thankfulness and find our peace in the mystery of God.

Jesus is our channel of the holy. Through his life, suffering, death, and resurrection, holiness becomes recognizable. When Jesus was physically present in the world, he was the outward and visible sign of holiness in humanness. Now Jesus prays that we will also be outward and visible signs of holy presence in the world. The baptismal celebrations and imagery of Easter are visible signs of God's grace. The power of the indwelling Spirit in us, and in the life we share together as "Christ's body," consecrate our humanness for service. We take up our life task and channel the holy through the Christ-life of justice and compassion. As channels of Spirit, we witness to divine healing.

Where Christmas spirituality moves through fullness to authentic selfhood, the spirituality of the Easter cycle moves through emptiness to authentic community. Together, the Christ-life cycles of self-fulfillment and self-emptying shape in us the strength and resilience of character which make for wholeness and capacity to love. The Christ-life brings together our proclamation of hope for the personal resurrection of individual human beings, for the transformation of communities into places of shalom, and the fulfillment of possibility for all creation.

Our new life in the Spirit comes into full consciousness when we gather in community to receive the holy gifts of the Spirit. Pentecost is our re-living of the outpouring Spirit – Christ in us and we in Christ and all in God together. This is the joy of our faith!

2. The beauty of Easter – colors, symbols, & art

The exuberance of Easter should be expressed both musically and visually. Textiles should be fine and elegant, and colors brilliant in contrast to Lent. The colors of Easter are white and gold, signifying purity, new life, rejoicing, and holiness. As the presence of the Spirit becomes more fully manifest through the seven weeks of Easter, tinges of red can be added to the white and gold, until red becomes the dominant color for Pentecost – the fiery festival which concludes the Easter season.

Easter decoration is resplendent with the glory of flowers. The rose represents the Messianic promise expressed in the first verse of Isaiah 35:1: "The desert shall rejoice, and blossom as a rose." The lily illustrates the inseparability of death and new life as its decaying bulb produces a new bulb, stem, leaves, and ultimately flowers.

The large, white Pascal candle, also called the Christ candle, is an important symbol of Christ's eternal life and of our eternal life with Christ. Lighted at the Easter Vigil (or the first worship service on Easter Sunday if there is no vigil), the Christ candle stays lighted through all the worship services of the season. (After Pentecost, place the candle near the baptismal font for the rest of the year, where it is lighted for baptisms, weddings and funerals to represent the joy of new life.)

Other symbols for the season include:

- The open tomb, reminding us that holy love conquers death.
- The cross drawn over the globe, signifying the victory of compassion over worldly ways.
- The circle, because it has no beginning or end, portrays the boundless love of God experienced in the Easter resurrection of Christ.
- The bursting pomegranate is a symbol of the resurrection of Christ, and also of the faithful, as the creative power of life in the abundance of seeds breaks open the skin of the fruit.
- The peacock is another early symbol of resurrection, because the molting peacock grows new feathers still more brilliant than the ones which were lost.
- The legendary Phoenix rises to new life out of the ashes of death.
- And the butterfly bursts from its death-like cocoon to soar into life with new wings.

Throughout the Season of Easter, adorn your worship space with Hallelujah and Resurrection banners. To beautify the worship space for Easter morning services, ask each family to bring one or more flowers, and after worship to deliver them to the sick and shut-in.

3. Celebrations during Easter & Eastertide

EASTER SUNDAY

On Easter Sunday, the reality of Christ's eternal presence is proclaimed by participants in the ongoing story of resurrection. Together, we touch ritual death and rebirth, to internalize its life-giving power.

As people grow into an inner knowledge of resurrection, it's important to encourage questions and even doubting. Indeed, no pat answers will suffice. Some will take the Easter truth as symbol and poetry while others will accept it as fact. Faith grows as we find ourselves living the story that is repeated and interpreted in faith community. The mysteries of the Spirit call us deeper and deeper into questions of faith, and the unfolding layers of meaning become our own truth.

The whole community should share actively in the experiences and feelings of the Easter liturgy. Even toddlers gathered on a quilt to draw or color while the liturgy unfolds all around them will absorb images and sensations which become deeply part of inner consciousness. The ancient cry is raised: "Hallelujah! Christ is risen! Christ is risen indeed! Hallelujah!" And all of human experience – its sorrow, joy, and anticipation – is captured in that great "Yes!" to life.

An outline of an Easter Vigil which can be adapted for worship at anytime on Easter Sunday is included in the section *Rituals for Easter and Eastertide.*

GOOD SHEPHERD SUNDAY

The fourth Sunday in the Season of Easter is called "Good Shepherd Sunday." The *Revised Common Lectionary* highlights each year a story of the "good shepherd" from the tenth chapter of John's gospel. Sheep and shepherds are important biblical images – from the ancient kings who were known as the "shepherds of Israel," through the 23rd Psalm, to the parables of Jesus. It's significant that scripture should view shepherds as models of caring concern, because shepherds were social outcasts in the ancient world. They were landless people with no fixed address.

Try building an all-age service around these themes.

ASCENSION OF JESUS

Jesus' ascension to heaven, as described in Acts 1:6–11, is celebrated on the Thursday after the sixth Sunday of Eastertide.

In the mystery of Christmas, holiness united with humanness and lived among us "in the flesh." Jesus' body suffered and died on a cross. And then in the mystery of resurrection he appeared again to his followers. Through the forty days which followed, Jesus prepared his followers to experience his presence in new and wondrous ways in the future. They would recognize the holiness of Christ in the "flesh" of the life they lived and shared as the church.

Following his ascension, Jesus' followers could no longer see the risen Christ directly. After a time, Christ's presence was marked more by feeling than by vision. The apostles "felt" the presence and power of Christ's Spirit.

Only when he left them bodily did they begin to understand that Christ's mission and ministry was to be re-embodied through their lives. The church celebrates this new experience of the Christ in the story of the Ascension – interpreted either literally as a vision shared by the disciples, or symbolically as a story which portrays the change in the disciples' experience.

In the mystery of Christ's ascension, we celebrate the continuing experience of Christ's presence among us. And we honor the sacredness of lives which are changed and empowered by the faithfulness of holy love.

In churches where it's not possible to worship on Thursday, celebrate Ascension on the following Sunday, the seventh Sunday in the Season of Easter.

Either way, build your liturgy around the texts of Luke 24:44–53, Ephesians 1:15–23, and Acts 1:1–11. Plan for a few participants to share experiences of the past year, when they were aware of Christ's presence.

DAY OF PENTECOST

In the days between the ascension of Jesus and Pentecost, we pray with the disciples for the coming of the Spirit. We pray for the Spirit to reverse the power of fear which disrupts communication and mutual understanding in our families and communities and world. We pray for an end to the pride and isolation represented by the tower of Babel (Genesis 11:1–9) and we pray for an end to the resulting estrangement which is described in that story as mutually incomprehensible languages.

Then comes the glorious festival of Pentecost, the climax and completion of Easter – the day the Spirit pours out like wind and flame on Christ's disciples so they can go to the world and share the gospel in ways that others understand. At Pentecost, we remember the fullness of God's promise of life in the Spirit with Christ.

In the Greek-speaking Roman world, the annual harvest festival for the Jews was known as Pentecost (from the Greek word for fiftieth) because it came fifty days after Passover. We call the festival which celebrates the church's birth "Pentecost" because Luke's dramatic account of the experience (Acts 2:1–21) tells us the disciples were gathered in Jerusalem during the Jewish feast of Pentecost. John's gospel provides an alternate version of the coming of the Spirit to the disciples. In John, Jesus simply breathes on the disciples with the breath of Holy Spirit (John 20:19–23) the evening of the day of his resurrection.

In both accounts, despite these differences, something amazing happens to a group of frightened people which sends them out proclaiming the mystery of resurrection and the wonder of continuing holy presence. And in both accounts, God comes again as Holy Spirit to become incarnate in human lives lived in Christ's image.

The poetry of Pentecost rests primarily on the multiple meanings of the Hebrew word *ruach* and the Greek word *pneuma*. Both *ruach* and *pneuma* can mean wind, breath, or spirit – the breath of life God breathed into humans at creation (Genesis 2:7), which gave new life to dry bones in Ezekiel's valley (Ezekiel 37:1–14), and which Jesus breathed anew into his beloved disciples (John 20:23). The Christian church was born on a day filled with wonder and delight in the power of Holy Spirit. So the themes for celebration on the festival of Pentecost are the windy spirit of the Holy Breath of God – and the flaming passion of the birthday of the church!

At Pentecost, we celebrate the Holy Spirit in our lives and our church. We remember how Jesus promised that a source of life-giving power would come to his followers when he was no longer physically present. So we celebrate the ministry for which the Spirit equips us, sending us into the world as apostles of Christ. The Spirit of God becomes incarnate in us as we manifest the teachings and Christ-life of Jesus, both through our commitment to personal transformation and through the life we share together as the church. Each of us is uniquely called to interpret divine meaning and purpose unfolding through our experience as a follower of Christ. And all of us are called to offer gifts to the world through the Christ-life of Christian community.

See *Rituals for Easter and Eastertide.*

4. Rituals for
Easter & Eastertide

The Great Fifty Days is the most festive season of the Christian Year, and the joy and celebration of Easter morning should continue through the seven weeks of Eastertide. These rituals and liturgies can be adapted for large gatherings like Sunday morning worship, for small-group gatherings, or for families at home.

Decide in advance who will lead, who will read, and who will take responsibility for actions.

THE EASTER VIGIL

The Easter vigil is also known as the Paschal vigil (from *pesah* or Passover.) Because it's more familiar and therefore easier to remember, we've chosen the name which comes from the Saxon goddess, Eastre, who was worshiped each spring. The Easter vigil has been part of the ritual of the church since the second century. Although in our time Easter Eve is a new experience for many churches, this is the service which should crown the Christian Year. Easter – not Christmas – is the central celebration of the church.

We're recovering in our day the power of Lenten preparations for baptism at Easter. At a midnight Easter vigil, or at dawn on Easter morning as we rejoice in the resurrection, baptism can be joyfully celebrated. Church members can express their common faith and commitment by renewing their own baptismal promises. And then the newly baptized can join the rest of the church in the symbolic meal of Holy Communion.

The Easter Vigil starts late on Saturday night or early on Easter Sunday morning. When the vigil begins at dawn, it is often called the "Sunrise" or "First Light" worship service, and can be followed with a community Easter breakfast. The traditional and most symbolic time for an Easter vigil is midnight. Families with young children, however, may not find this time practical. Check with the families in your faith community, and hold the service as late as you can and still have people come. It is a lasting and potent experience for a child to be wakened in the middle of the night to participate in a vigil. Check with your people – they might be willing to try it.

Before the service, invite everyone to place their Easter offering of breads and buns on the table for Communion. A pitcher of wine and as many chalices as will be needed for Communion should also be on the table. Although there has to be enough light for people to find their seats, leave the sanctuary as much in darkness as you can.

Begin the service with the lighting of "new fire." The tradition was that on Good Friday, at the moment of Jesus' death, all lamps, candles, and fires in every village were extinguished. All was dark and cold (like the tomb) until Easter Eve. Then a new fire was kindled in the church. After the service each family would take a taper, lit from the Christ-candle, to re-light their lamps and cooking-fires at home.

Preface your service with words like the following:

Grace and peace to you in the name
of God, the source of love,
in the name of Jesus, love in flesh,
and in the name of the Spirit,
love's power.
On this most holy night,
when Christ rose to life anew,
we gather to pray and watch
for the dawn.
With all of God's peoples
in heaven and on earth
we remember Jesus' victory
over every power of death,
our liberation from shadow,
into the light everlasting.

Then read John 1:1, 4–5 and light the new fire.

One: Light of Christ!
All: Thanks be to God!

A group of youth and young adults at a Toronto congregation worked with Louise to plan an Easter vigil. At a park across the street, they kindled "new fire" in a patio torch (fueled by lamp oil) on a tall bamboo pole. Then, carrying the Christ-light, they led the congregation across the street into the church, singing, "Light of Christ! Thanks be to God!" The Christ candle in the church was lighted from the "fire" and tapers for all the people were lighted from the Christ-candle flame. With the candle-light glowing, a worship leader prayed:

> **Eternal Love, through Christ**
> you have bestowed the light of life
> upon the world.
> Make holy this fire,
> and grant
> that our hearts
> might shine with the brightness
> of the rising of Christ. Amen.

You might conclude this "liturgy of light" part of the vigil with a hymn based on Philippians 2:5–11, *At the Name of Jesus.* When St. Paul wrote the words in Philippians, he was probably quoting from one of the earliest Easter hymns.

The "liturgy of the Word" part of the classic Easter vigil celebrates "The Mighty Acts of God" – the creation, exodus, the prophets, incarnation, and events leading up to the climax of the Easter story. In the early church, this recital represented the final instruction to the "catechumens," the people taking training for baptism. (In those days, candidates for baptism had already spent three years preparing!)

Keep this part of the vigil creative and dramatic so participants of all ages can enjoy it. If a homily is to be part of this section, be brief. Louise's youth group at Bellefair United Church in Toronto told the stories of "The Mighty Acts of God" in several voices, with an appropriate prayer and hymn between each section. Dancing or miming adds immensely. Nancy worked with a group of children who portrayed the story of creation, complete with sparkly, starry dust and stuffed animals.

If the sanctuary is still lighted only by candles (a beautiful and memorable way to worship), make sure there is a light shining on those who tell the story.

Next, invite everyone to stand for the Easter gospel. As a large white Christ-candle is lighted, proclaim the gospel truth with the ancient cry: "Christ is risen! Hallelujah!" to which all those gathered reply, "Christ is risen indeed! Hallelujah!" Turn the lights up enough for a rousing Easter hymn. Use trumpets, cymbals, and any celebratory instrument you can find!

The "liturgy of water" follows. Gather the children and youth to assist with baptism by helping to pour the water, pass out candles, etc. If there are no baptisms to celebrate, proceed directly to the congregation's reaffirmation of baptismal vows. Ask children to dip evergreen branches in the font, and then to sprinkle everyone with water while saying, "Remember your baptism and be thankful!"

At the liturgy of the Table, "the story" within the Great Prayer of Thanksgiving can be brief because the story has already been enacted. Use loaves from the table to "break Easter bread." Invite the people to come forward for Communion.

At the conclusion of the service, send each person home with bread or buns to share for Easter breakfast.

TABLE RITUAL FOR EASTER AND EASTERTIDE

The disciples recognized Christ when they broke bread with a stranger and shared a meal. Whenever you gather to share a meal through the Season of Eastertide, use the ritual which follows to celebrate the joy of the season and to reveal holy presence. Begin by lighting a large white Christ-candle. As the candle is lighted, share one of the following prayers:

Rejoice, heavenly powers!
Sing, choirs of angels!
Jesus Christ, the Morning Star,
is risen! Amen.

Gracious and loving God,
may the love with which you loved
Jesus be in us
that we may be one in the Spirit
of Christ,
and a sign for the world
of your presence. Amen.

PENTECOST SUNDAY

The Sunday celebration of Pentecost should be a great party, where all rejoice in the power of the Spirit – in scripture, story, poetry, dance, and song! If Communion is not celebrated every Sunday by your church, Pentecost is a marvelous opportunity to delight in sharing the ritual meal together. And it's a wonderful day for members of the faith community to reaffirm their baptismal commitment, and to celebrate the bestowal of the Spirit in the rite of confirmation.

Read Galatians 5:22–23 and 25 about the fruits of the Spirit, and the Pentecost story from Acts 2:1–21. You could read the Acts story first in English. Then dramatize it in the "Babel" of simultaneous reading in every language represented in the congregation, mirroring the Pentecost experience of the disciples which ends in the gospel being understood in many languages at once. We are one in the Spirit!

Delight in the lovely hymns and prayers about the Spirit which have been cherished through the ages by the church. And enjoy the beautiful prayers and hymns which have been written in our own era, as we rediscover the joy and mystery of Holy Spirit. Find creative ways to highlight the varieties of gifts which are given to the church, or share stories of the variety of ministries to which we are commissioned.

The evocative color for Pentecost is red, signifying the "tongues of fire" which rested on each disciple and transformed those who merely followed (known as disciples) into those who are sent forth (called apostles). Encourage everyone to wear red for Pentecost! Attach red crepe paper streamers to the congregation's worship orders so they can wave in the air like tongues of fire.

Fine textures are appropriate for Pentecost decoration. Pentecost symbols include tongues of flame, symbols of the church like a ship or a rainbow, and the descending dove which represents the Holy Spirit.

Some congregations choose to celebrate their own anniversary on Pentecost Sunday, to emphasize the coming of the Spirit to their midst rather than the opening of a building. If so, you might shape your worship service so people can share stories about how the Holy Spirit has come and is present in your particular faith community or denomination.

You could also combine Pentecost and the annual church picnic, lighting with sparklers a huge birthday cake for the church. Instead of competitive games at the picnic, play with images of wind and breath: blow bubbles, fly kites, and fold paper planes. Write messages of peace to send by "air" mail! If the celebration has to be held indoors, make pin-wheels and mobiles, and turn air into wind with a fan.

TABLE RITUALS FOR THE FESTIVAL OF PENTECOST

When you gather to share a meal, begin by lighting the Christ-candle. As the candle is lighted, share a versicle and response such as one of the following:

One: Come Holy Spirit, and fill the hearts
of your faithful.
**All: Kindle us with the flame of your
love!**

One: Spirit of Life, come to us,
All: So we can speak the truth of love.

One: Holy Spirit, bless us with tongues of
healing fire.
All: Make us a whole and holy people.

5. Sharing our story for Easter & Eastertide

The themes of suggested scriptures through the Season of Eastertide include the resurrection of Jesus and his subsequent appearances; the transformation of Jesus' community of disciples as witnesses to divine love and presence; and the contemplations of the early church on the meaning of Jesus' life, death, and new life in the Spirit. Easter scriptures describe the path of Christian discipleship as a unity of personal, social, and cosmic transformation. In the ancient world as now, "the way" of Christ embodies Christian hope.

The storytelling exercises which follow have been written for groups with one participant in the role of leader. They can be easily adapted for prayer partners or for personal use. Decide before you start who will read the scripture passages, and who will lead the storytelling for today.

When discussing stories located in a specific city in the ancient world, it will help to point out these locations on a map so that participants can connect the story's people and their problems with a particular place.

Remember to choose discussions which match the level of comfort and familiarity among those who are present, and remind participants they are always free to "pass." Let the stories and questions unfold as slowly as needed.

Close your session with prayer. You may find it helpful to hold hands in a circle as you pray. The leader can invite the group to offer the hopes and prayers of their hearts, and start the prayer with his/her own words. As the leader finishes, he/she squeezes the hand of the next person in the circle who either prays or passes on the "squeeze" to the next person.

Stories of Easter presence

TRANSFORMING EXPERIENCES

John 20:1–10, Mark 16:1–8, Luke 24:1–10, and Matthew 28:1–10 (four descriptions of the discovery of the empty tomb)

Read aloud the scripture passages. Reflect on each question and share responses. Reflect on these questions and share responses:

- What are the differences between the resurrection stories? What are the similarities?
- In the days between Jesus' resurrection from the dead and his ascension beyond the physical world, he prepared his followers to experience holy presence in new and wonderful ways. Can you think of historical or personal situations when people felt as if life had ended for them, and then discovered that the crisis led to a beautiful beginning?
- How can the way we respond to a crisis influence whether the experience will yield "new life" and growth, or "hell" on earth?
- What moments in your history have been experiences of "resurrection," when you and your life were transformed? We all experience times of crisis which are a lot like little deaths, holding both opportunity and loss. Why is it important to develop the strength to move through so-called failures, and be reborn into life again? How does faith in the promise of new life affect our attitudes and actions?

WOMEN AND THE RESURRECTION

Matthew 28:1–10 (the empty tomb), Mark 16:9–11 and Luke 24:1–12 (the male disciples don't believe the women), and John 20:11–18 (Jesus appears to Mary)

Read aloud the scripture passages. Reflect on each question and share responses.

- Several biblical stories tell us that Jesus appeared first to women after his resurrection. What does appearing first to women suggest about Jesus' connection to the women among his followers?
- Jesus asks Mary to wipe away her tears and recognize a new reality in the risen Christ. Then he asks her to share that truth with others. Why do you think the women followers of Jesus were not believed when they told what they had seen? Would male witnesses be considered more reliable by some in your community?
- How does it affect you personally to hear that Jesus appeared first to the women?

RECOGNITION IN EMMAUS

Luke 24:13–25 (two disciples meet a stranger on Emmaus Road, and later recognize him as by his actions)

Read aloud the scripture passage. Reflect on each question and share responses.

- In what ways is this story a model of how we meet the risen Christ? How does Christian worship mirror this pattern of revelation? How do ritual actions shape us for the Christ-life?
- Can you think of an "Emmaus Road" moment in your life when you recognized the Christ in a friend or stranger? How is the risen Christ recognizable when you share the bread and cup of Communion?

OVERCOMING DOUBT

John 20:19–29 (doubting Thomas)

Read aloud the scripture passage. Reflect on each question and share responses.

- Jesus comes back a second time, to reveal himself to Thomas in ways which overcome Thomas' doubts. How can we trust what we can't see with our own eyes? Or recognize with other senses? What other ways of seeing help us trust?
- How can we trust guidance that has no guarantee of outcome?
- When in your life have your doubts been eased by experience of the holy? Was this a physical experience of the senses, or something different? What was your response? How were you changed?

A SECOND CHANCE

John 13:33–38, John 18:12–17, 25–27 (how Peter denies knowing Jesus), and John 21:1–19 (Jesus gives Peter a second chance)

Read aloud the scripture passages and the following summary. Reflect on each question and share responses.

These three stories about Peter's relationship with Jesus end with his transformation from an expedient bumbler who characteristically gets things wrong to a committed successor of Jesus.

- Jesus describes the central task of discipleship as loving one another. How does Peter fail in this task in his relationship with Jesus? How are his self-deceptions shattered?
- Casting their nets in the Sea of Tiberius, the disciples took instruction from Christ and their empty nets were filled. In this story, how does Peter cleanse himself so he is ready to receive Christ's instructions? What other biblical event comes to mind

when Peter dresses? When he enters the water?

- When Peter shares a meal with Christ after swimming to shore, scripture tells us he knows for sure who Jesus is. What is the significance in Jesus asking three times if Peter loves him? How has Peter been changed?
- Peter learns about loving through failing and being forgiven. How does this story of boundless love and transformation speak to you? In what way is Peter's story your story? What can you learn from your experiences? How are you being strengthened and changed?

EMERGING FROM DARKNESS

Acts 6:8–7:2a and Acts 7:51–8:3 (the stoning of Stephen), and Acts 9:1–22 (Saul's conversion)
Read aloud the scripture passages and the following summary. Reflect on each question and share responses.

The stoning of Stephen eventually leads to the conversion of Saul, who will later be known as Paul.

- Name some times and places when violence and even murder have been rationalized in God's name by those with power. How were these situations similar to the stoning of Stephen?
- Paul's conversion emerged from the deepest shadows in his life. How was Christ the gateway to new life for Paul? How did the power of holy love release Paul from the past?
- What is the significance of Paul's period of blindness?
- Can you identify in your own life some experience of grief or shame through which you came to faith and new hope? What insights have emerged for you out of times of darkness?

THE BIRTH OF COMMUNITY

Jeremiah 31:1–6 (God's restoration of Zion), Acts 2:43–47 (the growth of the new church), and Acts 4:32–35 (caring for each other)
Read aloud the scripture passages. Reflect on each question and share responses.

- What are the marks of transformed community in these passages? In what ways are the seeds of transformation taking root in our community? In our nation? Around the world? How can we participate in the work of the Spirit in our community?
- If you could dream a new community into being, what would it look like? How does the biblical vision of community inspire you? In what ways are you embracing this vision in your lifestyle? What more could you do?

OPENING THE DOORS

Acts 8:26–40 (Philip converts the Ethiopian eunuch), Acts 16:9–15 (Paul initiates mission to Europe), and Acts 10:1–48 (Peter's vision)
Read aloud the scripture passages and the following summary. Reflect on each question and share responses.

Jewish tradition considered all Gentiles "unclean," and prohibited devout Jews from associating with them or eating with them. Those barriers came tumbling down under the influence of the Holy Spirit.

- The conversions in these stories demonstrate the radical inclusivity of followers of "the way." To what extent does our faith community live this same inclusivity? How do we fall short of this vision?
- How do you understand the role of radical inclusivity in healing and transforming community? What are the implications for you of inclusivity in faith community? How are you being asked to change? What steps could you take?

A NEW HEAVEN, A NEW EARTH

Isaiah 65:17–25 and Revelation 21:1–6 (visions of a new heaven and a transformed earth), and Acts 2:14–21 (Peter's vision). Also Ezekiel 37:1–14 (the valley of bones)
Read aloud the scripture passages and the following summary. Reflect on each question and share responses.

All these passages deal with prophecies about a new world, a transformation of heaven and earth.

- How does the biblical vision of God's future affect our experience of the present? How does trusting that good can come make a difference?
- How do you understand the role of the Christ in the transforming power of the Spirit? What difference does this make in your life?

THE WAY OF CHRIST

John 14:1–17 (Jesus promises the coming of the Spirit), John 15:12–17 (to lay down one's life for one's friends), John 17: 1–11, 20–23 (Jesus' prayer for his followers), and 1 John 3:16–24 (John's summary of Jesus' way)
Read aloud the scripture passages and the following summary. Reflect on each question and share responses.

Jesus defines the way, the truth, and the life which brings salvation – the way of life which transforms persons, communities, and the cosmos.

- If Christ embodies the Holy Spirit, how do you interpret the statement in John's gospel that no one comes to God except through Christ? How do people of other faith traditions embody Spirit?
- How do you interpret the teaching that believers who follow the way of the Christ will do even greater works of love than Jesus? What difference does this teaching make for you? How does Christ's way shape your lifestyle?

Stories of witnessing to divine power and meaning

THE PROMISE OF THE SPIRIT

Luke 24:44–53 and Acts 1:1–11 (Jesus' ascension), and Ephesians 1:15–23 (Christians as Christ's continuing body)
Read aloud the scripture passages and the following summary. Reflect on each question and share responses.

With the ascension of Jesus, the Spirit is to be incarnate in the followers of the Christ.

- What are the implications of the Spirit's incarnation in us? How can we stay conscious of our intimate relationship with the Spirit? How can we seek the inner guidance of the Spirit? What fears might we have about being guided by the Spirit? What truth can still these fear-driven voices?
- When have you experienced acts of caring, forgiving, and healing? How has Christ been present for you in these experiences? How can you open yourself to receiving gifts of Spirit?

THE COMING OF THE SPIRIT

Acts 2:1–42 (the Pentecost story)
Read aloud the scripture passage and the following summary. Reflect on each question and share responses.

In the first chapter of Acts, Jesus promised that the disciples would receive power when the Holy Spirit came upon them, and that they would be witnesses "to the ends of the earth." In the second chapter, that Spirit comes at Pentecost.

- In what ways is Jesus' promise fulfilled in the Pentecost event?

- What is the significance in the disciples speaking languages which can be understood by people from different lands? What does this say about the power of the truth revealed through Christ?
- How do you understand the ongoing mission and ministry of Christ in the world? What gifts of the Spirit have you been given with which to participate in this work? How can you share the gifts you have been given? To what life-task have you been called? What enables you to take the path of sacred service?

UPSETTING THE STATUS QUO

Acts 5:12–42 (the apostles' courage), Acts 9:32–42 (Peter heals in Christ's name) and Acts 16:16–40 (Paul heals a slave girl)

Read aloud the scripture passages and the following summary. Reflect on each question and share responses.

The new Christians disturbed the status quo with their enthusiasm. Opponents feared the apostles would arouse too much attention with their preaching and extraordinary healings. Both civil and religious authorities were afraid that stability and order would be threatened.

- Where in our time is the power of the Spirit disrupting the status quo in Christ's name?
- Where are Christians being persecuted? Why?
- What are the challenges and risks for you in sharing your faith? Have you felt penalized for being a Christian? How do you respond?

6. Embodied prayers for Easter & Eastertide

The Easter season is our springtime, when our bodies, minds, and spirits experience afresh the joy of being. In this time, the creativity of holy wisdom is revealed in creation as new life and hope. Our body prayers through Eastertide express our deep delight in the grace of God's unfailing love.

We long to feel the breath of Spirit in our bodies. The Hebrew word for Spirit also means "breath." The Bible tells us God breathed into the first human's nostrils and the creature became a living being. (Genesis 2:7) When we breathe *in* strength and courage, and breathe *out* fear and pain, God breathes new life into us.

Since all our life systems are interlinked in subtle ways, changing our breathing affects our whole self. Deep, slow breathing is the body's natural way of moving into relaxation, which in turn helps us attend to our experience. Combining breathing and prayer can help us focus and center on the presence of the Spirit, and deepen our awareness of that Spirit in our physical being.

INSTRUCTIONS

These prayers can be part of daily spiritual disciplines. They are written for groups, for prayer partners, or for personal use.

When used by a group, one participant will need to assume the role of guide. Decide in advance who will lead the prayers today, letting each prayer unfold slowly and gently.

For an effective pace, we suggest you take two full breaths whenever you see "…" before you start the next phrase. If a time frame is suggested, remember that one minute equals about eight full breaths. Give your group permission to breathe normally at any time, especially if they feel distressed or anxious. Tell the group never to strain or hold the breath. A deep breath is gentle and relaxed.

PREPARATION

Always begin embodied prayer sessions with this exercise. If you are practicing embodied prayers alone, read through the following instructions carefully before starting. If you are leading a group, read the following slowly and calmly aloud, with appropriate pauses.

Sit comfortably, with your spine fairly straight. Close your eyes. Without changing how you breathe, pay attention to the sensations of breathing ... Pay attention to the sensation of breath moving in and out of your nose or your mouth ... Can you feel the path of breath as it moves through your body into your lungs? ... Can you feel the breath move your chest and rib cage, and then release again as you breathe out? ... Continue to follow the flow of your breathing, without straining to do anything ...

Now breathe in and send the breath into your abdomen as though you are filling your stomach. Exhale, letting the stomach fall back to normal. Breathing in, your belly rises; breathing out, it falls back. Breathe this relaxed "belly breath" for one minute ... Don't strain or force your breath ... Relax as you breathe in and your belly rises, and relax as you breathe out ...

As you breathe quietly, begin to listen to the sounds in the room ... Move your fingers and your toes. Open your eyes when you are ready.

THE SIGN OF THE CROSS

Sit comfortably with your spine fairly straight. Close your eyes. Focus for a minute on how you are breathing. Allow your body to relax with your breathing for about one minute ... Feel the Spirit breath flowing into your body ... Feel how God breathes you ...

Shift your focus to your feet. Don't move them, but simply become aware of their presence. Feel the soles of your feet on your shoes and the pressure that you exert on the floor ... Move your attention to your legs. Become aware of the weight and volume of your legs ... Become aware of your torso. Feel your back against the chair and feel how your torso moves as you breathe ... Move your attention to your arms and hands. Feel their weight ... Now become aware of your head, its volume and weight ...

Now, see if you can become aware of your whole body at once, from head to foot. Fully sense your whole body ... Feel the wholeness of body and soul that God intends for us all ... Your body is a temple of the Holy Spirit ... feel it ... know it ...

Now, with a heightened sense of awareness, take your time and slowly, so slowly, make the sign of the cross. Slowly bring your hand to your forehead. Feel your whole body participate in this movement ... Pay attention to your whole body ...

Slowly, move your hand down to your heart. Sense the great distance between your head and your heart. Feel your motion drawing both together. Feel the movement with all of your body ...

Now, move your hand up and out to the far shoulder ... Take your time ... feel ... As you bring your hand back to the other shoulder, feel the arc of the movement ... Feel the blessing of Christ wrap around you ... Now slowly bring both hands in front of your body, palms up ... open ... Feel your whole body receiving grace ...

Slowly, repeat the sign of the cross in silence ...

As you breathe quietly, begin to listen to the sounds in the room ... Open your eyes when you are ready.

BREATHING HOLY WISDOM

Sit comfortably, close your eyes, and pay attention to the natural rhythm of your breath ... Let the breath flow in and flow out with ease ... Let the motion of the breath rock you gently from the inside ... helping you to relax ... Breathe and rock gently and let go of tension ... let go ...

Now, imagine that you can breathe through your forehead. Imagine your breath entering your forehead and filling your mind with calmness. As the breath leaves your mind it takes with it unwanted thoughts and chatter ... Let the breath flow in and out your forehead with ease ... Let the breath gently sway your mind's focus toward stillness ... You are clearing your mind for God's wisdom to enter ...With the breath imagine that God's thoughts enter and merge with your thoughts ... Imagine that God's understanding becomes your understanding ... God's peace becomes your peace ...

As you inhale through your forehead, silently say to yourself "Peace be with me" and fill your mind with God's peace. And as you exhale through your forehead silently say to yourself "Peace be with you," and spread the peace of holy wisdom to those around you ... From your forehead, inhale, "Peace be with me" And exhale, "Peace be with you" ... "Peace be with me" ... "Peace be with you" ...

Now, as you breathe through your forehead, imagine that your capacity to breathe God's peace and understanding is expanding. Imagine yourself able to breathe holy wisdom over your entire family ... It grows again as you imagine breathing holy wisdom over your community ... Your capacity expands further as you imagine breathing peace over the world ... Send the breath of peace and understanding to all ... The capacity of God's mindful love within you can encompass all of God's creation ... Love is infinite ...

As you breathe quietly, begin to listen to the sounds in the room ... Move your fingers and toes ... Open your eyes when you are ready.

SHARING THE TRUTH OF CHRIST

Sit comfortably and close your eyes. Begin by paying attention to your breath. Let the breath flow in and out with ease ... Let the breath release your tensions ... In rhythm with your breath silently say an ancient Aramaic word for holy presence that Jesus might have known ... *Alaha* ... Alaha ... Alaha ... You are clearing a place inside you where the oneness of God exists. You are clearing the inner temple of your heart ...

Imagine that inside the inner temple of your heart lies a beautiful crystal. It glistens with natural beauty ... The crystal lies at the heart of your soul ... Imagine that a ray of divine light enters from above through the center of your head, moves into the temple of your heart and fills your crystal with glowing light ... The crystal of your soul refracts the light into many rays of colorful light, sending these rays outward ... Imagine the many rays of divine light emanating from your heart, spreading outward ... The one ray of divine light fills your soul, and you turn the light into many rays reaching outward ...

Now, imagine other people receiving the rays that you are sending out ... Imagine that their hearts take in the divine light, and then in turn they send out many rays to others ... See the network growing and expanding ... Watch as you see more and more people connected together by rays of light ... See light pouring into your heart, into their hearts, sending and receiving ... Hearts touching hearts ... Souls touching souls ... The beautiful, intricate web of rays of divine light, of compassion, of love, of peace with justice for all ...

Imagine that you move the crystal from your heart to the middle of your forehead … Now the crystal lies at the inner eye of your soul … As the ray of divine light enters your crystal and radiates through your mind, feel how the essence of the light has shifted … The light enters your inner eye as divine truth …

Imagine divine truth filling your crystal with light, releasing the limitations of human reasoning, allowing trust in the Christ's greater purpose to shine within you … The light of divine truth merges with your own thoughts and banishes anxiety and doubt … Feel the peace of Christ's truth shining within you …

Know that when human logic seems to lead nowhere, you can look to the light of Christ's truth through the crystal of your inner eye … You can share the truth of the power of love in your interactions with others. Seek only the truth … Trust in the light of Christ's truth …

As you breathe quietly, begin to listen to the sounds in the room … Move your fingers and your toes. Open your eyes when you are ready.

HEART WALKING

Begin standing, and keep your eyes open. We are going to explore the relationship between tension in our bodies and how we extend love and comfort to others through our bodies. Start by walking slowly around the room. Shake out your arms as you walk, then have fun with shaking out your legs as you walk …

Now, place a gentle tension in your chin, jaw, and lips and slightly protrude your chin forward. Continue walking as though your chin is leading you. Feel what it is like to walk in the world with this posture, with this tension in your neck and jaw. What emotions or thoughts come to mind as you walk holding this posture? … Check the inner state that this posture creates in you … As you walk past other people in the room, how do you relate to them? … How difficult or easy is it to hold the other person in your heart? …

Relax your chin and limber up a bit …

Now, place a gentle tension in your buttocks and slightly push your pelvis forward. Walk as though your pelvis is leading you forward … How does it feel to walk in the world with this posture? … What emotions or thoughts come to mind? … Check the inner state created by this posture … As you walk past other people how do you relate to them? …

Relax your buttocks and limber up a bit …

Now, place a gentle tension in your shoulders and chest. Push your chest forward and walk as though your tight chest and shoulders are leading you forward … How does it feel to walk in the world with this posture? … What emotions and thoughts come to mind? … What inner state is created within you by holding this posture? … How do you relate to other people in the room as you pass by? …

Relax your chest and shoulders and limber up again …

Now, focus on relaxing the area around your heart. Each time you exhale, let tension release from your chest … As you walk, imagine that the area of your heart is softening and relaxing … Imagine that God's love flows in and out of your heart with your breath. God's love flows in as you inhale, and flows out as you exhale … Walk as though your soft, giving heart is leading you forward, as though the heart of Christ guides you … How does it feel to walk in the world with the heart of Christ leading? … What emotions and thoughts come to mind? … What inner state is created within you by holding this posture? … How do you relate to other people in the room as you pass by? … Hold this feeling in your body as you sit down.

Invite participants to discuss their experience with each other, as they feel comfortable.

WALKING IN THE PRESENCE OF CHRIST

Begin by taking off your shoes. Stand with your eyes open. Keeping your eyes lowered, watching the ground in front of your feet, begin to walk ever so slowly around the room. Pay attention to how your feet contact the floor … Walk in slow motion, being present with each footstep in this moment … Nothing else matters … Place your full attention on the sensation of walking … Feel the bottom of your feet. Feel the weight of your body … Feel how the foot rolls from the heel to the ball of the foot to the toes … Feel the moment that the weight shifts from one foot to the other … There is no judging here about a right way or wrong way to walk. This walk is about simply "being" …

Now, as you walk in slow motion, know that Christ walks with you … Know that as Christ walks with you, you are fully accepted just as you are … As you walk this simple walk, can you feel how you are completely accepted in the presence of Christ? … If a part of you resists, accept the part of yourself that resists … If unfocused thoughts intrude, embrace those thoughts and accept them. Let them go and bring your attention gently back to the sensation of walking with Christ … If emotions arise, embrace them … Feel yourself fully and completely accepted in the presence of Christ …

Gently bring yourself back to a normal pace and make your way to your seat …

Invite participants to share their experience with others, as they feel comfortable.

7. Written prayers for Easter & Eastertide

These written prayers can be a starting point for collective or personal devotions through the Season of Easter.

Prayers for delighting in God

When I found truth,
there I found my God who is the truth.
And there since the time I learned you,
you abide in my memory;
and there I find you, whenever I call
you to remembrance,
and delight in you. Amen.

(St. Augustine, 354–430, restated)

O sun, as you rise in the east
by God's power,
wash away the evils of the night.
Bless me, so my enemies
will not harm me or my family.
Guide me through my hard work.
O God, have mercy
on your suffering children.
Bring abundance at your rising;
Bring all good fortune today. Amen.

(Morning prayer from Kenya, restated)

O immeasurably tender love!

Who would not be set afire
with such love?
What heart could keep from breaking?
You, deep well of charity,
it seems you are so madly in love
with your creatures
that you could not live without us!
Yet you are our God,
and have no need of us.
Your greatness is no greater
for our well-being,
nor are you harmed by any harm
that comes to us,
for you are supreme eternal goodness.
What could move you to such mercy?
Amen.

(St. Catherine of Siena, 1347–1380)

O God, we are not worthy

to have a glimpse of heaven,
and unable with our works
to save ourselves.
Nonetheless you have given to us
your son, Christ,
who is far more precious
and dearer than heaven,
and much stronger than sin, death,
and hell.
For this we rejoice, praise,
and thank you, O God,
that without price and out of
pure grace you have given
this boundless blessing to us in your Son,
through whom you remove sin, death,
and hell from us
and give to us all that belongs to him.
Amen.

(Martin Luther, 1483–1546)

Blessed be the God and Father

of our Lord Jesus Christ!
By great mercy, God has given us
a new birth into a living hope
through the resurrection
of Jesus Christ from the dead,
and into an inheritance that is
imperishable, undefiled, and unfading,
kept in heaven for you,
who are being protected
by the power of God through faith
for a salvation ready to be revealed.
Amen.

(1 Peter 1:3–5)

I have calmed

and quieted my soul,
like a child quieted at its mother's breast:
like a child that is quieted is my soul.
Amen.

(Psalm 131:2 restated)

I arise today

Through the strength of heaven:
Light of sun,
Radiance of moon,
Splendor of fire,
Speed of lightning,
Swiftness of wind,
Depth of sea,
Stability of earth,
Firmness of rock.
I arise today
Through God's strength to pilot me.
Amen.

(St. Patrick, 389–461)

Prayers for transformation and renewal

Almighty God,
unto whom all hearts be open,
all desires known, and from whom
no secrets are hid:
Cleanse the thoughts of our hearts
by the inspiration of your Holy Spirit,
that we may perfectly love you,
and worthily magnify your holy name;
through Christ our Lord. Amen.

(Gregorian *Sacramentary,* restated)

Grant, O God, that we
who are baptized into Christ,
may die to ways of death,
and be reborn to joy daily,
living with Christ-like compassion.
Amen.

God of peace, grant us grace
so to follow the way,
that we may seek what you seek,
and love what you love,
and grow in the image of Christ,
who gave his body
to the rage of the world, trusting you.
Raise us into the new life of faith, in
Christ's name. Amen.

You are never weary, O God,
of doing us good.
Let us never be weary
of doing you service.
But, as you have pleasure
in the well-being of your servants,
so let us take pleasure
in the service of our Lord,
and abound in your work,
and in your love and praise, evermore.
O fill up all that is wanting,
reform whatever is amiss in us,
perfect the thing that concerns us.
Let the witness of your pardoning love
ever live in our hearts.

(John Wesley, 1703–1791, restated.)

O creator past all telling,
true font of light and wisdom,
primal source beyond all things,
pour forth a ray of your brightness
into my darkened places;
disperse from my soul sin and ignorance.
You, who make eloquent
the tongues of little children,
refine my speech and touch my lips
with graciousness.
Make me keen to understand,
quick to learn and remember;
make me delicate to interpret
and ready to speak.
Guide my going in and going forward,
and lead home my going forth.
You are true God and true human,
world without end. Amen.

(Thomas Aquinas, 1225–1274, restated)

Holy One, you sent Jesus
to be the cornerstone of our lives.
Open our eyes to the presence
of the Spirit
that we may see the living Christ
and be transformed by what we see.
Make us faithful instruments of peace
in the name of One
who loves us and frees us to serve.
Amen.

Teach me, O God,
not to torture myself.
Teach me to breathe deeply in faith.
Amen.

(Soren Kierkegaard, 1813–1855)

Holy God, who calls us
as followers of Christ,
grant that we may grow
in the humble self-knowledge
which opens to the gift of transformation.
Cleanse us and renew us
by the power of the Spirit,
that – like Peter – we may claim
the tasks of love as our ministry,
and live as Christ's body in the world.
This we pray in the name
of the one who sets us free,
now and forever. Amen.

Prayers of thanks and dedication

Holy One, we thank you
for your presence on the road,
and in the breaking of bread.
Stay with us, we pray,
until morning. Amen.

Gracious God, we give you thanks
for the springtimes of our lives,
for the beauty of your mercy,
and for the chance to start afresh,
every day.
Receive the gifts we offer
as signs of our commitment
to becoming living gifts for the world.
Through Christ, with Christ,
and in Christ,
in the unity of the Spirit,
our power and possibility is yours, God
most holy,
now and forever. Amen.

Gracious God, whose blessed Son
walked the way to Emmaus
and showed himself in the breaking
of bread,
we give thanks that the eyes
of our faith have been opened,
that we may walk with the stranger,
see you in the neighbor,
and share the holy food of compassion.
Amen.

Prayers for the world, ourselves, and others

Now may the God of peace
who brought from the dead
our Lord Jesus,
the great shepherd of the sheep,
by the blood of the eternal covenant,
make you complete in everything good
so that you may do the will of God,
working among us that which is
pleasing in God's sight,
through Jesus Christ, to whom be the
glory forever and ever. Amen.
(Hebrews 13:20–21)

O God, if there are people
who wish me evil
or do evil against me,
grant them rest and forgiveness.
Convert their hearts
to wholesome peace
and turn every malice into good.
And stand by me,
that with a pure heart I may be able
to love a friend in you,
and love an enemy for your sake.
Amen.

(15th century, restated)

8. Guided prayers & meditations for Easter

These prayer suggestions for Easter and Eastertide have been written for groups with one participant in the role of guide. They can easily be adapted for prayer partners and for personal use. Decide in advance who will read scripture, and who will lead the prayers today. Let each prayer unfold slowly and gently.

A MEDITATION ON RESURRECTION
1 Corinthians 15:35–58 (the mystery of Christ's resurrection)

Resurrection is not the same as resuscitation. The gospel writers understand the death of the physical body as a process of transition, leading to a new state of wholeness and harmony with God. Though we cherish our physical health on earth as a gracious gift of life, as "Easter people" we also live with the promise of ultimate resurrection.

Take a few moments to prepare. Sit or lie comfortably, eyes closed. Focus on your regular breathing pattern, to come fully into the present. Relax with your breathing … Feel the Spirit breath flowing into your body … Feel how God breathes you … As you listen for the word of God, listen for a word or a phrase which attracts you strongly...

Read the 1 Corinthians passage through, aloud.

Listen for the word of God … Choose a word or phrase from the passage which attracts you … Repeat the word or phrase in silence for a couple of minutes, in rhythm with your breathing …

Read the passage through again, aloud.

Reflect in silence on what your word or phrase means to you. How does it relate to your life? … To your dreams? … To your hopes for resurrection? …

Read the passage through again, aloud.

As you breathe, become aware of feelings which have been eased or aroused by your chosen word or phrase … Listen for what God may be saying to you … Is God speaking through a hope or a desire? … Is there something to release? … Is there something which calls for your attention? … How can you respond? …

Now rest quietly in God's presence, focusing only on the flow of your breathing, in and out … Stay open to God's possibilities …

Pray for yourself, for release from fear, and for joy in the promise of new life in Christ …

Pray for the person to your right, that he or she may know the joy of new life and holy presence … Finish with a prayer or a blessing you know by heart … Open your eyes when you are ready.

Other options
If you prefer, read one of the following short passages instead of the suggested reading from 1 Corinthians 15:35–58.

> **Do not remember the former things,**
> or consider the things of old.
> I am about to do a new thing;
> now it springs forth;
> do you not perceive it?
> I will make a way in the wilderness
> and rivers to flow in the desert.
>
> (Isaiah 43:18–19)

I am the resurrection and the life.
Those who believe in me,
even though they die, will live,
and everyone who lives
 and believes in me will never die.

(John 11:25–26)

Do not let your hearts be troubled.
Believe in God, believe also in me.
In my Father's house
there are many dwelling places.
If it were not so, would I have told you
that I go to prepare a place for you?
And if I go and prepare a place for you,
I will come again
and will take you to myself,
so that where I am, there you may be also.

(John 14:1–3)

I will not leave you orphaned:
I am coming to you.
In a little while
the world will no longer see me,
but you will see me;
because I live, you also will live.
On that day you will know
that I am in my Father,
and you in me, and I in you.

(John 14:18–20)

A MEDITATION ON HOLY PRESENCE
John 20:11–18 (Mary recognizes the risen Christ)

Take a few moments to prepare. Sit or lie comfortably, eyes closed. Focus on your regular breathing pattern, to come fully into the present. Relax with your breathing … Feel the Spirit breath flowing into your body … Feel how God breathes you … Listen for the word of God … Listen for the details in this story …

Read the biblical passage through two times slowly, aloud.

Imagine you are weeping at the tomb as Mary wept … Imagine that Jesus comes near to speak with you … Relive the whole scene as the gospel describes it … Hear Jesus speak your name … Hear the tenderness and love in Jesus' voice … Can you commit that voice to your memory?

Listen again to the sound of Jesus' voice, so you can hear it whenever you are in need of gentle comfort and certain knowledge that you are beloved …

Now rest quietly in God's presence, focusing only on the flow of your breathing, in and out. Stay open to the experience of holy presence …

Pray for yourself, for release from fear, and for joy in the promise and experience of life in the Spirit with Christ …

Pray for the person to your right, that he or she may know the joy of new life and holy presence … Finish with a prayer or a blessing you know by heart … Open your eyes when you are ready.

Lectio meditations on receiving the Holy Spirit

THE UPPER ROOM
John 20:19–23 (Jesus appears to the disciples)

Take a few moments to prepare. Sit or lie comfortably, eyes closed. Focus on your regular breathing pattern, to come fully into the present. Relax with your breathing … Feel the Spirit breath flowing into your body … Feel how God breathes you … Listen for the word of God … Listen for the details in this story …

Read the passage through two times slowly, aloud.

Imagine you are among the disciples in a room where all the doors are tightly closed … Imagine how you might feel when someone is suddenly with you, without coming through any entrance ... Hear him say familiar-sounding words: "Peace be with you" ...

What happens inside you when you see the wounds on this person's hands and side? ... How do you feel when Jesus tells you, "I send you"? ... When he tells you to "receive the Holy Spirit"? ...

What does it mean to you to be given authority to bring wholeness and forgiveness to others? ... To confront the power of evil when you encounter it? ... How will you respond to this gift? ...

Rest quietly in God's presence, focusing only on the flow of your breathing, in and out. Stay open to the experience of holy presence ...

Pray for yourself, for release from fear, and for joy in sharing the gifts of the Spirit ...

Pray for the person to your right, that he or she may be enabled to delight in the gifts of the Spirit ... Finish with a prayer or a blessing you know by heart ... Open your eyes when you are ready.

DOUBTING THOMAS

Substitute John 20:24–29, the continuation of the reading above. In the first part, Jesus appears to the disciples, not including Thomas. The second part is about Thomas's reaction.

Prepare as suggested above. Then read the passage through slowly and carefully, so you will remember the details.

Close your eyes, and imagine you are Thomas. You were not with the disciples when they thought they saw Jesus, and you just can't believe this wild tale. Tell them you will have to see the mark of the nails in his hands, and put your finger in the mark of the nails, and your hand in his side before you will believe ...

Now, imagine days have passed, and you are with the disciples in the house where they claim they saw Jesus. All the doors are shut

... Suddenly, Jesus is among you, and you hear him say the words, "Peace be with you." ... See Jesus reach out his hands to show the nail marks ... Hear him invite you to put your hand in the wound in his side ... Touch the places where the flesh is broken, where he bled ... Hear him say to you, "Do not doubt but believe."

Can you answer him, "My Lord and my God!"?

Complete the meditation as suggested above.

BREAKFAST BY THE LAKE

Prepare as recommended above. Then read John 21:1–19 (Jesus greets the disciples on the lakeshore) through twice, aloud. Read the passage through carefully, so you will remember the details.

- Close your eyes, and imagine you are Peter. Relive the scene as described. Are you embarrassed not to be the first one to recognize Jesus? Once you were the leader of the disciples, but now everyone knows that you denied you knew Jesus, when Jesus was most in need of friends. How do you feel? Exposed? Vulnerable? Why do you cover your body?
- How does the water feel when you dive in? Do you feel different by the time you reach the shore? How does it help you to pass through the waters on your way to the shore?
- Three times you denied Jesus before he was killed; now Jesus gives you three opportunities to pledge yourself to caring for his followers. What gift is Jesus giving you? What will it mean for you to follow Jesus in the next few days and weeks?

Complete the meditation as suggested above.

STRANGER ON THE ROAD

Luke 24:13–35 (the Emmaus road)
Read the Emmaus road story through twice, aloud.

Close your eyes. Imagine you are one of the two followers of Jesus on the road to Emmaus on Easter Sunday.

- How do the stories of God's love for humankind affect you as you hear them interpreted? How is your mood affected as you listen to the stranger?
- How do you experience the presence of Christ in sharing a meal and breaking bread? Can you invite Jesus to stay with you now?

BREAKING BREAD

Luke 24:36–49 (Jesus appears to the disciples)
Read the passage through twice, aloud.

Close your eyes. Imagine you are one of the disciples in Jesus' presence.

- Why is it significant that Jesus eats with you? What does this tell you about his spiritual body?
- How does Jesus open your mind and your heart to a new understanding of his presence? What does he promise will happen?
- When have you felt the power of the Spirit?

Complete the meditation as above.

DEATH ON A CROSS

1 Corinthians 1:25 (wisdom and foolishness), Galatians 6:14 (boasting of the cross), Philippians 2:5–8 (taking the role of a slave), Isaiah 53:11–12 (the suffering servant)
Read the biblical passages aloud.

Remembering the crowd who cried out, "Crucify him!" consider how Jesus returned blessing for evil.

- How does Jesus' willingness to die for a radically inclusive love change your heart?
- What does it mean to you to be loved, faults and frailties and all? How does the resurrection of Christ give you hope?
- Remember a time when you found a way to resist the temptation to return evil for evil. What blessing were you able to return? How was the situation changed by your blessing?
- Is there a situation in your life which might be eased by your blessing now? What blessing could you offer?

Complete the meditation as above.

FROM BLINDNESS TO SIGHT

Mark 10:46–52 (Jesus gives a man sight)
Read the biblical passage through twice, aloud.

Close your eyes. Imagine you are the blind Bartimaeus … Hear Jesus ask you, "What do you want me to do for you?" Reply to Jesus, "Rabboni, (teacher), I want to see."

Feel Jesus lay his hands upon you … Now, open your eyes, to see what you could not see before.

Complete the meditation as above.

A prayer for attentiveness – the Hebrew *Shema*

Take a few moments to prepare ... Sit or lie comfortably, eyes closed ... Focus on your breathing, to come fully into the present ... Relax with your breathing ... Feel the Spirit breath flowing into your body ... Feel how God breathes you ... Now, listen for the word of God ... Listen for words or phrases which attract you strongly ...

Read the following passage through two times, aloud.

> Hear, O Israel,
> Yahweh, our God, Yahweh is One.
> You shall love Yahweh your God
> with all your heart,
> and with all your soul,
> and with all your might.
>
> (Deuteronomy 6:4–5)

Leave a minute of silence.

Breathe slowly and quietly for a few minutes. Be still. Be open to your experience and your feelings ... Choose a word or phrase which attracts you strongly, and repeat it within you, in rhythm with your breathing ... Continue to breathe and repeat the word or phrase ... Listen for the word of God ...

Read the passage again. Leave a minute of silence after the reading.

As you breathe and repeat the word or phrase in your heart, become aware of what God may be saying to you ... What does this word or phrase mean to you now? ... How does it relate to your life? ... What is God inviting you to do or be? ...

Rest quietly in God's presence, focusing only on the flow of your breath, in and out ... Move your fingers and toes. Open your eyes when you are ready.

In past years, children and adults were expected to commit significant passages from scripture to memory. In your group, you might invite participants to memorize this passage from Deuteronomy 6:4–5. Next time you gather, you can pray the prayer for attentiveness again, but this time adding additional words:

> Keep these words that I command you
> today in your heart.
> Recite them to your children and talk
> about them when you are at home
> and when you are away, when you lie
> down and when you rise.
>
> (Deuteronomy 6:6–7)

9. Inner reflections for Easter & Eastertide

With fragrant myrrh
I come to the tomb
Even through my tears
I shall do
what I must
As I walk this dusty path
I run my list
of firsts and thens
But in one rolled stone
The old order is impossible
You cast
my best laid plans
to the wind
You empty the tomb
and fill my heart

Again, find your quiet spot, your candle, paper, pen, and pencil. During this retreat time, we invite you to explore your own Easter transformation.

EMPTY TOMB REFLECTION

You can do this reflection in one or several sessions.

Begin with a fragrant candle (or use potpourri, incense, a flower, or essential oil – any fragrance you love). Light your candle – sit in silence – breathe fully. Read Luke 24:1–12 (the women at the empty tomb).

Allow the fragrance and the story to guide your thoughts to memory or imaginings. Jot words or doodle images that reflect your thoughts.

Centre yourself with the candle flame. Imagine the profound love the friends of Jesus felt for him. Imagine their overwhelming fear and horror at his death. The act of anointing his body was an act of grieving and an act of love. Imagine the heavy-hearted expectation of this task.

Write as if you were the friend preparing to perform this loving, grieving act for your beloved Jesus.

Write a note to a loved one to explain where you are going and what you are about to do.

The initial shock of the empty tomb moves from disbelief to anger to sorrow.

- The angels speak: "Why do you look for the living among the dead?" How do you answer them? How do you wrestle with the word of the angels? Write your response.
- And the angels answer "He is not here, but has risen." Write your response.

ROAD TO EMMAUS REFLECTION

Luke 24:13–25 (two disciples meet Jesus on the road) Read the Emmaus road story.

On the dry dusty road to Emmaus, you encounter a stranger. The stranger seems unaware of your Jesus and all that has happened.

- Write what you tell the stranger about your beloved friend and his death.

The stranger listens and then responds, "Foolish ones – you are so slow to believe the prophets." And then he recounts the many prophecies about the suffering servant whose wounds are the wounds of the world. "The holy one – my servant – shall make many holy" (Isaiah 53:11b).

- How can Christ's holiness lead you to the holy? Write your response.

The disciples did not recognize their risen Christ on the road to Emmaus. Although their hearts were slow and their vision was muddied, they knew they wanted this stranger to stay with them through the night.

- Even when your heart is slow and your vision is muddied, can you invite Jesus to stay with you through this night? Write your invitation, starting, "My dear Jesus…"

STONES REFLECTION

"…but in one rolled stone
the old order is impossible."

Collect three stones. Choose ones you like in color, shape, and/or texture. Place your stones by your lighted candle. Center in silence …

Think of stones on your life path – past, present, and future. Ponder this – God's grace can turn tears to joy and death to resurrection. This is the promise of Easter.

Choose one of the stones to represent a stumbling stone on your path (something that "trips you" or challenges you). Hold this stone for as long as you need.
- What was/is this stone on your path? Name this stumbling stone.
- How can you move past this challenge? How is Christ present in your passage?

Choose another stone to represent a milestone on your path (something that marks an important event or revelation). Hold this stone for as long as you need.
- What was/is this stone on your path?
- Name this milestone. How can you acknowledge its significance? How is Christ present in your acknowledgment?

Take the last stone to represent a cornerstone in your life (something that gives you base and foundation). Hold this stone for as long as you need.
- Name this cornerstone. How can you honor this place of strength? How is Christ present in your knowing?

10. Activities for Easter & Eastertide

The activities of the Easter season reflect our intention to be signs of God's reign of love in the world through the joy of transformation and renewal.

EASTER EGG DELIGHTS
Easter eggs are symbols of transformation and new life – of breaking through our imprisonment into freedom. For children who are too little to participate in painting, decorate the eggs at night and surprise the children on Easter morning. With older children, make a festive occasion of decorating eggs, inviting friends and neighbors for a painting party.

Hide Easter baskets, Easter eggs, and/or small gifts around your church, house, or yard, and send the children out looking with a list of funny, rhyming clues to the whereabouts of the hidden treasures.

AN EASTER SIDE-LINE

Read the Easter story in the gospel of Luke, chapter 24.

In big letters, write the word "Easter" down the left side of page. Write words or phrases that follow from each letter in the word "Easter." When you're finished, decorate your side-line.

E   Empty tomb! *(and so on down the page).*
A
S
T
E
R

AN EASTER WALK

Take a brown paper bag on a nature walk. Collect symbols of life cycles – a lacy leaf shape from last year, a new green leaf or blossom, etc. Press them in waxed paper in a book.

AN EASTER COLLAGE

Press items from your nature walk overnight. Carefully glue them onto stiff paper to create either a card or a poster. Lay a sheet of clear plastic, sticky side down, over your collage and press it down.

NAME CARDS FOR YOUR EASTER FEAST

Glue an item collected during your Easter walk on a name card for each person who will be with you for Easter. Sometime before, during, or after your feast, have each person speak about the item on their card and its significance to them in this season.

EASTER CARDS

Create parchment-like paper by soaking plain white paper in strong tea for a few minutes. Dry flat. When your parchment paper is completely dry, paint or color on it an arrangement of blooming bulbs (such as tulips, daffodils, and crocuses) slightly smaller than the size of a greeting card you have selected. When your flower picture is completed and dry, carefully tear the edges of your picture so it looks very old. Glue your "flowers" onto the front of the card.

Tear another shape out of the blank tea-stained paper, and write an Easter greeting. Glue your greeting to the inside of the card.

Share your card and a cup of tea with someone.

AN EASTER SONG

Learn a new Easter song and share it. For example, try #166 in *Voices United*, the hymn book of The United Church of Canada – *Joy comes with the dawn!*

WAYS TO CARE

Always, Christ showed compassion for the most vulnerable ones in his world: the lonely, the ill, and the rejected. Who are the most vulnerable in our community?

Take an Easter card to someone who would otherwise be alone. Sing your Easter song for people who are sick or shutin. Make a point of encouraging others to share their stories of how the Spirit is at work in their lives and in the world. Share your own stories of the Spirit with someone needing fresh hope.

God's creation is also vulnerable. In this season of new life, could you reclaim a neglected lot for vegetation? Could you cycle instead of taking your car one or two days a week? Try altering your shopping patterns to purchase eco-friendly fabrics and cleansers. Could you eliminate toxic chemicals from the way you tend your garden and your lawn?

VI

THE
Pentecost
Season

I. The spirit of Pentecost
– an overview

The Season of Pentecost is also known as "ordinary time." However, nothing is ordinary for those Jesus sends to the world. Nothing is ordinary about letting God's healing breath blow us at will along the path to wholeness and community. Nothing is ordinary about letting the Spirit inflame our hearts with passion for mending the world that God loves. In fact, everything's *extra*ordinary when we let the Holy Spirit breathe into each and every moment.

The Pentecost season begins with Trinity Sunday (first Sunday after the festival of Pentecost) and lasts through to Reign of Christ (or Christ the King) Sunday which falls between November 20 and November 26

– the last Sunday before the start of Advent. Some traditions call this the "Kingdom-tide" season because we focus on making intentional contributions to the reign of holy love in the world. Other people call this "the season of the church," when we share what Jesus taught us and show our love for God by loving others.

In this season, we follow the followers of Jesus as they become the church. It seems the full significance of the ministry of Jesus was revealed to his friends only when his bodily presence was gone. In the fire and wind of Pentecost, the Spirit came among them as irrepressible life, and suddenly their experience with Jesus was inspired with new meaning – Jesus' mission was *their* mission! *They* were the hands and feet of Christ. Now they were to go to the world as apostles, a title which means "those sent out."

Jesus' followers were filled with burning passion and joy as they dashed out to share their wondrous tale. They said Jesus was "Christ," the long-awaited "Messiah," through whom a new creation would be born. They told how Jesus taught them to live every moment attentive to loving God and humankind. They told how Jesus suffered unjust violence and crucifixion but continued to love through it all. They told how Christ came to them after his death, and how the Spirit filled their hearts with holy abundance and sent them out to love as Christ loves.

All followers of Christ are part of God's creative unfolding through the power of the Spirit. As we journey together, our lives are marked by experiences of wonder and inspiration which serve as signs in our wilderness times. We start to see how the Spirit draws us out of captivity into our freedom to love. We come to know the Spirit as our source of excitement, confidence, connectedness, and insight. And we realize that, like the original apostles, we are receiving the Spirit so the transforming power of Christ will be revealed. As God sent Jesus Christ, so Christ sends us out to share, to heal, and to build true community.

In the Easter truth that holy love cannot be lost, we find confidence to relinquish our addictive attachments and also our need to control. Trusting God sets us free to recover our souls from judging other people and ourselves. By God's grace, we can come to inner peace with past and future, and risk living the Christ-life in the present. By grace, we can depend on God's continuing creativity. By grace, we are the hands and feet of Christ.

For the Season of Pentecost – fired by the Spirit – we focus on living the Christ-life together in ways that express God's yearning for the transformation of human lives and societies. We dream of joy, and Christ invites us to service. Then the blessing we find in serving *is* joy.

2. The beauty of Pentecost – colors, symbols, & art

In this Season of Pentecost, we focus on being the presence of Christ in a yearning world. By God's Grace we grow and heal, as individuals and communities, making whole what was broken or divided.

In this spirit of growth-to-wholeness, in ordinary time, the central color is green for banners and vestments. Some may choose to use red for the weeks immediately following the festival of Pentecost, in order to break the length of the season. White or gold can be used for All Saints' Sunday, and for the last Sunday of the season, Reign of Christ Sunday.

The tone of ordinary time is vibrant, communal, and active. Colors and textures could reflect this.

Symbols can include all the symbols for the Holy Spirit used to celebrate the festival of Pentecost which marks the end of Eastertide. As the Pentecost season moves through spring into summer and fall, images and decorations can reflect the many changes in nature's seasons. Growing flowers, bubbles, wind-socks, kites, and dandelion fluff are all appropriate to help us to understand the vibrant beauty and active spirit of the Season of Pentecost.

3. Celebrations in the Season of Pentecost

In a commendable effort to weave our faith with our lives, church leaders for centuries have woven a pattern of special feast days into the fabric of the seasons. Within the last two decades, a number of contemporary special celebrations have been integrated into the Christian calendar, and several fall in the Season of Pentecost. Some dates are fixed, and some may vary – check your calendar.

TRINITY SUNDAY

On the first Sunday after Pentecost, Christians celebrate the unity of God. Trinity Sunday was advocated by Pope John XXII in 1334 as a theological wrap-up to the Sunday observance of the life of Jesus Christ, and of the coming of the Spirit to the church. The doctrine of the Holy Trinity attempts to describe the unity of our human experience of holiness as "three persons" – as God, as Christ, and as Spirit. It is extremely hard to communicate in words what we comprehend of God in and beyond human history. For this reason, scripture describes the mystery of our experience by analogy, story, poetry, and symbol.

Language for God suggests God as source, creator, judge, shield, fortress, rock, father, mother, womb, and ruler of the universe. Jesus-language refers to God's anointed Messiah (Hebrew) or Christ (Greek), as Son of God, Son of Man (Child of the Earth), Lamb of God, Bread of Life, True Vine, Light of the World, Anchor, Never-failing Stream, Sun of Righteousness, Bright Morning Star, Living Water, Alpha and Omega, Redeemer, Suffering Servant, and Prince of Peace. References to the Spirit include Advocate, Guide, Comforter, Counselor, Transformer, wind, storm, flame, passion, dove, and wind or breath (both are meanings of the Hebrew word, *ruach*).

The inclusion in scripture of both gendered (feminine and masculine) as well as non-gendered images invokes a God beyond gender. We worship neither a male God nor a female Goddess, but the Holy Maker of all in whose image both male and female are created – who is, was, and ever shall be, who calls all things into being, who is wholeness and completeness, Yin and Yang, Adam and Eve.

ENVIRONMENT SABBATH

In early June, we remember the fantastic and the fragile nature of our environment. This Sunday offers a chance to focus on our beautiful world, as well as our human responsibility to care for it and conserve it.

FIRST NATIONS SUNDAY

In face of the pain of our First Nations people, in late June we focus on the sharing and caring that is called for. This Sunday directs our focus to those whose ancestors occupied this land before European contact.

HIROSHIMA SUNDAY

On August 6, or the Sunday closest, we remember the horror of nuclear war. Hiroshima and Nagasaki offer a bitter reminder of our conscience – or lack of it. We need to counteract our destructive capabilities with the reality of God's desire for healing.

Either on this occasion, or at Peace Sabbath in November (see below), you might wish to share the story of Sadako:

On August 6, 1945, an atomic bomb exploded on the Japanese city of Hiroshima. Sadako Sasaki was only two years old, and though her brother had been killed she seemed at the time to have suffered no effects from the explosion. Ten years later, however, when Sadako was 12, she developed leukemia – a disease often associated with radioactive contamination.

While she was ill, Sadako remembered an ancient Japanese legend about cranes bringing long life, health, and happiness. Using the Japanese art of paper-folding (called origami), Sadako started folding a thousand paper cranes in the hope she soon would be well. She told her cranes, "I will write 'peace' on your wings, and you will fly all over the world."

Sadako died before she could fold her 1000 cranes, but her classmates completed the folding. They also collected $25,000 worth of coins, to build a monument to Sadako and to all the children in Hiroshima who died as a result of the explosion. The memorial in the Peace Park in Hiroshima has a statue of Sadako on the top, holding a huge outline of a paper crane above her head. On the base of the memorial are these words: "This is our cry, this is our prayer: peace in the world."

LABOR DAY (CANADA)

In the 19th century, laborers often worked under terrible conditions for poor wages – and trade unions were illegal. In 1872, a printers' strike in Toronto forced the federal government to give official recognition to the trade union movement in Canada. The unions decided to hold annual parades to commemorate the achievement of political power and to mark the importance of workers' support for one another. In 1888, the Trades and Labor Congress asked the federal government for a national day to honor working people. Labor Day was declared a national holiday in 1894. All across the country, Labor Day celebrations on the first Monday in September also mark the end of summer vacations.

WORLD FOOD SUNDAY

World Food Day is observed on October 16 by over 150 nations. It commemorates the founding of the Food and Agriculture Organization of the United Nations in 1945. The world currently produces enough food to meet 125 percent of the world's need for food. Why then are so many people hungry? According to a World Bank Study, a mere three percent of the world's population owns or controls 80 percent of all the land that is good for growing crops. Almost all hungry people are also poor. What does hunger look like in our own communities or on the other side of the globe? Why do waste and want live side by side? This Sunday focuses on some important faith questions.

THANKSGIVING SUNDAY

Canada and the U.S. differ on their dates for celebrating Thanksgiving. In Canada, the Sunday before Thanksgiving Monday (second Monday in October) is often marked in Christian churches by services thanking God for providing us with so many blessings – including the abundance of the harvest. For most of Canada, the end of November is much too late to celebrate the gathering of crops. By that time, many fields are already under snow!

Like Christmas, Thanksgiving is both a congregational and a family festival. Either Sunday or Monday, families and friends gather to share a meal which often includes turkey and cranberry sauce, mashed potatoes, and pumpkin pie.

Because it's the best-known story, we tend to associate the festivities of Thanksgiving with Puritan celebrations in America in 1621. However, Canadians will be pleased to know that 53 years earlier, in 1568, Sir Martin Frobisher gathered English settlers together for a harvest feast in what is now Newfoundland.

PEACE SABBATH

On October 24, 1945, the United Nations charter was approved. In 1947, October 24th was designated United Nations Day. The Canadian Council of Churches and the National Council of Churches in the U.S. established Peace Sabbath to correspond with this date. In the context of faith community, we dream of and work for peace in the world.

ALL SAINTS' SUNDAY

The History of All Saints' Day really begins with the activities of Hallowe'en ("Hallowed Evening" or "All Hallows' Evening"), the night before October 31. In Britain and many other regions of northern Europe, Celtic peoples who lived more than 2,000 years ago gathered their communities on October 31 to honor their god of death, Samhain. While they feasted indoors, they believed that the spirits of those who had died were wandering outside in the cold.

So as not to offend these spirits, the feasters left gifts of food and drink for them outside on their doorsteps. And to guide them on their way, hilltop bonfires blazed and candles were lighted in windows. Those who dared to go outside disguised themselves to look like ghosts, so the "real" ghosts would not recognize them.

And everyone who braved the outdoors took a lantern, which gave rise to the Irish folk tale of "Jack-o'-lantern." Jack was said to be a mischievous trickster, who was so mean and stingy that St. Peter wouldn't let him into heaven when he died, and the devil wouldn't let him into hell. This accounts for why poor Jack has had to wander the earth, carrying his lantern, threatening tricks in his search for treats on Hallowe'en. In North America, Irish settlers used pumpkins to make lanterns, instead of turnips as they had previously done in Ireland.

Rather than trying to stop the Celtic Hallowe'en traditions, early Christian leaders used Christian ideas to re-interpret earlier practices. In the year 837 C.E., November 1 was proclaimed as All Saints' Day. On November 1 (or the Sunday which immediately follows), a special service is held in many Christian churches to celebrate the contributions of the saints of the church, especially those who do not have a specific day named in their honor.

These saints of the church are those (known and unknown) who have committed their lives to Christ's ministries, even at the cost of life itself. The New Testament refers to all who follow Christ as "holy ones" or "saints." We therefore celebrate All Saints' Day as a proclamation of the continuing relationship through Christ with those who have served God before us. Try praying for those related to the congregation who have died in the previous year, or those named by participants as having served for them as models of servanthood. Remember in love all those who are named, and rejoice in their presence in the communion of saints united in the Spirit with Christ.

Facing the reality of our human mortality helps to free us from fear so we are able to live more fully in the present. All Saints' Day is a good time to talk about the presence of God in our dying and death. Discuss with adults the importance of the funeral as an act of faith and a rite of passage. Encourage children to talk about people they have known who died, and how their lives have contributed to the lives of others. Who are the saints of your faith community? Who are the saints of your family? What makes them saints in your eyes? How does the presence of saints in our midst help to bring about the "new heaven" that is described by the words of Revelation. 21:1–6a?

REMEMBRANCE DAY

Remembrance Day (November 11) is not a celebration of war, but a remembrance of those who have given life for the sake of their country. Thousands of soldiers who died in World War 1 were buried in graveyards in Europe. In Belgium, wild red poppies blossom yearly in Flanders Fields where many young soldiers were buried. The poppy has become a vibrant symbol of sacrifice, and also of our resolve not to let this kind of violence be repeated.

On the eleventh hour of the eleventh day of the eleventh month of 1918, World War I came to an end. The temporary document that ended the war was called an armistice, which comes from Latin words meaning "weapons stand still." November 11 was known as Armistice Day for many years, until in 1931 the Canadian Parliament changed the name of the day to Remembrance Day. Since World War II, the day has been a memorial for those who died in both wars. Over 60,000 Canadian soldiers were killed in World War I, and another 42,000 in World War II. On the Sunday closest to the Remembrance Day holiday, many churches hold special services to honor those who have died as a result of war.

RESTORATIVE JUSTICE SUNDAY

Restorative Justice Sunday in late November is a time to recognize the pain of crime for perpetrators, victims, and the families of everyone involved. It is a time for us to remember our duties to the imprisoned, and to remember in prayer inmates, ex-inmates, their families, victims of crime, and all those who work in the field of corrections. With God's healing grace, we can open our eyes to the imbalances that lead to crime, and also to visions of abundant love.

Restorative Justice Sunday focuses especially on the differences between punitive forms of punishment and those forms of restitution that try to restore both victim and perpetrator to healed relationship in supportive community.

CHILDREN'S SUNDAY

November 20 is the anniversary of the UN ratification of the Convention on the Rights of the Child in 1989, a day designated by the Canadian government as National Child's Day. Close to the end of the Pentecost season, Children's Sunday reminds us to be present in God's grace with our children. It is not so much "stuff" that children need as our time and our hearts. In a time where so many children fall through the cracks of hurting families, we need to remember it does indeed "take a village to raise a child."

On a global scale, Children's Sunday is a time to consider how we can contribute to the health and well-being of children everywhere. What steps can we take to bring justice and safety to the world's most vulnerable citizens?

REIGN OF CHRIST SUNDAY

Reign of Christ Sunday falls between November 20 and November 26, the last Sunday before Advent. It's a transitional Sunday, as we shift from the Season of Pentecost into the beginning of the new church year. On this day we celebrate Jesus Christ as the Prince of Peace, the one in whom God's love rules – the "upside-down" leader who stands firm in solidarity with all of the "little ones" of the world.

4. Rituals for the Season of Pentecost

These rituals and liturgies can be adapted for large gatherings like Sunday morning worship, for small group gatherings, or for families at home. Decide in advance who will lead, who will read, and who will take responsibility for actions.

TABLE RITUALS

When you gather for a meal through the Pentecost season, use the ritual which follows to celebrate the Christ-life you share. Begin by lighting a large white Christ candle.

As the candle is lighted, join hands, as you are comfortable, and share one of the following prayers:

We give thanks for the healing
power of peace in our lives,
for release from fear, for patience,
and for courage to love as Christ loves.
Amen.

Dawn of Glory, we pray
for the healing of persons,
communities, and the world that you
love. Amen.

May the peace of Christ
be with us. Amen.

God of abundance,
we thank you for food
and we pray for the hungry.
We thank you for friends
and we pray for the friendless.
We thank you for freedom
and we pray for all prisoners.
We thank you for health
and we pray for the sick.
Bless us to service so that your gifts to
us may become gifts for others. Amen.

Holy One, you create us to be
Christ's companions
in communion with all of your saints.
Transform our hearts and lives
that we may serve you in joy
as makers of justice and peace. Amen.

RITES OF PASSAGE

As a people of God, we gather to mark passage points in the lives of individuals, families, and our community by affirming major moments in our personal and collective life journey. The birth or adoption of a child, baptism, confirmation, celebrations to mark various commitments to service, the blessing of marriage or acknowledgment of the end of a primary relationship, healing rites for the sick, and rites of passage for the dying and for those who mourn – all these are times for the community of faith to weave the journeys of individuals into the fabric of the journey we share. Preparing for and marking rites of passage as we deal with changes helps us grow in spiritual maturity.

Rites of passage remind us that we are not drifting aimlessly. We are beloved of God and created in God's image for a pilgrimage that leads towards wholeness. Each of us is a member of the Body of Christ. At each stage of the journey, our community gathers with us to celebrate our days, and to remind us we are never alone. As a people we are part of God's liberating action, and each of our stories – and our story together – expresses our unending quest for freedom, justice and peace.

Rites of passage are often designed for individuals or families in their own faith communities. Acts 13:2–3 tells us of just such a liturgy in the early church community as Saul and Barnabas are sent forth as apostles. When a family or person is going to leave the faith community, have their friends gather around them and lay hands on them to bless them, as the community did when Saul and Barnabas were leaving Antioch. In this way we give thanks for love already shared, and we commission one another into the future.

5. Sharing our story during the Season of Pentecost

In this Season of Pentecost we are especially "inspired" (a word based on "spirit") with the passion for wholeness, vision, and life that infuses the "good news" or "gospel" (from Old English "godspel"). The scriptures we read in the Season of Pentecost explore the core teachings that empower us for living the Christ-life:

- God is always present;
- God creates us in uniqueness and endows us with dignity;
- God loves us unconditionally;
- God continues to act in our lives to bring healing;
- God provides with abundance;
- God needs us as partners to help mend the world;
- God invites us to sacred friendship in community with others;
- God reveals for us a Spirit-guided "way" through communion with Christ.

The storytelling exercises which follow have been written for groups with one participant in the role of leader. They can be easily adapted for prayer partners or for personal use. Decide before you start who will read the scripture passages, and who will lead the storytelling for today.

When discussing stories located in a specific city in the ancient world, pointing out these locations on a map will help participants to connect the story's people and their problems with a particular place.

Remember to choose discussions which match the level of comfort and familiarity among those who are present, and remind participants they are always free to pass. Let the stories and questions unfold as slowly as needed.

Close your session with prayer. You may find it helpful to hold hands in a circle as you pray. The leader can invite the group to offer the hopes and prayers of their hearts, and start the prayer with his/her own words. As the leader finishes, he/she squeezes the hand of the next person in the circle who either prays or passes on the "squeeze."

Divine creativity

Biblical truth starts with the reality that the power of love we call "God" is the source of life. We take life for granted until something happens that threatens our sense of security – perhaps a crisis in health or relationship, or the loss of a loved one. Then we realize that, although we participate in our destiny, ultimately we cannot control it.

These life-changing moments are both frightening and humbling. We are tempted to despair or to trust in false sources of security. At the same time, we are invited to recognize God's power beyond the limits of time and life as we know it. We are invited to trust in God's boundless commitment to life – at our birth, in times of transformation and healing, and ultimately in "new life" through resurrection. The gift to us is certain hope in God. We can dare to believe that all is love, that God is good all the time.

THE SOURCE OF LOVE
Genesis 2 (God as source of life) and Genesis 3 (Adam and Eve displace God and learn about shame)
Read aloud the scripture passages and the following summary. Reflect on each question and share responses.

The second chapter of Genesis provides us with the Bible's second story of creation; the third chapter of Genesis interprets our human limitation. Creation stories shared within a society convey profound truths about the relationship between the creator and the created.

- Name some truths which are conveyed in each of these stories about the relationship between God, human beings, and the rest of creation. How have these truths been played out in human history as we know it?
- Through the course of human history, what kinds of things have happened when human beings have attempted to displace holy wisdom and rely on human knowledge instead?
- How have these two stories affected your own understanding of your relationship to God? To the rest of creation?
- Why would a loving God design a reality in which creatures are vulnerable to pain?
- When is it loving to permit another to experience pain? How can we trust that God loves us – even when we suffer?

SUPPLANTING GOD
Exodus 20:1–20 (God as source of social order) and Exodus 32:1–14 (the people displace God from the center of social order)
Read aloud the scripture passages. Reflect on each question and share responses.

- Name some sets of rules that have been helpful through the course of human history. What is the relationship between the freedom God gives us and our adherence to God-given guidance?
- How and when is the guidance of community norms a good thing?
- What happens when God's guidance is replaced by other kinds of communal norms?
- Describe a time when your faith gave you the guidance that helped you be constructive. Describe a time when social pressures (worshiping false idols?) distracted you from attending to God.

THE BURNING BUSH
Exodus 3:1–15 (Moses encounters God in the burning bush in the desert)
Read aloud the scripture passage and the following summary. Reflect on each question and share responses.

Fire has been a symbol for God through the ages. The flame of loving creativity burns continuously, without being consumed or consuming that within it which blazes.

- In an era of pluralism and accelerated change, how could the burning bush image be a blessing for relationships?
- When you are in a situation where people hold very different values and goals, how could the burning bush image help you trust that continuing dialogue is worthwhile? How could differences among participants contribute to God's unfolding creativity?
- Describe a situation within your own experience where God was present as persistent creativity through a process of dialogue. Was there a turning point in the discussion? What made the difference?

ABUNDANCE

Exodus 16 (God's abundance as food in the wilderness), Exodus 17:1–7 (God's abundance as water in the wilderness), and 1 Kings 19:4–8 (God's abundance as food for Elijah)
Read aloud the scripture passages. Reflect on each question and share responses.

- What are the essential similarities in these stories? Why do you think these stories were preserved and retold? What truth do they convey about God's relationship with human beings?
- What invitation do these stories hold for us? What steps could we take to share God's abundance with other peoples?
- Describe a situation where you were challenged to trust in God's abundance. How has this experience affected you? What steps can you take to distribute God's abundance more fairly in response to others' needs?

The power of love

MOSES

Exodus 1:6–2:25 (the origins of Moses), Exodus 3:18–21 (God promises to help the Israelites), Exodus 14:1–31 (crossing the Reed Sea), and Exodus 15:20–21 (Moses' sister Miriam rejoices)
Read aloud the scripture passages. Reflect on each question and share responses.

- In the story of Moses, how does God evoke strength through the experience of oppression? And freedom through the experience of bondage?
- Where else have you observed this pattern played out in human history?
- Remember a time when you experienced release as the past fell away and a new future opened before you. Describe this experience as you are comfortable.

- In baptism, Christians experience "new life" in Christ as a passage through "the waters" of re-creation, also symbolically a passage through the waters of the Reed Sea. Describe, if you can, a personal experience of renewal through faith. What does the story of Moses invite you to do or to be?

STEADFASTNESS

Daniel 3:8–30 (the fiery furnace) and Daniel 6:6–23 (Daniel survives the lion's den). Alternatively, 1 Samuel 17:1–18:16 (David and Goliath)
Read aloud the scripture passages and the following summary. Reflect on each question and share responses.

These stories were originally told to strengthen the courage and faith of the Jewish people in times of persecution.
- Share a real-life story in which power and vision safeguarded someone who remained loyal to God.
- Describe a time in your life when you were able to withstand a difficult challenge by holding fast to your faith. What inner qualities make this possible? How is God nourishing these qualities in you?

MIRACLES

1 Kings 17:8–24 (Elijah restores a widow's son to life), 2 Kings 4:1–7 (Elisha saves a child from slavery), and 2 Kings 4:8–37 (Elisha prophesies a son)
Read aloud the scripture passages. Reflect on each question and share responses.

- The women of the first two stories are peasants faced with poverty, but the faithful Shunammite woman lives among the ruling elite and still faces despair. How could these miracle stories empower the faithful of our time?
- Is there a detail or circumstance in one of these stories that speaks to you of your life?

Although miracles do not always unfold in the ways we could hope or expect, what promise do these stories hold for you?

Love in human flesh

Male-dominated cultures tend to produce male-oriented languages to interpret reality, and the English language has been no exception. Even the Judeo-Christian God of wholeness and completeness becomes, by default, more masculine than feminine. Still, scripture delights in many qualities of God which have typically been seen as feminine attributes.

In the Season of Pentecost, we recognize holiness in the feminine power that draws us into the creative process of the universe. She is the wisdom who nurtures our life and our healing from adolescence through to maturity. She is the priestess who teaches us how to draw boundaries that protect us from harm, who leads us from captivity into freedom of choice, who oversees justice and compassion in community, and is finally the midwife who leads us home to God, the womb of all.

THE FEMININE DIVINE
Genesis 49:25; Deuteronomy 32:11–13 and 18; Hosea 11:4 and Hosea 13:6–8a; Isaiah 42:14, 49:15, and 66:7–13; Jeremiah 31:15–22; and Psalms 17, 91, and 22:9–10 (all feminine images of God). Or consider the New Testament images of God as a homemaker (Luke 15:8–10) or as a baker-woman (Matthew 13:33)
Read aloud the scripture passages. Reflect on each question and share responses.
- List the feminine images in each of the biblical readings.
- How did you picture God when you were little? Were your early images of God most often characterized by masculine or feminine qualities?

- How has "inclusive language" affected your experience of God? What feelings arise in you when you hear feminine qualities ascribed to God?
- Nurturing mother, homemaker, sheltering womb, birthing woman, or midwife – choose a feminine image of God which interests or intrigues you. Spend two minutes imagining yourself in the presence and care of this feminine divine. What feelings does this presence evoke in you?
- Can you think of a time when experiencing God with you in this way might have been – or may yet be – refreshing and healing? What capacity could that "feminine" aspect of God empower in you?

LOVE THAT HEALS
2 Corinthians 5:17–21 (Anyone in Christ is a new creation), Mark 7:31–37 and 8:22–26 (Jesus cures the deaf and blind), and James 5:13–15 (healing prayer in community)
Read aloud the scripture passages. Reflect on each question and share responses.

- What are the differences between these stories of healing? What are the similarities? Describe how these different kinds of healing might be linked.
- Can you think of historical or personal situations when people experienced one or more of these kinds of healing?
- Realizing that healing is not always the same as curing, share your experience with love's power to "heal."
- What kinds of light have you been blind to? What can Jesus help you to hear? What does it mean to you to become a new creation in Christ?

TRANSFORMATION

Acts 7:55–8:3 (the stoning of Stephen), Acts 9:1–30 (Saul's conversion), and Acts 21:27–23:35 (Paul is imprisoned for his faith). Also 2 Timothy 1:1–5 (greetings to Timothy)

Read aloud the scripture passages and the following summary. Reflect on each question and share responses.

Paul's conversion to faith in God through Jesus Christ came about through an experience that changed everything. By contrast, Paul's second letter to Timothy suggests that Timothy has been surrounded by people of faith, and has therefore grown into faith gradually.

- Who among the people you know has experienced illumination in each of these ways?
- Describe the life of someone you know who has been deeply changed by faith. Would you describe yourself as being more like Paul or more like Timothy? Why?

LOVE THAT INCLUDES

Luke 17:11–19 (a Samaritan returns thanks), Luke 7:1–10 (Jesus heals a centurion's servant), and Luke 10:25–37 (a Samaritan models "The great commandment"). Also Matthew 15:21–28 (Jesus heals the daughter of a Canaanite woman)

Read aloud the scripture passages and the following summary. Reflect on each question and share responses.

At first, Jewish Christians believed that non-Jews (Gentiles) would have to become cultural Jews to belong to Christ's community. They wanted all of Jesus' followers to obey Jewish purity rules about food, ritual cleansing, and circumcision. Before long, the Holy Spirit set to work transforming the apostles' understanding of who is acceptable to God, and should therefore be accepted into the community of faith. Early Christians remembered how Jesus healed foreigners and outsiders.

- What impact do these memories have on our community life now? Who is excluded from our fellowship circle?
- What do these stories of Jesus invite us to do or be? What steps can we take?
- Who is it hardest for you to include? What would Jesus do in your situation? What steps could you take to let God's love flow more completely?

REMOVING BARRIERS

Acts 8:26–40 (Philip baptizes one who is not only a foreigner, but a eunuch as well)

Read aloud the scripture passage and the following summary. Reflect on each question and share responses.

The first Christians, who were Jewish, were amazed when both Jewish *and* non-Jewish listeners experienced the presence of the Spirit. Gradually they realized that baptism should be available to people they would formerly have excluded. They experienced a revolution in mindset as they gradually recognized that the blessings of Christ were also meant for non-Jewish peoples. Gradually they began to distinguish the difference between the rules and customs of a particular religious culture and sharing the heart of their faith.

- What implications does diversity of cultural expression hold for us in a pluralist era? What are the implications for unity among those who seek God?
- When several different generations within a single faith community can present different spiritual needs, what unites us in the midst of our diversity?
- How would you express the heart of your faith? How would you distinguish it from the religious culture in which you were raised?

CREATED BY GOD

Acts 10:44–48 (Peter's encounter with Cornelius)
Read aloud the scripture passage and the following summary. Reflect on each question and share responses.

Peter saw a vision of a cloth from heaven filled with all kinds of animals – including animals Jews considered unclean. Peter understood from the dream that nothing God considers clean should be called unclean by human beings.

- Whom has God created that human beings have reviled as unclean? Whom is God asking us to include? How could your faith community serve as a model of inclusive community for the world?
- What aspects of your own religious culture do you cherish most? What would be hardest for you to let go? Imagine a situation in which it would be faithful for you to let go of some attitude or standard you hold dear. Are there things now you could let go of for love of others? How can you go about doing this?

ONE PEOPLE, ONE BODY

Acts 15:1–35 (the council at Jerusalem)
Read aloud the scripture passage and the following summary. Reflect on each question and share responses.

Over time, the first Jewish Christians realized the implications of Jesus' teachings for inclusive faith community – that all are one in Christ Jesus. All who gather around the table of Christ are one people, united in Christ and Christ alone.

- How does your faith community invite, welcome, and integrate "outsiders"? What bonds unite your community of faith? Can the bonds that unite you capture the hearts of newcomers?

- How could your shared life in Christ inspire others to participate in mending God's world?
- How could you help to create space for outsiders to enter into faith community?

SHARING LEADERSHIP

Galatians 5:13–14 (freedom to love with self-discipline) and Matthew 23:1–12 (personal accountability and integrity)
Read aloud the scripture passages. Reflect on each question and share responses.

- How is freedom in a faith community distinct from freedom in secular culture? How does freedom differ from license?
- To what forms of guidance are we accountable in a community of faith? In what ways are we accountable to each other? As followers of the way of Christ, what are we modeling?
- To whom are you ultimately accountable for your integrity and conscience? How are you guided in these discernments? What kinds of guidance are you seeking? What is the role of prayer in your life? What would help you to deepen in commitment and spiritual discipline? How can you assist others?

GIFTS OF THE SPIRIT

Romans 12:1–8 (one body in Christ) and 1 Corinthians 12:4–11 (varieties of spiritual gifts)
Read aloud the scripture passages. Reflect on each question and share responses.

- How can we honor the diversity of gifts and function, and the importance of every contribution? What has worked and not worked in your experience?
- What happens when equality is treated as sameness? How should responsibility and authority be connected? What kinds of shared understandings are helpful in faith community?

- What is your experience with Jesus' upside-down approach to leadership? Describe an experience when the different gifts of members of the Body of Christ worked in harmony. What made this possible?
- What strengths and skills can you cultivate within yourself to contribute?

SENDING FORTH

Matthew 5:13–16 (Jesus' teaching about his disciples being the salt of the earth, and the light of the world) and Matthew 28:16–20 (the commissioning of disciples)
Read aloud the scripture passages. Reflect on each question and share responses.

- Describe a time when you were called to a particular role, or sent out to fulfill a certain goal. What were your fears?
- In response to our doubt, scripture assures us that God has given Christ authority, and that Christ sends us out to the world. In what parts of our life together do we need to place more emphasis on trusting in God, and less on our material concerns?
- Jesus promises to be with us to help us. How do you experience Christ's presence? How does Jesus' promise affect your capacity to trust?

PEACEMAKING

Ephesians 4:25–32 (do not grieve the Holy Spirit) and Matthew 18:15–20 (when someone has offended you)
Read aloud the scripture passages. Reflect on each question and share responses.

- Jesus teaches the principles of direct communication, peer support and community guidance. How does this pattern set the persons involved (as well as their community) free for change? If community is the locus of Spirit-guided support, how can faith communities establish patterns rooted in these teachings? How can we root this same pattern in relationships at home and in the workplace? How can the guidance of scripture be effectively shared?
- Describe how Jesus' teachings on dealing with differences preserve relationships and safeguard community.
- What feelings are evoked in you at the prospect of dealing directly with someone who has offended you? What strengths and skills would enhance your ability to deal constructively with that situation? How is God nurturing the strengths and skills that you need?

OVERTURNING OPPRESSION

Acts 5:27–40 (the apostles are flogged), Acts 7:54–8:1 (Stephen is martyred), Acts 12:1–5 (Herod kills James and arrests Peter), and Romans 8:38–39 (nothing can separate us from the love of Christ)
Read aloud the scripture passages and the following summary. Reflect on each question and share responses.

The Jesus movement was a threat to hierarchical society based on a system of status and rewards, polarization, domination, and oppression. Political and religious leaders used threats, imprisonment, torture, and death to try to stop it. Domination depends on evoking fear in order to gain control of peoples' lives.

- Describe how violence is disempowered in the Romans passage. What historical situations can you remember where active nonviolence stripped oppressors of their power?
- Describe a situation where you, or someone you know, exercised active nonviolence to defuse a conflict? What made those actions possible?

NON-VIOLENT POWER
Romans 12:14–21 (overcome evil with good)
Read aloud the scripture passage and the following summary. Reflect on each question and share responses.

Nonviolent suffering love does not ask victims to accept abuse passively. Nonviolent love is a powerful response to violence which refuses to return evil for evil.
- How does nonviolent love open up the possibility of transformation, reconciliation, and peace?
- Is it difficult for you to trust that active nonviolence is even more powerful than violence?
- To practice nonviolent love, what must you be willing to risk? What do we learn from Christ about the ultimate power of love?

SHARING THE WEALTH
James 2:1–17 (faith requires action) and 2 Corinthians 8:1–15 (Paul encourages his churches to give generously)
Read aloud the scripture passages and the following summary. Reflect on each question and share responses.

Christians in Palestine (mostly Jewish) were hungry because of a famine. Christians in Asia Minor and Macedonia (mostly Gentile) had more than enough to feed everyone.
- How does generosity contribute to peace? Share a story of generosity. In what way did the world become better?
- What confidence enables you to give with generosity? How does Christ empower you to do this? What steps can you take to give generously beyond yourself? What steps can you take to inspire others to share God's abundance?

A VISION FOR THE FUTURE
Revelation 21:1–6, and 22:1–5 (a new heaven and a new earth), 1 Corinthians 10:14–17 (one bread, one body), and 1 Corinthians 11:23–34 (the institution of the Lord's Supper)
Read aloud the scripture passages. Reflect on each question and share responses.

- In what ways does the "heavenly banquet" of Christ model peacemaking for the world?
- In what ways are we changed by rehearsing our roles as participants in the heavenly banquet?
- How is God's new earth and heaven real through us?

6. Embodied prayers for the Season of Pentecost

The Pentecost season is the summer flowering of faith, when our bodies, minds, and spirits come into the fullness of selfhood in communion with others. Our body prayers through Pentecost express wholeness of relationship with the self, with God, and all creation.

We long to feel the breath of Spirit in our bodies. The Hebrew word for Spirit also means "breath." The Bible tells us God breathed into the first human's nostrils and the creature became a living being. (Genesis 2:7) When we breathe *in* strength and courage, and breathe *out* fear and pain, God breathes new life into us.

Since all our life systems are interlinked in subtle ways, changing our breathing affects our whole self. Deep, slow breathing is the body's natural way of moving into relaxation, which in turn helps us attend to our experience. Combining breathing and prayer can help us focus and center on the presence of the Spirit, and deepen our awareness of that Spirit in our physical being.

INSTRUCTIONS

These prayers can be part of daily spiritual disciplines. They are written for groups, for prayer partners, or for personal use.

When used by a group, one participant will need to assume the role of guide. Decide in advance who will lead the prayers today, letting each prayer unfold slowly and gently.

For an effective pace, we suggest you take two full breaths whenever you see "…" before you start the next phrase. If a time frame is suggested, remember that one minute equals about eight full breaths. Give your group permission to breathe normally at any time, especially if they feel distressed or anxious. Tell the group never to strain or hold the breath. A deep breath is gentle and relaxed.

PREPARATION

Always begin embodied prayer sessions with this exercise. If you are practicing embodied prayers alone, read through the following instructions carefully before starting. If you are leading a group, read the following slowly and calmly aloud, with appropriate pauses.

Sit comfortably, with your spine fairly straight. Close your eyes. Without changing how you breathe, pay attention to the sensations of breathing … Pay attention to the sensation of breath moving in and out of your nose or your mouth … Can you feel the path of breath as it moves through your body into your lungs? … Can you feel the breath move your chest and rib cage, and then release again as you breathe out? … Continue to follow the flow of your breathing, without straining to do anything …

Now breathe in and send the breath into your abdomen as though you are filling your stomach. Exhale, letting the stomach fall back to normal. Breathing in, your belly rises; breathing out, it falls back. Breathe this relaxed "belly breath" for one minute … Don't strain or force your breath … Relax as you breathe in and your belly rises, and relax as you breathe out …

As you breathe quietly, begin to listen to the sounds in the room … Move your fingers and your toes. Open your eyes when you are ready.

THE TEMPLE OF THE HEART

Sit comfortably, close your eyes, and focus on your breath … Let your breath flow in and out with ease … Each exhalation releases tension ... Let your mind settle with each breath ... Relax and let each breath bring you into the present, focusing only on the breath moving in and out ... Let go ...

As you exhale, say in silence the word *Alaha* ... Alaha is an Aramaic word for holy presence that Jesus and his people might have used ... As you exhale, repeat the name "Alaha" ... Let Alaha lead you to stillness ... You are clearing the place where Alaha breathes in you ... where the Spirit is within you, and among us, and beyond us ... This is the center, the temple of your heart, where holy wisdom is embodied and available to you ... Rest in the peace and silence of the temple of your heart ...

We are now in the season after Pentecost, the season when we take Jesus' mission out into the world ... The season for living every moment attentive to loving both God and humankind ... This is the season to know the temple of your heart so well that you don't have to think about finding it ... Your whole being takes direction and action from your temple, from Alaha ... Can you imagine that you live in your temple always ... that God's work shines through your actions? ... You are the hands and feet of Christ in the world ... Think from the temple ... Move from the temple ... Act from the temple ... Be in the temple of your heart always ... Be the heart ... Be the Christ-life in the world ...

As you breathe quietly, begin to listen to the sounds in the room ... Move your fingers and your toes. Open your eyes when you are ready.

SUMMER PRAYER

Sit comfortably, close your eyes, and bring your attention to the breath ... Relax as you watch the breath flow in and out ... Consciously leave behind your busy day ... There is nothing more important to do than to be here now, praying ... For a couple of minutes watch the breath and let go ...

In this moment we celebrate the Season of Pentecost, the summertime of the Spirit. The seeds of service we planted earlier are now ripe with color and beauty. This is a time for cherishing the full bloom of the garden ... Imagine a beautiful summer garden ... Can you see a garden in your mind, full of flowers in bloom? ... Everyone's garden will be different, and all will be beautiful ... Imagine yourself taking the time to walk around your garden ... Walk slowly ... Notice the colors ... Reach out and touch a flower ... Can you feel the texture? ... Can you smell the fragrance of your garden, and let it fill your soul? ...

As the fragrance and the texture and the beauty fill your soul, know that God intends this beauty for you and all others ... These are the fruits of the Spirit ... You yourself are an important part of the garden's design ... You are God's instrument, creating a garden in the world through actions of love ... Through service your garden grows ... This is your authentic self and the flowers are your community of love ... This is the beauty ... This is the beauty ... Take a moment to cherish it all ... Feel the joy ... Feel the joy ...

As you breathe quietly, begin to listen to the sounds in the room ... Move your fingers and your toes. Open your eyes when you are ready.

RELEASE PARTNERS

Invite participants to pick partners of about the same size. Have them decide who will be the guide and who will lie on the floor (or sit in a chair if unable to lie down). They will switch places when they do the exercise a second time. The guide will begin standing. Be sure to remind the guides to bend their knees and relax their bodies and keep breathing as they manipulate their partners' limbs.

Take a moment to come into the present by bringing your attention to your breath ... Relax as you watch the breath flow in and out ... As you exhale, let tension flow out of your body ... Exhale and release ...

Now, if you are a guide, gently bring your attention back to the room. Activate your body by shaking your hands and gently tightening your leg and stomach muscles ... Move to a place where you can bend your knees and pick up the right hand of your partner ... Lift it up gently until the whole arm is off the floor and the arm is perpendicular to the floor ... Instruct your partner to give you the whole weight of their arm ... Lift the arm a bit more until the shoulder is raised slightly off the ground ... If your partner resists, tell them again to let go, to trust, to be fully supported ... Then gently lay the shoulder back on the floor ...

Gently lift the arm again till the shoulder rises from the floor, then place it back down ... Repeat this a few times, then carefully lay the arm back on the floor.

Repeat with the left arm ...

If the members of your group feel confident enough, invite them to try this exercise with the legs.

If you are a guide, straddle your partner with bent knees, and lift your partner's leg by placing both hands under the right knee. As with the arm, lift the leg gently, cradling the knee in both hands; gently sway the leg back and forth until your partner fully releases the weight of the leg and the guide can move the leg around without resistance. Then lower the leg. Repeat with the left leg.

Now, let your partner rest alone on the floor while those of you who are guides sit in meditative silence, while I read this text:

Just as you released the weight of your body to your partner, now release your weight to the earth ... Let your bones rest on the earth ... Feel where you hold yourself away from the earth and try to release this tension ... We all need to let go, to be able to be "present" to do God's work ... Just as we may hold our physical bodies away from the earth, we may also hold our spirit away from a person in need ... We need to let go so we can fulfill God's intention for simple here-and-now contact with each other ...

Trust in God's support ... Let go of your perceived limitations; God will hold you up ... Let go ...

As you let go of tension, imagine yourself letting go of patterns that hold you away from people, patterns that create pain ... Let go ... Physical release is spiritual release ... Let go and know how God calls you ...

As you breathe quietly, begin to listen to the sounds in the room ... Move your fingers and your toes. Open your eyes when you are ready.

Repeat the exercise, with the partners switching roles. Invite participants to share their experience as they feel comfortable.

WHOLENESS IS NOW

Sit comfortably, close your eyes, and bring your attention to your breath ... Relax as you feel the breath flow in and out ... There is nothing more important to do ... Just breathe in and out ...

As you continue breathing, bring your attention to your head, neck, and shoulders. Are you holding tension there? Do you feel any discomfort? ... As you exhale, release tension from your head, neck, and shoulders ... Release the tension in your forehead, your jaw, and your tongue ... Then bring your attention to your arms and legs. Are you holding tension there? Do you feel any discomfort? ... As you exhale, release tension from your arms and legs ... Let your arms release into your lap ... Let the tension of your legs fall into the floor ...

Now bring your attention to your whole body at once. Are there still areas of tension? What discomfort are you still sitting with? ...

Turn your attention to the thoughts in your mind ... What has been occupying your mind today? ... How have you been feeling? ... Has there been emotional discomfort in your day? ... Can you embrace whatever feelings and sensations you are currently sitting with? ... Can you embrace your discomfort? ... Can you carry these feelings deep within, to the center of your being, to the temple of your heart, where holy wisdom breathes within

you? ... Feelings and sensations, comfortable or uncomfortable, take them all in and feel them as being whole and complete in God's love ...

Now, say silently to yourself "Amen" and in the instant of saying "Amen" let all of yourself, spirit and body, come together, join in wholeness and healing, instantly in this moment of "Amen" ... "Amen" means "So be it" ... So be it ... This is the way it is for me right now ... Knowing that wholeness is always here, right now, "Amen" ...

As you breathe quietly, begin to listen to the sounds in the room ... Move your fingers and your toes. Open your eyes when you are ready.

7. Written prayers for the Season of Pentecost

These written prayers can be a starting point for collective or personal devotions through the Pentecost season.

Prayers for delighting in God

Holy One, whatever you choose
is my path.
Only this, I pray –
give me strength to trust
and courage to be present
every moment. Amen.

O Holy Creator, you have prepared
for those who love you
joys beyond all understanding.
Fill our hearts with such a faith that,
trusting you in all things,
we may give freely of your graciousness
and fulfill your dream of joy for all
creation. Amen.

Blessed are you, gracious God,
maker of earth and heaven;
we give you thanks for the mystery
revealed in the radiance of Christ
and the Spirit,
united with you in life-giving creativity,
undivided in beauty and power.
With the saints of all the ages
we lift our hearts to praise you forever.
Amen.

Power of love, we give you thanks
for your reign as truth and life,
for your reign as grace and wholeness,
for your reign as justice
for all of creation,
for your reign as Christ in the world.
Grant us grace to be the hands
and feet of compassion
that your glory may rule
earth and heaven. Amen.

Giver of joy, you surround us
with so great a cloud of witnesses
so that we may run with patience
the race set before us
and receive with them
the joy that never fades.
With all of creation and
with the saints of all the ages,
we gather as your people to praise you
in the name of Jesus Christ. Amen.

Blessed are you, gracious God,
holy maker of earth and heaven;
we give you thanks through Christ,
who is present with us,
whose rising from the dead
gives us hope of resurrection
and the promise of life eternal
in your light.
Unite us in joy
with all those who have loved
in that realm where every tear
is wiped away. Amen.

Holy God, our refuge,
defend us from despair when
the storms of life surround us,
and preserve us from the storms
of fear within.
Grant us grace to trust
and to follow Christ, our shepherd,
into peace. Amen.

Light of truth,
through Christ you teach us
that love fulfills the law of life.
May we love you with all our heart,
with all our soul, mind and strength,
and may we love our neighbor
as ourselves.
This we pray in Jesus' name. Amen.

Giver of all gifts,
in Christ Jesus you teach us
that what we do for those you love,
we do for you.
Grant us grace so to serve
in the image of Christ
that we too may be willing
to give our lives for love of others,
and in so dying be reborn
to life in you. Amen.

Almighty Creator, you heard
the cry of your people
and sent your servant to free them
from slavery.
By the guidance of your Spirit,
bring us in freedom
to our promised land
so that we can love and serve
in Christ's name. Amen.

Precious Love,
maker and keeper of souls,
fill us with such yearning
for the new life you promise
for ourselves and for all of creation,
that we reach for you and find you
in surprising ways and places,
following the way of Jesus Christ.
Amen.

In Christ, the love of God
can still every heart
that hammers with fear or doubt
or confusion.
The peace of Christ,
the warm mantle of peace
in our Creator,
covers all who are troubled or anxious.
Amen.

Prayers for transformation and renewal

Loving God, who calls us
together as disciples,
make our hearts willing
to care in Jesus' name
that we may know the peace of Christ
and find the meaning of joy
in loving service. Amen.

God who calls us from bondage
to the ways of devotion,
free our hearts for the joy
of new life in your service,
that we may speak to the pain
of our world in its turmoil,
and quell evil's rage with your love.
Amen.

God who gathers us together
in the Spirit of Christ,
let this house of prayer
be a place of renewal,
of powerful compassion
and compassionate power,
so the light of your love is revealed
through our life,
as the Body of Christ in the world.
Amen.

God, you call us to life
as the Body of Christ,
bound by water and the Spirit
to one another.
From our fears and anxieties,
draw us into wholeness
with hearts and minds ready
for the path which is open before us.
Amen.

Dawn of glory, we beseech you
to help and defend us.
Deliver us from our oppressions
so that we may free others.
Lift up our fallen spirits
so that we may show mercy.
Speak to our inner need
so that we may comfort others.
Prepare our hearts for the peace
that comes of reconciliation,
and for service that gathers all
into one human community.
Power of Love, make us whole
and holy for Christ's sake. Amen.

**Gracious God who guides us
from fear into freedom,**
speak through the ancient story
to show us your way
for our lives and the earth that you love,
that transformed as one body,
we may serve in the world,
united in the joy of the Spirit. Amen.

Ever faithful God, by whose will
we walk by faith
in a wondrous and mysterious universe,
increase now our trust in you,
that in the midst of the many things
we cannot understand,
we may not doubt your love
or miss your delight,
of fail to offer you our thanksgiving.
Amen.

Spirit of Life, all too often
we forget who and whose
we really are.
We accept, without thinking,
ways of being and doing
which thwart your intentions
for our lives.
We give ourselves over
to other, smaller gods,
and shore up our inner frailty
with arrogance, rigidity, and illusion.
Power of Love, speak into our hearts
the truth of Christ.
Unite us in the Spirit
as holy members of one body,
that we may cherish both
what we share and how we differ,
and honor each gift and contribution
as your blessing for community.
In silence, Holy Presence,
we seek you... Amen.

Holy Maker, in whose image
all peoples are created,
we live among those whose ways
are different from our own,
whose tongues we do not understand,
whose worship and songs
are not the same.
Help us to remember
that all are beloved,
that all faiths reach for you,
that the yearnings of other hearts
are known to you.
Help us see you
and reveal you in beauty,
and in actions of love.
Help us see in others
the image of Christ,
to whom no one is ever a stranger.
Amen.

As the earth turns and turns
and dawn breaks from land to land,
let us hold in our hearts one creation,
one world,
one humanity, one Spirit,
one Peace. Amen.

Eternal God, you knit your people
into mystical communion
with the body of Christ.
Give us grace so to follow
the example of your saints,
in justice and kindness and humility,
that when our days on earth
have ended,
we may come into the presence
of Christ with all who love,
in the realm of joy where tears
are wiped away. Amen.

Prayers of thanks and dedication

Blessed are you, O Power of Peace,
for the abundance of mercies
that grace our lives
and enable us to share.
Receive these gifts with the beauty
of your tender compassion,
even as you receive us.
Accomplish through these gifts
and our grateful commitment,
the work of love
for the sake of creation.
With Christ, in Christ,
and through Christ
in the unity of the Spirit,
all power and possibility is yours,
God most holy,
now and forever. Amen.

Morning Star, we give you thanks
for all good things which bless us.
We give you thanks
for the gift of selfhood,
for hearts and minds
to see your miracles,
and for relationships through which
we are challenged
to growth and new life. Amen.

We give you thanks, gracious God,
for the gift of compassion
which empowers us to be
the church of Christ.
We give you thanks for the gifts
of identity and belonging
which enable us to be
Christ's disciples.
And we give thanks for the teachers
and learners in our midst,
who show us how to be your new
community.
Receive these gifts we offer
at the table of Christ,
that our lives and these gifts
may be turned to your purposes,
for the sake of the world you so love.
Amen.

Holy Creator, giver of all good gifts,
open our hearts and reshape our wills
so in thankfulness we give freely
of all you have given
for love of you, for love of Christ
and your world. Amen.

Blessed are you, O God,
for your gracious gifts to us.
You sent Jesus among us
to teach and heal and show us
what it means to give of self
for love of others.
You send the Christ among us now
to teach and heal and show us
what is possible
in the light of your love.
So with all of creation, and
with the church around the world,
we give you thanks. Amen.

Gracious God, you nourish us
in times of greatest need.
You free our hearts
and light the path we walk.
We give thanks for the abundance
of your mercy every moment,
and for every opportunity for new life.
Receive our gifts as symbols
of commitment to your purposes,
that all we have, all we are,
and all you call us to become
may reveal your loving presence
in the world. Amen.

Holy God, you call us
to prayerful thanksgiving,
united in the Spirit of Christ.
Embody within us
your holy word of wisdom
that our lives and your world
may be shaped for compassion,
and all creation may know the joy
of your love. Amen.

Prayers for the world, ourselves, and others

Holy God of mercy,
who daily stands with those
who are in danger,
from the depths of our being,
we cry for those who have suffered
the devastation of violence,
for those whose lives and homes
and communities have been ravaged,
for those who bear the loss
of ones they love.
May their spirits not be broken
by grieving or bitterness.
May their livelihoods and health
be restored.
May they be released from fear
to find freedom in love,
and may the justice
you have promised be theirs.
From the depths of our being, we cry.
Amen.

God of comfort and strength,
let the power of your Spirit
to breathe life anew
be more real in our hearts
than our fear,
so we each find our peace
with the past and the future
and freedom to love in this moment.
Amen.

God of compassion,
grant us courage to risk
and share the gospel of hope,
that your Spirit may turn
our vulnerabilities to strengths
and heal every soul in the world.
Amen.

God of Hope, as we journey
and your meaning unfolds,
grant us open minds
that our hearts may be converted
and we find our part
in mending your world.
This we pray in the power
of the living Christ among us. Amen.

Holy Mystery, Wind of God,
Creator of all,
you speak through the prophets,
heal through the Christ,
and live in us as the power of love.
Open our hearts
and set us free in your grace,
that we might be instruments
of your blessed peace,
and menders of your holy world.
Amen.

Holy God, who watched over
the shaping of our souls,
shape us as learners
and free us as lovers,
that we may listen for your truth
and be a blessing to others,
and share in the healing of the world.
Amen.

Blessed Potter, you turn
the mortal clay of our being
into moments of sacred opportunity.
Call us into holy freedom
through our human limitations
that we may daily choose the path
you hold open before us,
the open-hearted path
that leads to you. Amen.

O eternal wisdom,
you have laid the earth's foundations
and breathed into your creatures,
making us in our variety
to cherish your world
and seek your face.
Let us find you and know you
in the mighty crash of thunder,
in the laughter of a child,
and in the simple act
of breathing out and in,
so every moment of our lives
is transfixed by your presence
and by yearning to fulfill your joy
on earth. Amen.

Holy God,
what is your yearning for us?
Where are the places
for us to place ourselves
to bring about the future you intend?
Here, in the space
where new visions are born,
we listen in hope,
we listen in readiness,
we listen as pilgrims again. Amen.

Precious Love, who sends us out
to the world in Jesus' name,
help us to share the joy
of new life in Christ
in ways an aching world longs to hear.
Amen.

8. Guided prayers & meditations for the Season of Pentecost

These prayer suggestions have been written for groups with one partici-pant in the role of guide. They can easily be adapted for prayer partners and for personal use. Decide in advance who will read scripture, and who will lead the prayers today. Let each prayer unfold slowly and gently.

A MEDITATION ON WRESTLING WITH GOD
Genesis 32:22–32 (Jacob wrestles with God)
Remind everyone before you start that all are responsible to pray for one another, and that each will be particularly responsible for praying for the person immediately to their right. Encourage all to feel free either to share or remain quiet at the close of the prayer.

Take a few moments to prepare. Sit or lie comfortably, eyes closed. Focus on your regular breathing pattern, to come fully into the present. Relax with your breathing … Feel the Spirit breath flowing into your body … Feel how God breathes you … Listen for the word of God …

Read the biblical passage through three times slowly, aloud.

Listen for the word of God … Take a few moments to imagine how Jacob must have felt as he struggled … Reflect in silence on ways you are struggling with God … Why is God struggling to change you? … What do you fear in this struggle? … In what ways have you been wounded? … What new identity is God giving you? … What blessing do you crave? … How will you bless the generations which will follow after you? … Pray for the grace to embrace your struggle with God …

As you breathe, listen for what God may be saying to you … Is God speaking through some hope or desire? … Is there something which calls for your attention? … How can you respond? …

Rest quietly in God's presence, focusing only on the flow of your breathing, in and out … Stay open to God's possibilities …

Pray for yourself, for release from fear … for courage to struggle … for opportunities to grow in strength and wisdom … for purpose and meaning in your journey …

Pray for the person to your right, that he or she may be blessed by the struggle with God … Pray for the community of Christ's followers in this new time … for release from fear … for courage to struggle … for wisdom to recognize holy blessing … Finish with a prayer or a blessing you know by heart … Open your eyes when you are ready.

RECEIVING FORGIVENESS, AND FORGIVING

Luke 15:1–10 (the twin parables of the lost sheep and lost coin), Luke 15:11–32 (the parable of the lost son), Matthew 9:9–13 (Jesus and the tax collector), Matthew 18:21–35 (the unforgiving servant), John 8:1–11 (the woman caught in adultery)

Remind everyone before you start that all are responsible to pray for one another, and that each will be particularly responsible for praying for the person immediately to their right. Encourage all to feel free either to share or to remain quiet at the close of the prayer.

Take a few moments to prepare. Sit or lie comfortably, eyes closed. Focus on your regular breathing pattern, to come fully into the present. Relax with your breathing … Feel the Spirit breath flowing into your body … Feel how God breathes you … Listen for the word of God …

Read one of the biblical passages through three times slowly, aloud.

Reflect in silence on a time in your life when you experienced forgiveness … What burden was lifted from your heart? … How was your sense of yourself altered? … How was your relationship with God affected? … What new possibilities opened up for you as a result of being forgiven? …

As you breathe, become aware of feelings which have been either eased or aroused by your reflections … Listen for what God may be saying to you … Is God speaking through a hope or a desire? … Is there something which calls for your attention? … Are you feeling in need of forgiveness now? … Have you been honest with God about your need for forgiveness and your desire to restore broken trust? … Have you shared your regret, your willingness to make things right, and your hope for healed relationship with the someone you have wronged? …

Is there someone whose life could be changed by your forgiveness? … Has the time come for you to do this? … What steps can you take? … How will your heart be freed when you forgive? …

Rest quietly in God's presence, focusing only on the flow of your breathing, in and out … Stay open to God's possibilities …

Pray for yourself, for release from fear and pride … for courage to speak lovingly the truth of your feelings … for humility and willingness to make restitution … for hope in the restoration of right relationship … and for opportunities to share the blessings of the Christ-light …

Pray for the person to your right, that he or she may be empowered to receive forgiveness and to forgive … for the community of Christ's followers in this time … for opportunities to share the joy of confidence in God's mercy … Finish with a prayer or a blessing you know by heart … Open your eyes when you are ready.

THE HUMILITY OF A CHILD

Mark 9:33–37 (whoever welcomes one such child)
Prepare as above. Then read the passage through three times slowly, aloud.

Reflect on what Jesus might mean when he says that we welcome him whenever we welcome a little child … What Christ-like qualities are characteristic of childhood? … How are these qualities important in our relationship with God? … How do these same qualities help us love and serve others? … How does our Creator nurture these qualities in our lives? …

Rest quietly in God's presence, focusing only on the flow of your breathing, in and out … Stay open to God's possibilities …

Pray for yourself, for the deepening of those Christ-like qualities you most need … for release from fear and pride … for release from arrogance and self-pity … for opportunities to love and serve … and for opportunities to share the blessings of the Christ-light …

Pray for the person to your right, that he or she may be free to live the Christ-life in the power of humility … free to love and serve … free to share the blessings of the Christ-light … and free to share the joy of faith … Finish with a prayer or a blessing you know by heart … Open your eyes when you are ready.

PUTTING FIRST THINGS FIRST

Matthew 10:37–42 (those who lose their life will find it)
Remind everyone before you start that all are responsible to pray for one another, and that each will be particularly responsible for praying for the person immediately to their right. Encourage all to feel free to either share or be quiet at the close of the prayer.

Take a few moments to prepare. Sit or lie comfortably, eyes closed. Focus on your regular breathing pattern, to come fully into the present. Relax with your breathing … Feel the Spirit breath flowing into your body … Feel how God breathes you … Listen for the word of God …

Read the biblical passage through three times slowly, aloud.

Now reflect in silence on what distracts you from putting the light of Christ at the center of your life … What would it mean for you to take up your cross and follow Christ? … What costs would you need to bear to do this … What would it mean for you to find your life by losing it? … What inner strengths from God would enable you to do this? …

As you breathe, become aware of feelings which have been either eased or aroused by your reflections … Listen for what God may be saying to you … Is God speaking through a hope or a desire? … Is there something which calls for your attention? … How can you respond? … What inner quality would enable you to respond to God more fully? …

Rest quietly in God's presence, focusing only on the flow of your breathing, in and out … Stay open to God's possibilities …

Pray for yourself, for the personal strengths you need most … for release from anxiety and self-absorption … for grace to hold the Christ-light at the center of your life … for courage to bear your crosses … for purpose and meaning in your journey … for the grace to follow Christ …

Pray for the person to your right, and for the community of Christ's followers in this time … for release from fear … for courage to carry out God's work in Christ's name … for opportunities to share the joy of faith … Finish with a prayer or a blessing you know by heart … Open your eyes when you are ready.

Lectio prayers

A LECTIO PRAYER ON HUMILITY

Luke 18:9–14 (the Pharisee and the tax collector)
Matthew 7:1–5 (the log in your eye)
Luke 14:7–11 (sit in the lowest place)
Remind everyone before you start that all are responsible to pray for one another, and that each will be particularly responsible for praying for the person immediately to their right. Encourage all to feel free either to share or to remain quiet at the close of the prayer.

Take a few moments to prepare. Sit or lie comfortably, eyes closed. Focus on your regular breathing pattern, to come fully into the present. Relax with your breathing ... Feel the Spirit breath flowing into your body ... Feel how God breathes you ... Listen for the word of God ... Listen for a word or phrase or image which attracts you strongly ...

Read one of the following passages through slowly, aloud:

Listen for the word of God ... Choose a word or phrase or image from the passage which attracts you ... Repeat the word or phrase or image in silence for a couple of minutes, in rhythm with your breathing ...

Read the passage through slowly again, aloud.

Reflect in silence on what this word or phrase or image means to you. How does it speak to your heart? ... How does it relate to your life? ...

Read the passage through slowly again, aloud.

As you breathe, become aware of feelings which have been either eased or aroused by your chosen word or phrase or image ... Listen for what God may be saying to you ... Is God speaking through a hope or a desire? ... Is there something which calls for your attention? ... How can you respond? ...

Read the passage through slowly again, aloud.

Rest quietly in God's presence, focusing only on the flow of your breathing, in and out ... Stay open to God's possibilities ...

Pray for yourself, for release from fear and pride, from arrogance and self-pity ... for opportunities to love and serve ... and for opportunities to share the blessings of the Christ-light ...

Pray for the person to your right, that he or she may be free to live the Christ-life in the power of humility ... free to love and serve ... free to share the blessings of the Christ-light ... and free to share the joy of faith ... Finish with a prayer or a blessing you know by heart ... Open your eyes when you are ready.

A LECTIO PRAYER ON SERVING

Matthew 9:36 (compassion for the crowds)
Matthew 28:16–20 (the great commissioning)
Matthew 5:13–16 (the salt and the light)
Remind everyone before you start that all are responsible to pray for one another, and that each will be particularly responsible for praying for the person immediately to their right. Encourage all to feel free either to share or to remain quiet at the close of the prayer.

Take a few moments to prepare. Sit or lie comfortably, eyes closed. Focus on your regular breathing pattern, to come fully into the present. Relax with your breathing ... Feel the Spirit breath flowing into your body ... Feel how God breathes you ... Listen for the word of God ... Listen for a word or phrase or image which attracts you strongly ...

Read one of the biblical passages through three times, aloud.

Listen for the word of God ... Choose a word or phrase or image from the passage which attracts you ... Repeat the word or phrase in silence for a couple of minutes, in rhythm with your breathing ...

Reflect in silence on what this word or phrase or image means to you. How does it relate to your own life? ... To your presence in the world? ... To the work of your community of faith? ...

As you breathe, become aware of feelings which have been either eased or aroused by the word or phrase or image you have chosen ... Listen for what God may be saying to you ... Is God speaking through a hope or a desire?... Is there something which calls for your attention? ... How can you respond? ...

Rest quietly in God's presence, focusing only on the flow of your breathing, in and out... Stay open to God's possibilities ...

Pray for yourself, for release from fear, for purpose and meaning in your journey ... and for opportunities to share the blessings of the Christ-light ...

Pray for the person to your right, that he or she may be empowered to love and serve in the world ... Pray for the community of Christ's followers in this time, for opportunities to share the joy of faith ... Finish with a prayer or a blessing you know by heart ... Open your eyes when you are ready.

A LECTIO PRAYER ON LOVING ACTION

James 2:14–26 (faith and works)
Luke 16:19–31 (the rich man and Lazarus)
Remind everyone before you start that all are responsible to pray for one another, and that each will be particularly responsible for praying for the person immediately to their right. Encourage all to feel free either to share or to remain quiet at the close of the prayer.
Take a few moments to prepare. Sit or lie comfortably, eyes closed. Focus on your regular breathing pattern, to come fully into the present. Relax with your breathing ... Feel the Spirit breath flowing into your body ... Feel how God breathes you ... Listen for the word of God ... Listen for a word or phrase or image which attracts you strongly ...

Read either of the two biblical passages through slowly, aloud.

Listen for the word of God ... Choose a word or phrase or image from the passage which attracts you ... Repeat the word or phrase or image in silence for a couple of minutes, in rhythm with your breathing ...

Now reflect in silence on what this word or phrase or image means to you. How does it relate to your own life? ... To your presence in the world? ... To the work of your community of faith? ...

Read the passage through slowly again, aloud.

As you breathe, become aware of feelings which have been either eased or aroused by your chosen word or phrase or image ... Listen for what God may be saying to you ... Is God speaking through a hope or a desire? ... Is there something which calls for your attention? ... What loving action(s) are you called to? ... How can you respond? ...

Read the passage through slowly again, aloud.

Rest quietly in God's presence, focusing only on the flow of your breathing, in and out. Stay open to God's possibilities ...

Pray for yourself, for release from fear ... for freedom to love and serve ... and for opportunities to share the blessings of the Christ-light ...

Pray for the person to your right, that he or she may be empowered to love and serve in the world ... Pray for the community of Christ's followers in this time, for opportunities to share the joy of faith through loving actions ... Finish with a prayer or a blessing you know by heart ... Open your eyes when you are ready.

A LECTIO PRAYER ON COURAGE

Matthew 10:26–33 (courage for Christ)

Remind everyone before you start that all are responsible to pray for one another, and that each will be particularly responsible for praying for the person immediately to their right. Encourage all to feel free either to share or to remain quiet at the close of the prayer.

Take a few moments to prepare. Sit or lie comfortably, eyes closed. Focus on your regular breathing pattern, to come fully into the present. Relax with your breathing ... Feel the Spirit breath flowing into your body ... Feel how God breathes you ... Listen for the word of God ... Listen for a word or phrase or image which attracts you strongly ...

Read the biblical passage through slowly, aloud.

Listen for the word of God ... Choose a word or phrase or image from the passage which attracts you ... Repeat the word or phrase or image in silence for a couple of minutes, in rhythm with your breathing ...

Reflect in silence on what this word or phrase or image means to you. How does it relate to your own life? ... What are your fears for your ministry? ... For the work of your community of faith? ... What are your fears for the Church? ... Of whom are you afraid? ...

Read the passage through slowly again, aloud.

As you breathe, become aware of feelings which have been either eased or aroused by your chosen word or phrase or image ... Listen for what God may be saying to you ... Is God speaking through a hope or a desire? ... Is there something which calls for your attention? ... How can you respond? ...

Read the passage through slowly again, aloud.

Rest quietly in God's presence, focusing only on the flow of your breathing, in and out. Stay open to God's possibilities ...

Pray for yourself, for release from fear ... for strength and courage in the face of adversity ... for purpose and meaning in your journey ...

Pray for the person to your right, and for the community of Christ's followers in this time ... for release from fear or persecution ... for courage to carry on God's work in Christ's name ... for opportunities to share the joy of faith through Jesus Christ ... Finish with a prayer or a blessing you know by heart ... Open your eyes when you are ready.

A LECTIO PRAYER ON "NEW LIFE"

John 3:1–17 (born of the Spirit, for God so loved the world), Ezekiel 37:1–14 (Spirit breathed into dry bones) , Jeremiah 6:16 (stand at the crossroads)

Remind everyone before you start that all are responsible to pray for one another, and that each will be particularly responsible for praying for the person immediately to their right. Encourage all to feel free either to share or to be quiet at the close of the prayer.

Take a few moments to prepare. Sit or lie comfortably, eyes closed. Focus on your regular breathing pattern, to come fully into the present. Relax with your breathing ... Feel the Spirit breath flowing into your body ... Feel how God breathes you ... Listen for the word of God ... Listen for a word or a phrase or image which attracts you strongly ...

Read one of the biblical passages through slowly, aloud.

Listen for the word of God ... Choose a word or phrase or image from the passage which attracts you ... Repeat the word or phrase or image in silence for a couple of minutes, in rhythm with your breathing ...

Read the passage again, slowly, aloud.

Now reflect in silence on what this word or phrase or image means to you. What does it mean to your life? ... To your presence and work in the world? ... To the presence and work of your faith community? ... How have you experienced new life? ...
Read the passage again, slowly, aloud.

As you breathe, become aware of feelings which have been either eased or aroused by the word or phrase or image you have chosen ... Listen for what God may be saying to you ... Is God speaking through a hope or a desire? ... Is there something which calls for your attention? ... How can you respond? ...

Rest quietly in God's presence, focusing only on the flow of your breathing, in and out. Stay open to God's possibilities ...

Pray for yourself, for release from fear, for purpose and power in your faith, and for the joy of new life ...

Pray for those you love, for the person on your right, and for the community of Christ's followers, for opportunities to share the joy of new life ... Finish with a prayer or a blessing you know by heart ... Open your eyes when you are ready.

THE PRESENCE OF CHRIST
Matthew 16:13–19 ("Who do you say that I am?")
Remind everyone before you start that all are responsible to pray for one another, and that each will be particularly responsible for praying for the person immediately to their right. Encourage all to feel free either to share or to be quiet at the close of the prayer.

Take a few moments to prepare. Sit or lie comfortably, eyes closed. Focus on your regular breathing pattern, to come fully into the present. Relax with your breathing ... Feel the Spirit breath flowing into your body ... Feel how God breathes you ... Listen for the word of God ...

Read the biblical passage through three times slowly, aloud.

Reflect in silence on who Jesus is to you ... How do you relate to the historical Jesus? ... What aspects of Jesus' ministry hold most promise and meaning for you? ... How often would you think of him through the course of an ordinary day? ... Do you sometimes sense the presence of the risen Christ? ... What part does the risen Christ play in your day-to-day life? ... What more could you do to hold Christ at the center of your desires, your thoughts, words, and deeds? ... What part do you play in Christ's continuing work in the world? ...

As you breathe, become aware of feelings which have been either eased or aroused by your reflections ... Listen for what God may be saying to you ... Is God speaking through a hope or a desire?... Is there something which calls for your attention?... What is God's invitation to you through Christ? How can you respond?...

Rest quietly in God's presence, focusing only on the flow of your breathing, in and out. Stay open to God's possibilities ...

Pray for yourself, for release from fear and resistance ... for courage to seek healing and hope in God through Christ ... for comfort and joy in the presence of Christ ... for meaning and purpose in sharing the blessings of the Christ-light ...

Pray for the person to your right, that he or she may be empowered to receive Christ's healing presence ... pray for the community of Christ's followers, that they may continue to be the body of Christ in this time ... for opportunities to share the joy of confidence in holy presence and power ... Finish with a prayer or a blessing you know by heart ... Open your eyes when you are ready.

THE EXPANDING POWER OF FAITH

Luke 17:5–6 (faith the size of a mustard seed), Matthew 13:33 or Luke 13:20–21 (the kingdom of heaven like yeast)

Remind everyone before you start that all are responsible to pray for one another, and that each will be particularly responsible for praying for the person immediately to their right. Encourage all to feel free either to share or to be quiet at the close of the prayer.

Take a few moments to prepare. Sit or lie comfortably, eyes closed. Focus on your regular breathing pattern, to come fully into the present. Relax with your breathing ... Feel the Spirit breath flowing into your body ... Feel how God breathes you ... Listen for the word of God ... Listen for a word or a phrase or image which attracts you strongly ...

Read either of the biblical passages through slowly, aloud.

Listen for the word of God ... Choose a word or phrase or image from the passage which attracts you ... Repeat the word or phrase or

image in silence for a couple of minutes, in rhythm with your breathing ...

Now reflect in silence on what this word or phrase or image means to you. What does it mean to your life as a seeker of faith? ... To your presence and work in the world? ... To the presence and work of your faith community? ... How have you experienced the expanding power of faith? ...

Read the passage through slowly again, aloud.

As you breathe, become aware of feelings which have been either eased or aroused by the word or phrase or image you have chosen ... Listen for what God may be saying to you ... Is God speaking through a hope or a desire? ... Is there something which calls for your attention? ... How can you respond? ...

Read the passage through slowly again, aloud.

Rest quietly in God's presence, focusing only on the flow of your breathing, in and out. Stay open to God's possibilities ...

Pray for yourself, for release from fear ... for willingness to receive ... for capacity to trust in God's presence and power ... for purpose and meaning in your life ... and for opportunities to grow in faith ...

Pray for the person to your right, and for the community of Christ's followers in this time, for opportunities to grow in faith ... and for opportunities to participate in the power of faith through Jesus Christ ... Finish with a prayer or a blessing you know by heart ... Open your eyes when you are ready.

A MEDITATION ON ABUNDANCE

Matthew 14:13–20, Mark 6:30–44, Luke 9:10–17 (feeding the 5,000)

For this meditation, you will need a whole loaf of bread, preferably round, on a table in the center of the group.

Remind everyone before you start that all are responsible to pray for one another, and that each will be particularly responsible for praying for the person immediately to their right. Encourage all to feel free to either share or be quiet at the close of the prayer.

Take a few moments to prepare. Sit or lie comfortably, eyes closed. Focus on your regular breathing pattern, to come fully into the present. Relax with your breathing ... Feel the Spirit breath flowing into your body ... Feel how God breathes you ... Listen for the voice of Jesus, saying "You give them something to eat" ...

Read one of the biblical passages through three times, aloud.

Repeat the words "You give them something to eat" in silence for a couple of minutes, in rhythm with your breathing ...
Invite participants to continue inwardly to hear and repeat the words of Jesus as they tear a piece of bread from the loaf, give the piece of bread to their neighbor to eat, and then pass the loaf along.

One of you could pick up the loaf of bread from the table now. Break off a piece, and pass it to your neighbor to eat, but continue to hold the bread until he or she has eaten ... Now pass the bread to your neighbor, to continue the process ...

The idea is to feed your neighbor first, and then pass the bread, so that the participants continue to feed each other until all have been fed.

Having fed each other, reflect in silence on the meaning of this story ... What does this story say to you about God's abundance? ... What does it say about sharing? ... About hoarding? ... How have you experienced the abundance of God in your life? ... What do Jesus' words, "You give them something to eat" mean in your life? ... For your presence and work in the world? ... For the presence and work of your faith community? ...

As you breathe, become aware of feelings which have been either eased or aroused by Jesus' words, your actions, and your reflections ... Listen for what God may be saying to you ... Is God speaking through a hope or a desire? ... Is there something which calls for your attention? ... How can you respond? ...

Rest quietly in God's presence, focusing only on the flow of your breathing, in and out. Stay open to God's possibilities ...

Pray for yourself, for release from fear ... for capacity to trust in God's presence and power ... for willingness to receive ... for willingness to give ... for opportunities to grow in faith and share it ...

Pray for the person to your right, and for the community of Christ's followers in this time ... for life-giving opportunities to deepen in trust ... for willingness to receive ... for willingness to risk ... for opportunities to participate in God's work by sharing ... and for opportunities to participate in the power of faith through Jesus Christ ... Finish with a prayer or a blessing you know by heart ... Open your eyes when you are ready.

A MEDITATION ON TRUSTING

Matthew 14:22–33, Mark 6:45–51, John 6:16–21
(Jesus walking on water)

Remind everyone before you start that all are responsible to pray for one another, and that each will be particularly responsible for praying for the person immediately to their right. Encourage all to feel free either to share or to be quiet at the close of the prayer.

Take a few moments to prepare. Sit or lie comfortably, eyes closed. Focus on your regular breathing pattern, to come fully into the present. Relax with your breathing ... Feel the Spirit breath flowing into your body ... Feel how God breathes you ... Listen for the word of God ...

Read one of the biblical passages through three times slowly, aloud.

Remember a particular time in your life when you felt the winds of life were against you ... when you felt battered and far from shelter ... when you feared you wouldn't make it back to shore ... Be in that moment, with those feelings ... When help comes to you, are you able to recognize Christ? ... Can you trust in Christ's power to help you? ... Can you trust that Christ can help you to do what seems to be impossible, to "walk on water"? ... How do you feel when Christ is with you and the winds die down around you? ...

As you breathe, be aware of the feelings which have been either eased or aroused by your reflections ... Listen for what God may be saying to you ... Is God speaking through a hope or a desire? ... Is there something which calls for your attention? ... How can you respond? ...

Rest quietly in God's presence, focusing only on the flow of your breathing, in and out. Stay open to God's possibilities ...

Pray for yourself, for release from fear ... for trust in the power of holy presence ... for courage to believe that you too can walk on water, with the help of God ...

Pray for the person to your right, and for the community of Christ's followers in this time ... for release from fear ... for trust in holy presence ... for courage to believe in God's power to make things possible ... Finish with a prayer or a blessing you know by heart ... Open your eyes when you are ready.

PEACEMAKING – OPTION 1

Psalm 46 (the Lord makes wars cease)

Remind everyone before you start that all are responsible to pray for one another, and that each will be particularly responsible for praying for the person immediately to their right. Encourage all to feel free to either share or be quiet at the close of the prayer.

Take a few moments to prepare. Sit or lie comfortably, eyes closed. Focus on your regular breathing pattern, to come fully into the present. Relax with your breathing ... Feel the Spirit breath flowing into your body ... Feel how God breathes you ... Listen for the picture-images in this psalm ... Listen for the word of God ...

Read the Psalm through three times slowly, aloud.

Now imagine or remember a turbulent situation of which you are aware in real life ... Place yourself within the situation ... See the physical surroundings, and each of the persons involved in the situation ... Note body language, words and facial expressions, and the energy between those who are present ... What is each person feeling? ... Is he/she sad or grieving? Is she/he angry? What could each one be fearing? What does each one need? ...

Consider the difference which has emerged as a "mountain" between the persons involved ... How would each person name the mountain between them from his/her perspective? ... How would you name the mountain for yourself? ... Consider the invitation in accepting responsibility for sharing your own perspective with others ... What invitation lies in viewing the mountain from the perspectives of other persons involved? ...

What forces, like roaring waters, are at work here? ... In shaking the mountain at the heart of the sea, what healing opportunity is God offering? ... In what ways is God at work in trembling mountains and foaming seas to bring peace? ... In the midst of this trouble, what would it mean to honor God at work in the tumult? ... How can you express your trust in God? ...

Imagine the peace of God as a river of light streaming into each person involved ... Begin with yourself as you too are experiencing the turbulence ... Feel the light streaming through you as a shower of healing from several feet above you ... Receive the light into the center of your head ... from where your inner eye perceives an "insight" ... Feel the light calming ... releasing fear ... illuminating perspectives ... revealing possibilities ...

From the center of your head, let the light flow through your body, empowering and steadying ... uniting with the energy of the earth ... From the center of your head, let it flow through you as Christ-light, revealing the truth of God in this experience ... From the center of your head, be aware of the Christ-light all around you and around every person ... From the center of your head, see God as refuge and strength, even though the earth changes and mountains tumble into the sea ...

Let the Christ-light shine within you as ultimate safety ... Let it awaken within you the courage to love in this moment, and patience with yourself and with others ... Let it awaken within you the strength to hold emptiness as open space for hope in God ... Let the Christ-light shine through you as healing presence ...

Now rest quietly in the peace of God, focusing only on the flow of your breathing, in and out. Stay open to your experience of holy peace ... Listen for the voice of Christ, "My peace I leave with you" ... Give thanks for the healing power of peace in your life, for release from fear, for patience, for courage to love ...

Pray for the persons involved in the situation you have named before God ... Pray for the person to your right, that he or she may be freed from fear, patient with self and others and strengthened to love in the present moment ... Finish with a prayer or a blessing you know by heart ... Open your eyes when you are ready.

PEACEMAKING – OPTION 2
Matthew 5:21–26 (on anger and reconciliation) and John 2:13–17 (Jesus cleanses the temple)
Prepare as above. Then read the biblical passages through twice slowly, aloud.

Reflect on the differences between holding onto anger against another and actively resisting wrongdoing which desecrates God ... How are we to deal with our anger in the first situation? How are we to deal with anger in the second situation? ...

What inner strengths will you need? Pray for the grace to deal constructively with a situation about which you feel angry ... Listen for what God may be saying to you ... Is God speaking through a feeling or a hope or desire? ... Is there something which calls for your attention? ... How can you respond? ...

Rest quietly in God's presence, focusing only on the flow of your breath, in and out ... Stay open to God's possibilities ...

Pray for yourself, giving thanks for the healing power of peace in your life, for release from fear, for patience, for courage to love …

Pray for the persons involved in the situation you have named before God, that each one may be freed from fear, patient with self and others, and strengthened to love in the present moment … Finish with a prayer or a blessing you know by heart … Open your eyes when you are ready.

PEACEMAKING – OPTION 3

Matthew 18:15–20 (on direct communication)
Prepare as in Option 1 above. Then read the passage through three times slowly, aloud.

How does direct communication preserve good faith and honor in relationships? … What is the best possible outcome of communicating one-to-one? … When a relationship is strained for you, in what ways are you tempted to avoid the stress of communicating directly? … What is the hardest part for you? … What feelings do you experience? … Whatever others may do or say, what gift could God strengthen within you that would help to bring peace? … Pray for this gift …

Now, imagine or remember a distressing situation in which you are (or have been) involved in real life … Place yourself within the situation … See the physical surroundings, and each of the persons involved in the situation … Note body language, words and facial expressions, and the energy between those who are present … What could each person be feeling? … Sad or grieving? … Angry? (If angry, is there fear behind the anger?) … What could each one be fearing? … What does each one of you need? …

What acknowledgment or action by other persons would restore harmony to the relationship? … Have you shared this need directly with the person(s) involved? … If not, what steps could you take to do so? … What action or acknowledgment could you offer? …

If you have attempted to discuss the matter directly and it remains unresolved in your heart, who could assist you constructively in supporting this relationship? …

If you have tried to communicate directly and also with the support of wise companions, what guidance can you receive from your community of faith? … Have you asked for community guidance in restoring this relationship? … Has the time come for you to do so? … What steps could you take at this time? …

Rest quietly in God's presence, focusing only on the flow of your breath, in and out … Stay open to God's possibilities …

Pray for yourself, giving thanks for the healing power of peace in your life, for release from fear, for patience, for courage to love …

Pray for the persons involved in the situation you have named before God, that each one may be freed from fear, patient with self and others, and strengthened to love in the present moment … Finish with a prayer or a blessing you know by heart … Open your eyes when you are ready.

A MEDITATION ON BEARING BURDENS

Matthew 16:21–26 (Jesus foretells his death)
Remind everyone before you start that all are responsible to pray for one another, and that each will be particularly responsible for praying for the person immediately to their right. Encourage all to feel free either to share or to remain quiet at the close of the prayer.

Take a few moments to prepare. Sit or lie comfortably, eyes closed. Focus on your regular breathing pattern, to come fully into the present. Relax with your breathing … Feel the Spirit breath flowing into your body …

Feel how God breathes you … Listen for the word of God …
Read the biblical passage through three times slowly, aloud.

Take a few moments to imagine how Jesus must have felt about the future he anticipated … Now reflect in silence on what it would mean in your life to follow in the footsteps of Jesus …

What crosses are yours to bear? … How is your attitude toward suffering and sacrifice similar to Peter's? … What could it mean for you to "find your life" by losing it for the sake of a greater love? … What inner strengths from God will enable you to do this? … Pray for the grace to embrace your crosses as opportunities …

As you breathe, listen for what God may be saying to you … Is God speaking through a hope or a desire? … Is there something which calls for your attention? … How can you respond? … What inner quality would enable you to respond to God more fully? …

Rest quietly in God's presence, focusing only on the flow of your breathing, in and out. Stay open to God's possibilities …

Pray for yourself, for release from fear … for courage to grow in strength and wisdom … for purpose and meaning in your journey … for the grace to follow Christ in your life …

Pray for the person to your right, that he or she may receive the courage and strength to bear burdens … Pray for the community of Christ's followers in this new time … for release from fear … for courage to carry on with God's work in Christ's name … for opportunities to share the joy of faith … Finish with a prayer or a blessing you know by heart … Open your eyes when you are ready.

A MEDITATION ON INTEGRITY
Matthew 10:34–36 ("I have not come to bring peace, but a sword")
Remind everyone before you start that all are responsible to pray for one another, and that each will be particularly responsible for praying for the person immediately to their right. Encourage all to feel free either to share or to remain quiet at the close of the prayer.

Take a few moments to prepare. Sit or lie comfortably, eyes closed. Focus on your regular breathing pattern, to come fully into the present. Relax with your breathing … Feel the Spirit breath flowing into your body … Feel how God breathes you … Listen for the word of God …

Read the biblical passage through three times slowly, aloud.

Reflect in silence on what distinguishes the kind of "peace" that Christ dismisses in this passage from the inner peace that Christ promises … Have you experienced a disruption of peace for the sake of acting with integrity out of love? … What has this meant for your presence and work in the world? … What inner strengths will you need to support you in participating in God's work with integrity? …

As you breathe, become aware of feelings which have been either eased or aroused by these reflections … Listen for what God may be saying to you … Is God speaking through a hope or a desire? … Is there something which calls for your attention? … How can you respond? …

Rest quietly in God's presence, focusing only on the flow of your breathing, in and out. Stay open to God's possibilities …

Pray for yourself, for release from fear … for the courage and integrity to live in ways that are congruent with your ultimate commitments

... for clarity of purpose and humility in relationships ... for opportunities to serve, and opportunities to grow in faith ... Pray for the grace to follow Christ in your life ...

Pray for the person to your right, that he or she will find the courage to carry on the work of love with integrity... Pray for the community of Christ's followers in this time, for integrity in service ... for release from fear ... for release from persecution ... for opportunities to share in the power of faith through Jesus Christ ... Finish with a prayer or a blessing you know by heart ... Open your eyes when you are ready.

A CENTERING MEDITATION ON LISTENING
1 Samuel 3:1–10 (God calls the child, Samuel, who replies, "Speak, for your servant is listening"), Matthew 13:3–9 (the parable of the sower, which ends, "Let anyone with ears listen!")

Take a few moments to prepare. Sit or lie comfortably, eyes closed. Focus on your regular breathing pattern, to come fully into the present. Relax with your breathing ... Feel the Spirit breath flowing into your body ... Feel how God breathes you ... Listen for the word of God ...

Read one of the biblical passages through three times slowly, aloud.

Repeat these words within yourself, in rhythm with your breathing ... "Speak, for your servant is listening" ... "Speak, for your servant is listening" ...

Or repeat, "Let anyone with ears listen" ... "Let anyone with ears listen," if the Matthew passage was read aloud.

As you continue to repeat the words in rhythm with your breathing, stay open to your feelings and invite the Holy Spirit to fill your being ... Sustain this pattern of inner speaking and listening so that every breathing in and breathing out, whether conscious or not, becomes your prayer ...

As you breathe quietly, begin to listen to the sounds in the room. Outside the room ... Move your fingers and toes. Open your eyes when you are ready.

9. Inner reflections for the Season of Pentecost

In this spring sunshine
seeds are sown
one by tiny one
abundant visions
glow quietly
Through the mud
of fertile furrows
Through the beauty
of unfolding blossoms
Through the riches
of ripening harvest
Through the crystals
of frosted panes
And brilliance builds
from beginnings
so easily overlooked
so very ordinary

In the rhythm of the Seasons of the Christian year, the Season of Pentecost invites us into God's perfect timing of right now. We are invited to enter into the challenge and the gift of living in right relationship with God, ourselves, each other, and our world.

The beauty of nature's parade through this season is amazing. In each of the following reflections we draw from nature's beauty and let the simple and ordinary introduce us to the profound.

THIS AMAZING CREATION

Go for a short walk with the aim of collecting five examples of nature's amazing creation to put beside your candle. Arrange your items around your lighted candle and read.

One by one hold each item. As you hold each one, write how you came to choose it as an example of God's amazing creation.

Write how you are an example of God's amazing creation.

FALLING LEAVES

Collect colored leaves and arrange them around your candle. Just as trees let go of their leaves, so in time there will be room for new growth. We too need to let go of those dried ideas and habits so we also will have room for new growth.

- What do you identify as dried or withered places in your life that need to be let go?
- What is your dream of new growth?

RECONCILIATION

In this Pentecost season we are called to be the hands and feet of Christ in the world. Christ is very clear about our responsibilities for forgiveness and the restoration of right relationship.

The Hebrew word *shalom* means peace – but even more, it means wholeness and justice for all. In our families, friendships, and work lives we sometimes experience brokenness that is beyond our ability and/or desire to mend. At times when the hurt or rift is bigger than us, God's grace can move in like cool, healing waters.

Get a jug of cool water and a bowl to pour the water into (bring a hand towel). Light your candle. In the quiet of this moment, slowly pour the water into the bowl. Listen to its gentle splash and watch the candle light play on its surface.

As you let your fingers play in the bowl of cool water, think of an incident or person that has made you angry or hurt.

Slowly and gently cool your brow with wet fingers.

Dry your hands. Write a note that tells of the incident or person that caused you to feel distressed.

From a voice beyond your hurt and anger write a grace-filled response to your note.

Sit in the candlelight; reread your note and your shalom-filled reply. Cool your brow one more time.

FALLOW TIME

In our busy lives, "down time" is often looked upon as non-productive. We are constantly doing and making. Nature has an important lesson for us in the season after harvest. The lesson is fallow time – the time of resting and regrouping, replenishing ourselves before we attempt to blossom and create.

Collect a gathering of twigs/grasses/dried flowers from a post-harvest growing space. Bring them into your reflection writing space. Arrange them in a vase or basket.

Light your candle; center in the quiet of the moment.

In your candlelight, write thoughts of your own fallow time, and how God's grace can be part of your rest and replenishment.

A THANKFUL HEART

Get a small notebook to record your lists.

Light your candle. Sit in your candlelight, and allow your heart to fill with thanksgiving for all the gifts that are part of your life.

Choose a number for your list – 4, 5, 6, whatever. Number down your notebook page and write an item of thanksgiving for each number. Keep your items simple and specific. Make a decision that at sometime each day for the next month you will work on a list of thanksgivings to help you focus on God's abundance in your day.

10. Activities for the Season of Pentecost

The Season of Pentecost lasts many days, through many changes in our natural world. We move from late spring, to summer, to fall, to the first edges of winter. This season holds a variety of events and special days that can be pulled deliberately and meaningfully into our faith journey – a journey of awareness, reconciliation, and thanksgiving.

In the following activities we invite you to explore and celebrate the extraordinary that is around and inside each one of us during these "ordinary days."

BUG WATCHING

Our own "nature special" is as close as our backyard or a spot in the park. Go to the library and get a book on insects common to your area. Lie on your stomach in the grass and see what you can find. Try drawing the bugs you find.

CLOUD WATCHING

Some summer days have blue skies and amazing clouds. Get some people to play cloud shapes with you. Lie on a blanket and imagine wonderful things going by in the clouds. See if anyone else can see what you see.

PAINT A PICTURE

Set up an outside painting spot. Use water- colors and allow the colors to flow into each other. Don't worry about coloring "within the lines" – whether those lines are real or only in your head. Be an impressionist – impressed with the beauty around you. Share your picture with someone.

WRITE A POEM

Sit outside and allow your senses to be filled. Close your eyes, open your ears, listen for a wee while, then jot down things that you hear. Repeat this process with each of your senses. Arrange your words into a poem, and send it to someone special.

GO FLY A KITE

Make sure you are in an open field away from power lines and kite-eating trees. (Those 99- cent plastic bats work amazingly well!) Be a kid again.

BUBBLES IN THE WIND

Small bottles of bubble mix cost very little, and give hours of fun watching bubbles form, drift, and shimmer. Blow bubbles and enjoy.

WIND IN THE TREES

Listen to the rustle of leaves. Do different trees make different sounds? Learn to read your tree leaves. Gather as many different leaves as you can. Get a tree book to help you. Find ten trees that live near you – get to know them.

MAKE A WIND CHIME

Using wood, shells, rocks, etc., and fishing line, create your own wind chimes. Hang your chimes in a friendly tree.

WATCH BIRDS IN THE WIND

Use a bird book, and keep a list of birds you see. Notice how each bird has a different pattern of flying. Some beat their wings busily; some glide. Some stay level; some swoop up and down.

PAPER BOATS

Get an origami book from the library. Make a simple paper boat. Find a long stick for boat steering. Float your boats. (Don't forget to take your boats out of the water when you're finished).

RUN THROUGH THE SPRINKLER

...together – just do it!

SAND CASTLES

Collect non-glass containers that will make interesting molds. Make a plan – or simply create a castle in the sand.

GLOAMING PICNIC

When the world is golden, the sun has gone but not quite tucked in. It can be the nicest time of the day. Enjoy eating your favorites in this magic light. Invite friends.

WATCH A SUNSET (OR MOONRISE)

Choose an evening and make a point of watching the sun set (be careful not to stare directly at the sun). Toast the day and say aloud the blessings it has brought. Be quiet and drink in the colors and sounds and smells of this sunset time.

MAKE A SUNSET CARD (OR MOONRISE CARD)

Cut a small piece of white cotton about 7 cm by 9 cm.

Cut a piece of 100 grain sandpaper the same size. Use wax crayons to create sunset shapes and colors on the sandpaper. Iron the sandpaper sunset onto the white cotton.

Attach the decorated cotton to a blank card or paper. Write a note sending sunshine (or moon shadows) to someone.

WALK IN THE AUTUMN LEAVES

Open your senses. Walk in the leaves and deliberately scuff your feet. Listen to the crackle, smell the autumn air. Look at the amazing colors. Let your heart and memory bank be filled.

COLLECT SOME BEAUTIFUL LEAVES

Preserve the glory of autumn leaves! Gather leaves from several different brightly colored trees. Place them between sheets of waxed paper, and put the wax sheets between the pages of a large, heavy book. After at least a week, check the results!

You can use dried pressed leaves in pictures, on cards, on candles, and in letters.

GO FOR A WIENER ROAST

Prepare a feast, invite some friends, build a fire (safely!), and enjoy.

PLANT SOME BULBS

Before the ground gets too hard, choose a special spot and plant your bulbs carefully. Write a letter about planting day, and about your dreams and wishes for the spring flowers. Put your letter in a safe spot to read next spring.

CHECK OUT THE STARRY HEAVENS

Can you find the Big Dipper, the North Star, Cassiopeia, or Orion's Belt?

Get an astronomy book to help you identify some of the more visible stars and constellations. Make up your own names for the groups of stars that you can see. What do they look like? What do they remind you of?

SAY "THANK YOU!"

Note five things from each day for which you are especially grateful. Say, "Thanks be to God" for each one.

Glossary

Advent – The preparatory season immediately before Christmas. From the Latin *advenire*, to come to.

Alaha – an Aramaic word for "holy presence." Jesus and his companions spoke Aramaic.

Amen – a word that concludes a prayer and means "so be it."

Apostle – The special title given in the gospels to followers of Christ who were sent out to spread the "good news." From the Latin *apostolo* or messenger.

Ascension – The vision of Christ ascending into heaven as witnessed by his followers.

Ash Wednesday – The first day of Lent, 6 1/2 weeks before Easter. On this day, through the ages, people marked themselves with ashes as a sign of penitence.

Asperges – In a recent recovery of ancient tradition, the sprinkling of water from the font over the congregation (with evergreen boughs, where available!) in celebration of baptismal faith.

Atonement – From atone, to make amends, to reconcile and restore relationships; in Christian theology, the reconciliation between God and humans, brought about by the life and death of Jesus Christ.

Beatitudes – Christ's promises of blessing found in the Sermon on the Mount.

Christ – The title given to Jesus of Nazareth (not his last name!). The word derives from the Greek equivalent of the Hebrew "Messiah."

Christ candle – A single candle, usually tall and white, lit to celebrate the blessing and presence of Jesus.

Christ-life – The life of Christ shared. The possibilities of living with Jesus as example.

Communion – the symbolic meal, sharing bread and wine, derived from Jesus' last supper with his disciples. Also known as the Eucharist or Mass.

Covenant – A relationship based on commitment which includes both promises and obligations, that is both reliable and durable. Like a contract, only stronger.

Crucifixion – Specifically, the death of Jesus of Nazareth on a cross in Jerusalem; figuratively, punishment for the sake of one's beliefs.

Disciple – One of the 12 followers Christ called during his lifetime. Also, a professed follower of the risen Christ now. From the Latin *discere,* to learn.

Divina meditation – A meditation directed towards the divine.

Easter – the day of Christ's resurrection. The name comes from Eastre, a Saxon goddess who was worshiped each spring.

Embodied prayer – A prayer expressed in bodily form. A physical posture for prayer.

Epiphany – The feast of the Christian church which celebrates the presentation of the Christchild to the Sages who travelled by starlight from afar. From the Greek *epiphaneia*, to show.

Eucharist – A central act of Christian worship involving bread and wine, by which we symbolically receive the gift of Christ, give thanks, and unite in offering our own lives as Christ's "body." Also known as Communion and the Lord's Supper.

Gospel – Literally, "good news." Any of the four biblical narratives of the life, death, and resurrection of Jesus.

Grace – The blessings and abundance of God's love, unearned and unending.

Hallelujah – An expression of praise and thanks. "Hallelujah" means "praise the Lord;" it comes from a combination of two Hebrew words, *hillel*, to praise, and *Yah*, a shortened form of Yahweh.

Hosanna – In the Bible, a word shouted by the crowds when Jesus rode into Jerusalem on the day we call Palm Sunday. "Hosanna" means "Save us now!"

Ignatian – from St. Loyola of Ignatius, the founder of the Roman Catholic Jesuit order.

Incarnation – The unity of divinity and humanity in physical form. The Christian belief that Jesus is the personification of the Spirit of God on earth. From the Latin *incarnare*, to make flesh.

Indwelling Spirit – The Christian spirit abiding within a person, a guiding source of motivation, power, and insight.

Intercession – Prayer on behalf of others.

Kyrie – A prayer, usually sung, for holy mercy.

Lectio – Related to the reading of scripture.

Lectio Divina – Prayerful contemplation of God and God's intentions after reading of scripture.

Lectio meditation – Meditation inspired by a passage of scripture.

Lectio prayer – Prayer inspired by a passage of scripture.

Lent – The preparatory period of 40 days (excluding Sundays) before Easter, observed as a season of self-examination and repentance.

Liturgy – The pattern of service used in public worship.

Maundy Thursday – The Thursday preceding Good Friday, traditionally associated with the Last Supper and the ritual of foot-washing.

Messiah – In Jewish theology, the leader destined to appear as one anointed by God to save and rule the people of Israel.

Paschal – from the Hebrew *pesah*, meaning Passover. More commonly Easter.

Pentecost – The "50th day" falling originally on the 50th day after the Jewish Passover; also referred to later as Whitsunday.

Quantum physics – The theory of the relationship of atoms, molecules, and other physical systems as bundles of energy.

Redeem – To transform tragedy to blessing.

Reproaches – A series of laments directed by the crucified Christ towards his ungrateful people, traditionally forming part of the Good Friday liturgy.

Resurrection – The rising of Christ in "new life" on the third day after his crucifixion and burial.

Salvation – Deliverance to joy beyond the powers of darkness; to be found in the safety of God's redeeming love.

Shaker – A branch of the Quaker sect (Society of Friends). Founded in England in 1747.

Tenebrae – Meaning "darkness" or "shadows," a liturgy sung or read during Holy Week in anticipation of the crucifixion.

Transfiguration Sunday – The feast celebrating the divine radiance of Jesus during his earthly life, as witnessed by Peter, James, and John and recorded in three of the four gospels.

Yahweh – the name of God. When Moses encountered the burning bush in the desert (Exodus 3:13–14) he asked for God's name. The Hebrew letters for God's reply – "I am who I am" – are YHWH. Because of some confusion between the Roman letters Y and J, and W and V, earlier transcriptions rendered the letters as JHVH, which, with vowels added, came out as Jehovah.

Index

Scripture Index

About the Authors

LOUISE MANGAN, B.A., MDiv., has served as a member of the Worship Focus Group for the Division of Mission of The United Church of Canada, and also of the Inter-Faith Dialogue Committee of the Division of World Outreach. She has served as pastoral minister of four Ontario congregations, and is currently serving with the congregation of Oakridge United Church in Vancouver, BC. Her passions are worship, spiritual formation, and social action – and bringing all three together!

NANCY WYSE is a mother and elementary school teacher, and has been involved in church life since her early childhood. Her deep and personal faith has been constant and sustaining and her church communities have also provided many rich opportunities and relationships. She believes in the importance of connecting with the stories and meaningful heritage of her roots... this book has been an integral part of that connection.

LORI FARR has a B.A. in dance/kinesiology, and a certificate in Stress Management Education.She is the President of Farr Reach Training and Development. She works with her unique Personal Leadership coaching process which helps individuals to clarify values, focus on goals, enhance joy and productivity, and live everyday life in alignment with spiritual purpose.